PEACOCK
his Circle and his Age

Peacock, aged seventy-two: from a photograph

PEACOCK

his Circle and his Age

HOWARD MILLS

Lecturer in English
University of Kent at Canterbury

CAMBRIDGE
AT THE UNIVERSITY PRESS
1969

Published by the Syndics of the Cambridge University Press
Bentley House, 200 Euston Road, London, N.W.1
American Branch: 32 East 57th Street, New York, N.Y.10022

Library of Congress Catalogue Card Number: 68–23183

Standard Book Number: 521 07262 X

Printed in Great Britain
at the University Printing House, Cambridge
(Brooke Crutchley, University Printer)

FOR MARY

Contents

vii

CONTENTS

Illustrations

Acknowledgements

This study developed from my Cambridge Ph.D. dissertation, and I am grateful to my research supervisor, Mr L. G. Salingar, for his help and patience. Mr Charles Cudworth and Dr Nicholas Temperley have been generous with their time and knowledge in discussing nineteenth-century music, and in letting me test out on them my estimate of Peacock as a music critic. In addition, Mr Cudworth not only let me use but served as an enthusiastic guide to the Pendlebury Music Library at Cambridge.

Among the many friends and former teachers who have helped I wish in particular to thank Mr H. A. Mason and Mr Charles Page for their encouragement throughout my work on Peacock and their radical suggestions at crucial stages.

Mr Joseph Barrell kindly help to compile the index.

Chronological Table

1785   Born at Weymouth, spent first three years of life in London.

1788   Father died: Peacock and mother move to Chertsey, Surrey.

1791   Went to school at Englefield Green, Surrey.

1798   Left school and became a clerk in London.

1804   *The monks of St Mark* printed, but probably not published.

1806   *Palmyra, and other poems* published. Walking tour of Scotland in autumn.

1807   Affair with Fanny Falkner.

1808–9   Worked as secretary on board H.M.S. *Venerable*: wrote several pieces of verse and *The genius of the Thames*, part I.

1809   Left *Venerable*; walked from Chertsey to source of Thames.

1810   In Wales; met future wife. *The genius of the Thames: a lyrical poem* published.

1811–13   *The dilettanti* and *The three doctors* (farces) written.

1812   *The philosophy of melancholy: a poem in four parts* published. *The genius of the Thames, Palmyra and other poems* published (revised versions).
October: met Shelley.

1813   April: second meeting with Shelley; then second tour of Wales.
July: returned to Marlow, Bucks: Shelley and Harriet now living nearby at Bracknell.
October and November: went with the Shelleys to Scotland.
Sir Hornbrook; or Childe Launcelot's expedition. A grammatico-allegorical ballad, published. 'Ahrimanes a mythological poem', written 1813–14.

1814   July: Shelley and Mary eloped to the Continent.
September: they returned to London; Peacock and mother moved to London.
Peacock's affair with Marianne St Croix.
Sir Proteus: a satirical ballad 'by P. M. O'Donovan' published.

1815   Moved from London to Marlow; Shelley and Mary moved to Bishopsgate, within walking distance, then to Marlow itself.
Headlong Hall published (post-dated 1816).

1817   *Melincourt* and *The Round Table: or King Arthur's feast* published.

1818   Shelley and Mary left England.
Nightmare Abbey and *Rhododaphne: or the Thessalian spell* published. 'An essay on fashionable literature' written, and *Maid Marian* begun.

1819   Began work at East India House.

1820   Married Jane Gryffydh.
'The four ages of poetry' published in *Ollier's literary miscellany*.

1822   Shelley drowned.
Maid Marian published.

1827   Review of Moore's *Epicurean* in *Westminster review*.

1829   *The misfortunes of Elphin*.

1830   Review of Moore's *Letters and journals of Lord Byron, vol. I*; of *Memoirs, correspondence and private papers of Thomas Jefferson*; and of *Chronicles of London Bridge*: all in *Westminster review*.

1831   *Crotchet Castle*.

1833   Mother died.

1834   Contributed to *Report from the Select Committee on steam navigation to India*.

1835   Review of Mount Edgcumbe's *Musical reminiscences* in *London review*.
Article on 'French comic romances' in *London review*.

1836   Articles on 'The *Epiciere*' and Bellini in *London review*.

1837   'The Legend of Manor Hall' and 'Recollections of Childhood', in *Bentley's Miscellany*.
Headlong Hall, *Nightmare Abbey*, *Maid Marian* and *Crotchet Castle* reprinted in Bentley's *Standard novels and romances*. *Paper money lyrics* published.

1849   Daughter married George Meredith.

1851   'Gastronomy and civilization', written with his daughter, published in *Fraser's magazine*.

1852   'Horae dramaticae: Querolus; or the buried treasure' and 'The Phaëthon of Euripides' in *Fraser's magazine*.

1856   Retired from East India House.

1857 'Horae dramaticae: The flask of cratinus', in *Fraser's magazine*.

1858 Daughter left Meredith. 'Memoirs of Percy Bysshe Shelley', in *Fraser's magazine*.

1859 Review of Müller and Donaldson's *History of Greek literature*, in *Fraser's magazine*.

1860 'Memoirs of Shelley' (second paper), 'Unpublished letters of Shelley' and Postscript in *Fraser's magazine*. *Gryll grange* serialised in *Fraser's magazine*.

1861 *Gryll Grange* published in book form.

1862 'Memoirs of Shelley. Supplementary notice', in *Fraser's magazine*.
Gl'*Ingannati*. *The deceived: a comedy performed at Siena in 1531: and Aelia Laelia Crispis*.

1866 Died.

1

Introduction

What does Peacock offer the general reader, and what is the justification for a book about him?

He is not a 'seminal mind', a creative thinker. Nor is it appropriate to call him a great creative artist. For, even in a successful imaginative work like *Nightmare Abbey*, he strikes us primarily as a keenly intelligent mind responding to and offering us insight into outstanding men who rank above him in his age, as well as the minor talents and the ephemera below him. This book about Peacock is therefore equally about Shelley, Coleridge and Byron.

His response to his age has a striking variety—variety of quality, of the subjects he engaged with, and of the media of letters, memoirs, reviews, poetry, novels. Yet with all this variety one rejoices to find a distinct and tangible central object: Peacock's relationship with Shelley. Instead of stumbling vaguely over Peacock's 'Response to Romanticism', for instance, we can study a tangible example of that response. In Shelley, the personality and the writer, many aspects of Romanticism are embodied. 'Embodied' here does not mean 'personified' in any abstract sense. Quite the reverse: what in the period we have to study as 'trends' or 'currents' or 'spirits', we find in Shelley as flesh and blood and nerves. When Peacock himself rejoiced in this palpable study he won his great advantage over any abstract History of Ideas. This is acknowledged in Humphry House's comment on a scene in *Nightmare Abbey*, that 'a whole long chapter of Professor Irving Babbitt says little more'.[1]

This book will argue that the friendship *made* Peacock: it was the central fact in his development, the central condition of his quality. Before 1812 he was in the pejorative sense what Hazlitt calls 'a pure emanation of the Spirit of the Age'.[2] The

[1] H. House, 'The novels of Thomas Love Peacock', *The listener*, XLII (8 Dec. 1949), 998.   [2] *Complete works*, ed. P. P. Howe, 21 vols. (London, 1930–4), XI, 86.

friendship, which coincides with the Regency decade, made him find himself, and gave authenticity to his criticism of the Romantic personality and more widely of the literature and society of the Regency.[1] Humphry House rightly says that 'it is the true focus... to think of him as... the intimate friend of Shelley ...Not only in his reading, but in this friendship most of all, Peacock lived through the major phases of romanticism, and he speaks of it with that intimate knowledge.'[2]

The three novels of the 1810s centre on a response to a different aspect of Shelley and, through and around that, to Shelley's age. After that friendship—with Shelley's last period abroad and his death—Peacock's work declined into a more rigid conservatism of attitude that dominates 'The four ages of poetry' and colours the later novels although relaxed in his later literary and musical reviews.

The chapters bringing this out will cut slightly across chronology, surveying Peacock's life, poetry and critical essays up to 1820 before returning to concentrate on the friendship with Shelley. An appeal to experience will show why this is so. When we look back on our own life, or our relationship with someone, it presents itself as a number of strands, each involved with the others, but each demanding to be followed separately along its full length before we return to pick up another. And often it is only in retrospect, and even then only in following the other strands, that we realise which one was crucial. The reader who feels that this is all very well, but who for clarity wants for Peacock the kind of chronological summary which he can supply for his own life, may consult the table on page xiii.

To get our bearings on Peacock's relative position, and give a fairer and more subtle reading of his mind and his friendship with Shelley, we need to apprehend him as one of a group of friends with their balanced and changing relationships. The main figures are Shelley, Peacock, Leigh Hunt and

[1] 'The Regency decade' refers in this book to the decade 1811–20, which are exactly the years in which George acted as Regent. However the term 'Regency' is often used with traditional latitude for the rough period 1800–30. It also usefully provides a more neutral and more comprehensive label for the period than does 'the Romantic Age'. Where anything more is implied, the context will make it clear.

[2] 'The novels of Thomas Love Peacock', p. 997.

Hogg. Thomas Jefferson Hogg, Shelley's Oxford friend, and co-editor of the defence of atheism that led them both to be expelled, will be a frequently used 'third term' as we chart Peacock's position in relation to Shelley. For Hogg is the simple Regency figure that Peacock is often mistaken for. He can with little unfairness be nailed down by the ringing finality of M. Mayoux's Gallic epithets:

Hogg, le solide, le positif, l'épais, à côté de qui Peacock est plus que raffiné, est plus que délicat, presque éthéré...Solide, égrillard, érudit, bon vivant, mais vivant, c'est une figure typique de l'ancien barreau anglais, présentant un mélange curieux de personnalité et de convention, de curiosité intellectuelle et d'essentielle matérialité.[1]

Peacock should also be compared much more freely than is usual with other critics of the Regency. Three major ones—Crabb Robinson, Hazlitt and Byron—are considered at length in chapter 7. Specific comparisons with other writers are made when they are called for: thus, for instance, the treatment of society in *Melincourt* calls for comparison with treatments by Southey, Samuel Bamford, Cobbett and others. The provision 'when called for' applies also to my account of the age. This book avoids opening with a general social history but (for instance), where Peacock invites us in *Melincourt* to consider Malthus, an investigation will be made of what he stood for in the age, as help in judging Peacock's interpretation. This practice arises from an important principle. Peacock is often condemned by the obtuse method of laying down a dogmatic account of his period and noting that he does not share that account. To complain that he does not see his age as we do, nor mentions Karl Marx,[2] is no better than the old chestnut about Jane Austen and the French Revolution.

The first justification for a new book on Peacock is dissatisfaction with previous ones, a feeling that the accepted view of him has gradually become more and more crude.

[1] J.-J. Mayoux, *Un Epicuréan anglais: Thomas Love Peacock* (Paris, 1933), p. 123. Mayoux also characterises Leigh Hunt and his family: 'Les Hunt...exubérants, sentimentaux, cajoleurs' (p. 129).
[2] See for example R. Mason, 'Notes for an estimate of Peacock', *Horizon*, LX (1944), which still turns up in 'Select Bibliographies' on Peacock.

Shelley's admiration[1] should guard us from thinking Peacock was out of touch with the Regency: he praised the novels in terms resembling his praise of *Don Juan*, 'Something wholly new and relative to the age'. And, although no considered appraisal appeared until the 1830s,[2] the Reviews took it for granted that Peacock should be discussed as an informed critic of his period. The *Westminster review* in 1831 admitted that the attack in *Crotchet Castle* on its own Utilitarian ranks had hit home.[3] Spedding's article in *The Edinburgh review* of 1839 is one of the best accounts of Peacock ever written, in its subtle discussion of the sense in which he is 'serious', and of the development in technique and understanding from one novel to another. Saying that Peacock began as a court jester, 'the disturber-general of favourite systems', the review argues that after *Headlong Hall* 'the humour seems to run deeper; the ridicule is informed with a juster appreciation of the meaning of the thing ridiculed; the disputants are more in earnest, and less like scoffers in disguise; there is more of natural warmth and life in the characters...'[4]

The change in attitude to Peacock (corresponding, incidentally, to that towards Crabbe) can be picked up in the scanty Victorian references, and in Lord Houghton's Preface to the 1875 edition. Standing at the same distance from his subject as Leslie Stephen's distance from Crabbe a year later,[5] Lord Houghton has lost all the sharpness and fine detail we noted in these views of the 1830s. Peacock has become a harmless eccentric just as Crabbe became a Parson Adams. His novels, like Crabbe's tales, are blurred together. His treatment of the ideas of his time was only for the sake of 'the intellectual gaiety to which the follies, inconsistencies, exaggerations, conceits and oddities of other men supply a continual fund of interest'.[6] And, 'although brought...in contact with the best influences and most powerful impulses of the nineteenth century, he belonged in all his tastes, sentiments, and aspects of life to the

---

[1] In letters to be quoted in chapters on the relevant novels.
[2] Apart from an attack (mainly political) on *Melincourt* in *The British critic* in 1817, reviews did little more than tell the story and give extracts, in the manner of *The literary gazette*. [3] xxix (July 1831), 208 ff. [4] Lxvii (Jan. 1839), 432.
[5] In his essay in *Hours in a library*, 2nd series (London, 1876).
[6] *Works of Peacock*, ed. H. Cole, 3 vols. (London, 1875), I, vii.

eighteenth, the age pre-eminently of free fancy and common sense.'[1]

There have been isolated and uninfluential hints of a subtler account in our century. J. B. Priestley in 1927 questioned Lord Houghton and distinguished (much too arbitrarily) between Peacock the 'humorist, expressing a universal mockery', and the serious 'satirist'.[2] But this is not elaborated in his anecdotal general guide. From the six hundred pages of J.-J. Mayoux's French study[3] can be extracted a cautious and just account of Peacock; but he relies on exhaustive detail rather than judicious inferences. At the other extreme Humphry House's acute judgement covers only two pregnant pages.[4] Largely for the reasons suggested, these three accounts have not been influential; and how much cruder the common view has become since 1875 can be seen by comparing the quotations from Lord Houghton made above with the following sample from 1965: 'For the truth of the ideas, Peacock seems to care very little; it is their quaintness, their picturesqueness, their absurdity that catches the eye . . . To make the ideas amusing, and therefore impossible, is the sole intent.'[5] That this is the official view is indicated by its closeness to Dr Jack's chapter in *English literature 1815–32* (Oxford, 1963). The simplification is not in Dr Jack but in the modern opinions which it is the policy of the *Oxford history of English literature* to summarise instead of venturing independent insights. But, if, as the series claims, 'all the contributors are acknowledged authorities on their periods, and each volume incorporates in text and bibliography the results of the latest research',[6] then Peacock is badly in need, if not of research, of critical study. Hence the present book.

To re-open the case of Peacock, like any other, calls for fresh evidence. Many previously unpublished letters by Peacock, Shelley and Hogg, and new biographical research,[7] have

---

[1] *Ibid.* pp. viii–ix.
[2] *Thomas Love Peacock*, 'English Men of Letters' (London, 1927), p. 32.
[3] *Un Epicuréen anglais: Thomas Love Peacock.*
[4] *The listener*, XLII (8 Dec. 1949), 998.
[5] A. E. Dyson, *The crazy fabric, essays in irony* (London, 1965), pp. 58 and 62.
[6] See the advertisements and dust-jackets.
[7] Notably *New Shelley letters*, ed. W. S. Scott (London, 1948), which contains many by Peacock and Hogg; *Shelley and his circle*, 1773–1822, the Carl H. Pforzheimer Library, ed. K. N. Cameron (Oxford, 1961); *The letters of Shelley*,

appeared since the last books on Peacock and the last complete edition,[1] and largely modify those previous verdicts. Yet the most recent book on Peacock is a reprint, without any alteration, of the one Priestley wrote in 1927 before even the later Halliford volumes had appeared.[2]

But I shall also attempt a fresh and more scrupulous weighing of previous evidence. For instance, 'The four ages of poetry' will be balanced against the usually ignored 'Essay on fashionable literature'. *Melincourt* will be given much more attention, and the representation of Coleridge in *Nightmare Abbey* entertained more seriously, than is usual. Fuller credit will be given to the 'Memoirs of Shelley', and to the music reviews and articles. The latter particularly deserve extended treatment because literary critics give them only a passing mention, and because they appear not to be known by music historians—who, however, when introduced to them are impressed by Peacock's intelligence and knowledge.[3]

The established idea of Peacock will be taken for granted as the background of this study, and so Priestley, Van Doren and Freeman rarely cited—or reiterated. Above all this study, unlike theirs, will present the complexity of Peacock in preference to fixing a clear-cut judgement.

Dealing with a writer like Peacock calls for a particularly strong sense of proportion and tact; so that two instances of

ed. F. L. Jones (Oxford, 1965). I found minor help in the unpublished letters of Peacock in the Broughton papers (British Museum unplaced manuscripts 47225). The works on Shelley by Cameron, White and Notopoulos (see bibliography) belong to the 1940s and 1950s, as does Lady W. Scott's biography *Jefferson Hogg* (London, 1951).

[1] Benvenuto Cellini's study appeared in 1937; the Halliford Edition from 1924 to 1934. The only strictly new book, by O. W. Campbell (1953), is hardly longer than a pamphlet-monograph like J. I. M. Stewart's.

[2] Priestley makes this bland comment in a brief new preface: 'I must regret that the concluding volumes of Messrs. Constable's fine Halliford Edition of the complete works, volumes that may possibly contain a little new material, were not to hand while I was writing these chapters. I can hardly imagine, however, that such material would interfere with any judgment on Peacock's character or work to be found there' (London, 1966, p. vii).

[3] I have been able to use Peacock's own copies of the music periodical *The harmonicon* and of Lord Mount Edgcumbe's *Musical reminiscences*, the latter bearing Peacock's pencilled marginal marks and personal index of topics and page-references inside the back cover. These books are in the Pendlebury Library at Cambridge.

these qualities may be pinned up, as it were, as exemplary reminders. The first was written by Spedding in 1839. While my own general estimate of Peacock will be pitched higher, Spedding is enviable for the tact and nicety with which he balances Peacock's human understanding and wide intellectual grasp against the relative lack of depth 'which only deeper purposes can impart'. Spedding attributes to him

An eye and a heart open enough to impressions and opinions of all kinds, so that vanity be the end of all; a perception of the strangeness and mystery which involves our life,—keen enough to enliven the curiosity, but not to disturb or depress the spirit; with faith in some possible but unattainable solution just sufficient to make him watch with interest the abortive endeavours of more sanguine men, but not to engage him in the pursuit himself; a questioning, not a denying spirit;—but questioning without waiting for an answer; an understanding very quick and bright,—not narrow in its range, though wanting in the depth which only deeper purposes can impart; a fancy of singular play and delicacy; a light sympathy with the common hopes and fears, joys and sorrows of mankind, which gives him an interest in their occupations just enough for the purposes of observation and intelligent amusement; a poetical faculty, not of a very high order, but quite capable of harmonizing the scattered notes of fancy and observation and reproducing them in a graceful whole.[1]

Spedding's portrait is one of intelligence and curiosity qualified by an ultimate reserve and unadventurousness: the range of Peacock's perceptions is remarkably wide, yet he is seldom deeply disturbed, or disturbs the reader, by what he perceives.

There is a different kind of balance in my second 'exhibit', written by F. R. Leavis in 1948. It conveys how Peacock, while being limited, within those limits is valid and inexhaustible: 'In his ironical treatment of contemporary society and civilization he is seriously applying serious standards, so that his books, which are obviously not novels in the same sense as Jane Austen's, have a permanent life as light reading— indefinitely re-readable—for minds with mature interests.'[2] The sense of proportion—the sanity—of a book on Peacock will depend on its never losing sight of what that passage acknowledges: the way in which Peacock is at once 'serious' and 'light'.

[1] *Edinburgh review*, VII (Jan. 1839), 438.
[2] *The great tradition* (London, 1948), p. 18 n.

2
Peacock in the Regency

The aim of this and the following chapter is to use Peacock's biography, letters and critical essays so as to give a setting to the Regency novels: to evaluate his way of life in the 1800s and 1810s, and to evaluate his mind as it responded to the classics and to contemporary literature.

In chapter 3 the key subject will become Peacock's standards as they engaged with the literary practice of his age. But it takes time, a certain maturity and self-knowledge, to achieve any standards or coherent point of view, conservative or otherwise. Until this happens Peacock, like us all, is the mere receptacle of current habits and feelings, watered down and mingled from Augustan and Romantic, eighteenth and nineteenth centuries alike. To try another metaphor: if the swamp of current fashions is one of the things we mean by the 'spirit of the age', then Peacock takes time to emerge from that swamp and to look down on it critically. Hence the crude distinction in the chapter-headings, to be refined by the chapters themselves, of 'Peacock in the Regency' and 'Peacock on the Regency'.

The overlapping concepts of 'the spirit of the age', *Zeitgeist*, and 'fashion' have never been clearly distinguished. The first is a literal translation of the second, yet the second has acquired (certainly since Matthew Arnold) a pejorative meaning much nearer that of the third. 'The spirit of the age' can indicate the important movements of the time which are worthy of influencing great creative minds and to which those minds can in turn contribute and give a direction. The apparent paradox in the relation between individuals and this kind of 'spirit' can be analysed no further than it is by Shelley in his Preface to *The revolt of Islam*:

There must be a resemblance, which does not depend upon their own will, between all the writers of any particular age. They cannot

8

escape from subjection to a common influence which arises out of an infinite combination of circumstances belonging to the times in which they live; though each is in a degree the author of the very influence by which his being is thus pervaded.[1]

But an age also has its ephemeral fashions, which may be quite independent of literature or at least have their centre of activity elsewhere. For instance, the fashion for tours of the Lake District, which was growing around the turn of the century, *may* have helped Wordsworth's reputation and *may* in time have been helped by it; but this is no reflection on Wordsworth nor credit to that fashion. *Lyrical ballads*, and the trip to the Lakes, belong to different spheres and to different levels. Yet there is a good deal of verse on mountains and solitude—by Wilson, for example, or Byron in *Childe Harold's pilgrimage*— where the realm of fashion is dictating to the realm of literature.

The relation of the talented writer, rather than the genius, to the fashions by which he is influenced, comes out very clearly in Regency verse. A brief survey of this verse will give us a contemporary setting for Peacock's own early poems and his tastes as a reader of poetry.

Dr Johnson himself unwittingly provided a description of the violent flood of literary change that was to follow his own age:

Imagination, a licentious and vagrant faculty, unsusceptible of limitations, and impatient of restraint, has always endeavoured to... burst the inclosures of regularity...every new genius produces some innovation, which, when invented and approved, subverts the rules which the practise of foregoing authors had established.[2]

Despite the Romantic poets, the eighteenth century still stands. Yet for most modern readers their flood has swept away and drowned those lesser figures of the Regency who tried to uphold the Pope tradition. It has swept away the opinion of Byron who, in *English bards and Scotch reviewers* (itself a desperate exhumation of Pope applied to the world of 1809) reserved his praise of contemporary poetry for Rogers, Campbell and Crabbe. But it is essential to distinguish between these three, for each represents a different kind of conservatism.

---

[1] *Poetical works*, ed. Mary Shelley, 4 vols. (London, 1839), vol. I, 149.
[2] *The rambler, 125*, in Samuel Johnson, *Works*, Oxford English Classics (1825), VI, 344–5.

Scott wrote to Rogers in 1820: 'As you have made the most classical museum I can conceive, I have been attempting a Gothic.'[1] He was in fact referring to their houses: as Scott designed Abbotsford, so Rogers designed his house in St James's Square, London, in a mode more ultra-classical than any Georgian building, as is the case with all self-conscious revivals or pastiches. But Scott's remark applies equally well to their verse. Rogers's fastidious technique, enervated couplets and 'philosophical' sentiments in the Regency poem 'Human life' (1819) show no development from 'The pleasures of memory' (1792) —or from the stock of reflective verse of the previous half-century. His work is mere dead conservatism, a classical museum.

Byron's second figure, Campbell, belonged to a group of which Rogers was in fact the 'father' and host, and Moore, Luttrell and the early Byron the other chief members. Each mixed conservatism with one kind of 'development'. The result is a loose combination of the worst of both qualities that would better be labelled as 'derivative but fashionable'. In his chapter on 'The London society poets', F. E. Pierce writes that:

As a literary phenomenon, the chief mark of this group was the close union of romantic medievalism, Orientalism, and Wertherism with the most unadulterated type of the Pope tradition. Every member of it except Rogers and Luttrell wrote poetry that according to any possible definition would be called wildly romantic. Every member of it without exception wrote a considerable amount of verse in the most servile imitation of Augustan models.[2]

Sometimes they drifted to and fro unconsciously with the *Zeitgeist*; more often they consciously cashed in on fashion.

Stick to the East [Byron advised Moore in 1813], the oracle, Stael, told me it was the only poetical policy. The North, South and West have all been exhausted; but from the East we have nothing but Southey's unsaleables...The little I have done in that way...if it has had any success, that also will prove that the public are orientalising, and pave the path for you.[3]

[1] P. W. Clayden, *Rogers and his contemporaries* (London, 1889), I, 305.
[2] *Currents and eddies in the English romantic generation* (Yale and Oxford, 1918), p. 129.
[3] Byron, *Works...letters and journals*, ed. R. E. Prothero (London, 1903), II, 255.

And so Moore wrote 'Lalla Rookh'. As F. E. Pierce says,

Wordsworth's return to nature, Scott's return to feudalism, grew out of emotions that had been deeply felt from boyhood...About the 'romantic' elements in the work of the London society poets there is frequently a made-to-order atmosphere. We feel too often that they wrote with their ears open for the applauses or hisses of the audience. We detect the rouge on their odalisques and the false beards on their druids.[1]

We recognise each overlapping wave of Regency fashionable taste, orientalism, hellenism and medievalism, as we recognise the corresponding succession of modern cinema *décors*. But we cannot easily distinguish each poet's individual brand of fashionableness-with-derivativeness. Here the contemporary sketches in Hazlitt's lecture *On the living poets* are of great help. Yet his particular contrast of Scott, 'the most popular of all the poets of the present day', with Wordsworth, 'the most original poet now living', surely sums up a general contrast of authentic and false.

Scott...has none of Mr. Wordsworth's *idiosyncrasy*. He differs from his readers only in a greater range of knowledge and facility of expression. His poetry belongs to the class of *improvisatori* poetry. It has neither depth, height, nor breadth in it; neither uncommon strength, nor uncommon refinement of thought, sentiment, or language. It has no originality...this author has no research, no moving power in his own breast...He has just hit the town between the romantic and the fashionable; and between the two, secured all classes of readers on his side. In a word, I conceive that he is to the great poet, what an excellent mimic is to a great actor. There is no determinate impression left on the mind by reading his poetry. It has no results. The reader rises up from its perusal with new images and associations, but he remains the same man that he was before. A great mind is one that moulds the minds of others. Mr. Scott has put the Border Minstrelsy and scattered traditions of the country into easy animated verse. But the Notes to his poems are just as entertaining as the poems themselves, and his poems are only entertaining.

Mr. Wordsworth is the most original poet now living. He is the reverse of Walter Scott in his defects and excellences.[2]

---

[1] *Currents and eddies*, p. 139.
[2] Hazlitt, *Complete works*, ed. P. P. Howe, 21 vols. (London, 1930–4), v, 154–6.

Here is a cutting account of the kind of 'novelty' or 'development' Scott shared with the London society poets: 'he has just hit the town between the romantic and the fashionable'. Whether or not they were cynically exploiting taste for money, they could never be genuine, for they had no inner centre from which to write, no 'idiosyncrasy' in the sense of authentic individuality. Nor had they that idiosyncrasy in language: we remember the criticism made by Peacock, Arnold and T. S. Eliot of Byron's linguistic inertia. 'This imperceptiveness of Byron to the English word. . . indicates for practical purposes a defective sensibility.'[1] The opposition of the authentic and the fake is absolute: opposed to Wordsworth and Coleridge, fashionable developers like Scott or Campbell stand with mere conservatives like Rogers.

But another group remains. Crabbe—the last of Byron's true 'English bards'—is out of place with Rogers and Campbell. His youth belongs to the age of Johnson, and the Pope tradition is his element. But his Regency poems at their best make his own creative development of that tradition, with the extension of vision that interpreting the new age demanded. This extension of vision makes his verse as free from Regency as from Augustan conventions. In this his position relative to Rogers is indicated by Rogers's blindness to Crabbe's creative struggle: 'Crabbe's early poetry is by far the best, as to *finish*. The conclusion of 'The library' is charmingly written. . .'[2]—he merely saw the later Crabbe as a clumsy conservative. Similarly Rogers could not appreciate how the Byron of the later satires was making a creative development from the Augustan and from his earlier Regency-fashionable self.

Peacock's way of life

'I did not go to any University or public school', Peacock told Thomas L'Estrange in 1862; 'I was six years and a half at a private school in Englefield Green. I left it before I was thirteen. The master was not much of a scholar; but he had the art of inspiring his pupils with a love of learning, and he

[1] T. S. Eliot, 'Byron', *On poetry and poets* (London, 1957), p. 201.
[2] Samuel Rogers, *Table-talk*, ed. M. Bishop (London, 1952), p. 203.

Peacock, aged eighteen: from a miniature
(*National Portrait Gallery*)

had excellent classical and French assistants'.[1] On leaving
school in 1798, he worked as a clerk. But he continued to study,
probably using the British Museum Reading Room or the
'Oriental Repository' Library of East India House, and under
the guidance of his well-read and intelligent mother, with whom
'I passed many of my best years...taking more pleasure in
reading than in society'.[2] He took even more pleasure in
walking along the Thames or in Windsor Great Park, near
his mother's home at Chertsey.

When he was reading, he told L'Estrange, 'I took to...the
best books, illustrated by the best critics; and amongst the
latter I feel especially indebted to Heyne and Hermann':[3] we
cannot penetrate beyond the bland vagueness of 'the best
books', but feel uneasy that in the age of Porson 'the best
critics' were for Peacock one whom classicists have long forgotten and another only remembered because his theories were
once thoroughly demolished by Porson himself.

While 'the best books' would have been mainly classical,
they included a varied bunch of curious period pieces that
caught Peacock's attention when published around the turn of
the century. One specimen is Horne Tooke's *The diversions of
Purley*, a grammatico-etymological treatise at once mechanical
in its theory of language and fanciful in its scholarly proofs,
underlining for us the distinction and novelty of his contemporary Coleridge's concept of language. Published earlier but
still current were Lord Monboddo's *Origin and progress of
language* and *Ancient metaphysics*—for which the notes to *Melincourt* give sufficient introduction. Another work was Sir William
Drummond's *Academical questions* (1805), a history of philosophy invoking Aristotle in order to attack (and misunderstand)
Kant; and the same year appeared Forsyth's *Principles of moral
science*. Forsyth, like the early Peacock, was a dabbler: it is
significant that he also brought out in 1805–8 *The beauties of
Scotland...embellished with engravings*, cashing in on the rage
Scott's poems were producing for Scottish scenery—a rage to
which Peacock on a Scottish walking tour in 1806 duly responded.

[1] *Works*, Halliford Edition, ed. H. F. B. Brett-Smith and C. E. Jones, 10 vols.
(London, 1924–34), VIII, 259.
[2] *Ibid.*   [3] *Ibid.*

To these writers who left their mark on his later essays and novels, we should add one who helped form the character of Peacock's early poetry: le Comte de Volney. What Scott did for the historical remains of Scotland, Volney did for the Middle East in his *Les Ruines, ou, méditation sur les révolutions des empires* and *Voyage en Syrie et en Egypte*. It is on the basis of the descriptions by Volney and others of the ruins of Palmyra that Peacock, in the poem bearing its name, 'works himself up into a soliloquy of philosophical pathos, on the vicissitudes of empire and the mutability of all sublunary things'. That comment is in fact a quotation from *The misfortunes of Elphin*; to apply it to 'Palmyra' forms the first of many illustrations which show the early Peacock a prey to literary habits that the mature Peacock came to criticise in others.[1] One stanza will convey the theme and the manner:

> Yes, all are flown!
> I stand alone,
> At ev'ning's calm and pensive hour,
> 'Mid wasting domes,
> And mould'ring tombs,
> The wrecks of vanity and pow'r.
> One shadowy tint enwraps the plain;
> No form is near, no sounds intrude,
> To break the melancholy reign
> Of silence and of solitude.
> How oft, in scenes like these, since TIME began,
> With downcast eye has CONTEMPLATION trod,
> Far from the haunts of FOLLY, VICE and MAN...[2]

—and so on: the reader of minor Augustan verse can almost make up the remaining lines of such a stanza, if given their basic props: GOD, FATE, WAR, DEATH, and OBLIVION.

It is in 1807, a year after the success of the 'Palmyra' volume, that the surviving adult letters begin. To Edward T. Hookham, son of his publisher Thomas Hookham, he writes from Chertsey where he is walking in Windsor Forest, planning another long poem ('as I have no better occupation I will return to the "idle trade" of writing verses'[3]) and falling in

---

[1] *The misfortunes of Elphin*, ch. 13: in Halliford, IV, 101.
[2] Stanza 11: Halliford, VI, 13. I have restored Peacock's original capitals.
[3] Halliford, VIII, 160.

love with a girl with whom (true to his period again) he has rendezvous in the 'romantic' ruins of Newark Abbey. Characteristically Peacock here makes light of what was probably his first disturbing adult experience. Family tradition tells of a near-engagement, of a locket with her hair that Peacock wore until his death, and of his dreams of her that 'for some weeks frequently recurred' just before he died.[1] And the poem 'Newark Abbey, August 1842: with a reminiscence of August 1807' implies strong feeling and hints at a forced separation. Certainly it looks as if he was hustled off to sea for a year. But none of this comes through the contemporary letters or poems: the second letter to Edward Hookham (28 Nov. 1808) merely presents the *fait accompli* of Peacock on board H.M.S. *Venerable* as Captain's clerk, and projects an impersonal 'period' image. He envies Hookham's Scottish tour which 'went over the same ground on which I wandered alone in the autumn of 1806': Peacock is here again an indistinguishable part of the age, 'playing the sentimental tourist' as the Halliford biography puts it, 'and enjoying the scenery made fashionable by Scott's narrative poems'.[2] The scenery is indeed Scott's, but the idiom takes one back earlier, to Marianne Dashwood's period:

Is not the Esk a most delightful stream? Did you see that enchanting spot where the North and the South Esk unite? Did you think of the lines of Sir Walter Scott?...Did you visit the banks of the sweet river Teviot, and that most lovely of rivers, the indescribably fascinating Tweed? Did you sit by moonlight in the ruins of Melrose?[3]

The last sentence alludes to the Regency reading public's favourite passage from 'The lay of the last minstrel', which begins

If thou wouldst view fair Melrose aright,
Go visit it by the pale moonlight...[4]

So far Peacock is the perfect 'fashionable reader', ordering Lewis's *Romantic tales*, Scott's *Minstrelsy of the Scottish border*, 'and something very elegantly *romantesque* in the poetical department'; and asking

What news in the republic of letters? Is another volume of Miss Baillie's tragedies forthcoming?...What is Walter Scott about? Is

[1] See especially his granddaughter's memoir, *Works*, ed. Cole, 3 vols. (London, 1875), I, xxviii–xxix.
[2] Halliford I, xxv.   [3] *Ibid*. pp. 161–2.   [4] Canto II, stanza 1.

anything new expected from the pen of the incomparable Southey? How is poor Campbell? His lyre breathed the very soul of poetry... Is Wordsworth sleeping on his bed of mud in the profundity of the Bathos?...[1]

Besides keeping to fashionable names and opinions, this passage ends with one of the fashionable 'standard jokes' that Peacock himself was to expose in his 'Essay on fashionable literature'.

'As to writing poetry, or doing anything else that is rational, in this floating Inferno,' he told Hookham, 'it is almost next to a moral impossibility.'[2] But despite the pose of Poet Blighted by an Alien Environment, Peacock produced enough odds and ends of verse on board. The 'Stanzas written at sea' treat his painful separation in a style impervious to individual feeling:

> Thou white-rolling sea! from thy foam-crested billows,
>   That restlessly flash in the silver moon-beam,
> In fancy I turn to the green-waving willows,
>   That rise by the side of my dear native stream.
> There softly in moonlight soft waters are playing,
>   Which light-breathing zephyrs symphoniously sweep;
> While here the loud wings of the north-wind are swaying,
>   And whirl the white spray on the wild-dashing deep.[3]

He also obliged the officers with Prologues for their amateur theatricals, and by March 1809 could report to Hookham that 'I have a number of miscellaneous pieces by me, sufficient, with a classical ballad or two now in embryo, to make a volume the size of *Palmyra*.'[4] Besides this rag-bag he had written the first part, mainly historical–panegyrical, of *The genius of the Thames*; and after ending his year's service in May 1809 he walked the length of the Thames to get material for the second, more topographical part of the poem, which he then wrote at Chertsey. Letters to Hookham ask for works of curious speculation and exploration like Kurwan's *Metaphysical essays* and Mungo Park's *Travels in Africa* 'for the purpose of manufacturing notes' and for working up the 'philosophical' digressions:

[1] Halliford, VIII, 163–4.   [2] *Ibid.* p. 162.
[3] Halliford, VI, 95. Other separation poems written on board are printed and discussed in K. N. Cameron's *Shelley and his circle*, the Carl H. Pforzheimer Library (Oxford, 1961), I, 421–8.
[4] Halliford, VIII, 165. Some of the theatrical pieces are printed and discussed in *Shelley and his circle*, I, 467–74.

I have thought of several subjects for an episode, but cannot hit on anything to suit my fancy, unless, in my reflections on the mutability of empire, I were to introduce one on the fall of Carthage. I think this subject highly susceptible of poetical ornament.[1]

This is exactly the kind of thing the mature Peacock came to attack in Southey's epics.

The end-product can be fairly represented by its 'Analysis', the relation of which to its 'poetical ornaments' is that not of bones clothed with flesh but of a skeletal scarecrow hung about with well-worn out-of-fashion cast-offs.

First Part. An autumnal night on the banks of the Thames. Characters of several rivers of Great Britain. Acknowledged superiority of the Thames. Address to the Genius of the Thames. View of some of the principal rivers of Europe, Asia, Africa, and America. Pre-eminence of the Thames. The port of London. The naval domination of Britain and extent of her commerce and navigation. Tradition that an immense forest occupied the site of the metropolis. Episode of a Druid, supposed to have taken refuge in that forest, after the expulsion of Mona.

Second Part. Return to the banks of the Thames. The influence of spring on the scenery of the river. The tranquil beauty of the valleys of the Thames contrasted with the sublimity of more open and elevated regions. Allusion to the war on the Danube. Ancient wars on the Thames. Its present universal peace. View of the course of the Thames. Its source near Kemble Meadow. Comparative reflections on time. Ewan, Lechlade...[*etc. etc.—see map*]...Comparative adversion to the ancient state of the Euphrates and Araxes, at Babylon and Persepolis. Present desolation of those scenes. Reflections on the fall of nations. Conclusion.[2]

The poem came out in 1810: it was not perfect, Peacock admitted, but self-effacingly enough he would 'defer my corrections till I learn the opinion of the critics'.[3] Meanwhile he had moved on to Wales, first settling in Merionethshire and then walking home through central Wales.

The Welsh letters reflect a slightly changed 'spirit of the age' from the earlier effusions on Scotland. The *picturesque* is overtaken by the *wild* and *romantic*. 'The view from the top of this mountain [Cader Idris] baffles description. It is the very

---

[1] *Ibid.* pp. 176 and 174–5.   [2] Halliford, VI, 108 and 132.
[3] *Ibid.* VIII, 185.

sublimity of Nature's wildest magnificence.'[1] But they are the letters of a tourist, not of a poet: the Romantic poets are already becoming watered down to the hiker's exhilaration expressed typically in Hazlitt's essay 'On Going a Journey'. The formula for happiness is a day's solitary walk ending up at an inn with a good fire and dinner, and a rattling good book for company. The outdoor philosophy of *mens sana in corpore sano* has set in. Peacock writes: 'I am in high health and spirits...I feel how happy a man may be with a little money and a sane intellect, and reflected with astonishment and pity on the madness of the multitude.'[2]

He brought back for his publisher a drastically re-written and reduced 'Palmyra', and *The philosophy of melancholy: a poem, in four parts*. Once more the General Analysis will do as a guide:

The contemplation of the universal mutability of things prepares the mind to encounter the vicissitudes of life. The spirit of philosophical melancholy which delights in that contemplation, is the most copious source of virtue, of courage, and of genius. The pleasures arising from it...[are] felt in every sense and sound of nature; more especially, in the solemn grandeur of mountain scenery, and in the ruined magnificence of former times...[it] dwells on scenes of our childhood and on the memory of departed friends.[3]

This is an odd muddle of Stoicism and Tourism. The 'philosophy' of the opening is an excuse for the sketchbook that follows, the most vivid pages of which present (to quote the Analysis again) 'Scenery of Merionethshire—A cataract in flood:—in frost'.

The philosophy of melancholy came out in 1812: it is a shock to remember we have reached the year when Peacock met Shelley, and so the year from which we date the emergence of the mature Peacock, Peacock the satirist. It is worth stressing that the lack of centre or coherence we have noted in his youth was still as glaring in 1812. One can say 'variety' of the Welsh letters' mixture of awe at the scenery with satirical sketches of the locals that remind us of what was to come in *Headlong Hall*. But incoherence is the only word for the muddle in *Melancholy* of lugubrious ruminations and hiker's gusto. And,

---

[1] Halliford, VIII, 190.   [2] *Ibid.* p. 191.   [3] *Ibid.* VI, 186.

while *Melancholy* and the revised 'Palmyra' were appearing, Peacock was writing a couple of stage farces. Only through contact with Shelley did he find his own identity and direction as a writer.

There is, however, a direct and unbroken line in his *way of life* from the first decade of the century to the second; his habits at Chertsey and later at Marlow fit his own description: Hermit of the Thames. By 1812 he had some right to Shelley's respect for him as a classical scholar: but books still took their place with boating and walking. In summer, Charles Clairmont reported in 1815, 'he owns he cannot apply himself to study, and thinks it more beneficial to him, as a human being, entirely to devote himself to the beauties of the season, while they last'. Peacock wrote to Shelley in 1818:

For the most part my division of time is this: I devote the forenoon to writing; the afternoon to the river, the woods and classical poetry; the evening to philosophy—at present the *Novum Organum* and the *Histoire Naturelle*, which is a treasury of inexhaustible delight. My reading is as usual, at this season, somewhat desultory.[1]

A year earlier he wrote to Hogg, 'Perhaps a due mixture of tea, Greek and pedestrianism constitute the summum bonum'.[2]

Tea, Greek and pedestrianism: this, on the face of it, is also the common ground on which Peacock, Shelley, Hogg and Leigh Hunt spent so much of their time together in the 1810s. Yet how common was the ground?—one must now begin to distinguish between the friends. How vigorous and how serious was their reading of classical and contemporary literature? We can first ask (without pedantically belittling those normal pleasures) how far their *Greek* was an intellectual interest that will stand up to serious inspection when isolated from its context of *tea and pedestrianism*.

Before discussing the value of Peacock's classicism we need a factual indication of its mere strength. This strength, or power of emission, can be registered most dramatically in terms of its impact on the mind of Shelley. So that the theme in

---

[1] *Ibid.* VIII, 203.
[2] *New Shelley letters*, ed. W. S. Scott (London, 1948), p. 101.

hand conveniently allows us to take up the beginnings of their friendship. For, while Shelley had wanted to meet Peacock because he admired Peacock's poetry, the most obvious and rapid effect of their meetings was to re-convert Shelley to the study of the Greek classics.

To avoid exaggerating Peacock's powers of arousing enthusiasm, we need to see their first meetings as coinciding with a lucky receptive stage of Shelley's development: he was feeling the need for release from a constricted circle of friends and a constricted intellectual world shared with Harriet. He began to find this release when he got to know some friends of Godwin's called the Newtons and the Boinvilles. While their circle, as we shall see later, sparked off Peacock the satirist and inspired *Headlong Hall*, they gave Shelley the habit of shared study with congenial companions, and were responsible for his wide reading of Italian literature in the original. But Shelley's booklists show that Peacock had the greatest and quickest effect on his reading. In July 1812 Shelley was more Godwinian than Godwin, such a disciple of *Political justice* that he could not take Godwin's own advice to widen his studies and read the Classics. Still smarting from his experiences at Oxford, he protested that

the evils of acquiring Greek and Latin considerably overbalance the benefits...In the first place, I do not perceive how one of the truths of *Political Justice* rests on the excellence of ancient literature. That Greek and Latin have contributed to form your character it were idle to dispute, but in how great a degree have they contributed?...Was not the government of republican Rome, and most of those of Greece, as oppressive and arbitrary, as liberal of encouragement to monopoly, as that of Great Britain is at present? And what do we learn from their poets? as you have yourself acknowledged somewhere 'they are fit for nothing but the perpetuation of the noxious race of heroes in the world'...Nor can I help considering the vindicators of ancient learning as the vindicators of a literary despotism, as the tracers of a circle which is intended to shut out from real knowledge, to which this fictitious knowledge is attached, all who do not breathe the air of prejudice, and who will not support the established systems of politics, religion and morals.—I have as great a contempt for Cobbett as you can have, but it is because he is a dastard and a time-server; he has no humanity, no refinement; but were he a classical scholar would he have more? Did Greek and Roman literature refine the soul of Johnson, does it extend the thousand narrow bigots educated in the very bosom of classicality?[1]

In October Shelley first met Peacock. On 1 December he wrote to Thomas Hookham for copies of Herodotus, Thucydides, Xenophon, Plutarch, Marcus Aurelius, Seneca and Plato, with translations; and a week later he asked another bookseller for works by seventeen classical authors. J. A. Notopoulos points out that, although these and later lists include many of Godwin's recommendations, they also include Peacock's favourites Lord Monboddo, Horne Tooke and Sir William Drummond, together with many minor classical authors that of Shelley's friends only Peacock could have known at that time.[2] One should add that Peacock would have endorsed Godwin's recommendations of the major classics. More important, the new friends studied and translated together in 1813 during Shelley's stay at Bracknell (within walking distance of Chertsey) and on their visit to Scotland that autumn. Towards the end of their stay in Edinburgh Shelley wrote to Hogg that he had read Homer, Tacitus, Cicero's philosophical works, Laplace and Hume, and had translated Greek with Peacock, 'a very mild and agreeable man, and a good scholar'.[3] This shared study continued while Shelley was in England, living within reach of Peacock's new home at Marlow until the elopement with Mary, and then in Marlow itself. The 'Memoirs of Shelley' tell us that: 'The whole of the winter 1815–16 was passed quietly at Bishopgate. Mr. Hogg often walked down from London; and I, as before, walked over from Marlow. This winter was, as Mr. Hogg expressed it, a mere Atticism. Our studies were exclusively Greek.'[4]

With Shelley's general enthusiasm went the desire to learn to read Greek in the original; the habit, inspired partly by Peacock's translations in 1812 of choruses from Sophocles, of

[1] 29 July 1812: *Letters*, ed. F. L. Jones, 2 vols. (Oxford, 1964), I, 316–18 (throughout this book, I have normalised minor points of spelling and punctuation in Shelley's letters).
[2] J. A. Notopoulos, *The platonism of Shelley* (Duke University Press, 1949), pp. 40 ff. For Shelley's reading at this time, see also K. N. Cameron, *The young Shelley* (London, 1951), chapter 6; and *Shelley and his circle 1773–1822*, ed. Cameron.
[3] 26 Nov. 1813: *Letters*, ed. Jones, I, 380.
[4] Halliford, VIII, 99–100

21

translating works such as Plato's; the effect of Greek thought and Greek society on Shelley's political ideas; and the use of Greek myths and legends in his poetry. One does not have to share Notopoulos's uncritical respect for Shelley's 'platonism', or overlook his frequently self-dramatising use of Greek myth, to acknowledge Peacock's part in widening Shelley's mind from its narrowly early-Godwinian interests.

Once the scholar has collected quite straight-faced this detailed evidence, the critic in him is bound to look at it more quizzically, with the critic's curiosity and doubts about the value of the classicism. It is difficult to satisfy this curiosity, because Peacock rarely bothered to justify his studies: he himself is a scholar and perfectly straight-faced about it. For all one can tell from those scholarly details, Peacock and Shelley might have been ordering bottles of medicine. In fact they spoke of Greek as such: 'I have employed Greek in large doses,' wrote Shelley to Hogg, 'and I consider it the only sure remedy for diseases of the mind.'[1] And any bottle will do: it is difficult to get past the idea of Greek as a homogeneous commodity merely bottled and labelled by different classical authors.

Peacock was in fact a scholar, conscientious but unreflecting. Like Hogg he hated textual and lexical pedantry, but like Hogg believed in a careful reading of the original. This seriousness had a limited distinction in a self-taught man in an age when such seriousness was neglected even at the universities (a favourite hobby-horse of Peacock's). But the typical pride of the self-taught man diverted him from reflecting enough on the value or relevance of what he had taught himself. One reads right through Peacock's articles on Greek literature[2] and through Hogg's classical contributions to the *Edinburgh review* and elsewhere,[3] without finding a glimmer of the doubts which Nietzsche so strongly expressed about his own classical training. Nietzsche's criticisms have inwardness and authority because he himself had been a Professor of Classical Philology. Because of this his varied points, of which a convenient cross-section has

[1] 2 Oct. 1821: *Letters*, ed. Jones, ii, 360.
[2] See Halliford, x, especially the review of Müller and Donaldson's *History of Greek literature*, 163 ff.
[3] W. Scott, *Jefferson Hogg* (London, 1951), p. 279, prints a full list.

been translated by Professor William Arrowsmith,[1] may be used as a framework for appraising Peacock's classicism.

Nietzsche's first criticism was that the nineteenth century's notion of the Greek spirit was really a reflection of its own *Zeitgeist*. Here Peacock at least had the negative virtue that he was immune to the popular, Romantic Hellenism of his age. That popular taste grew when Byron returned from his Greek tour with the sun, ruins and battlefields of the first cantos of *Childe Harold's pilgrimage*. About the same time Lord Elgin brought to England his Marbles, which in 1816 were exhibited in the British Museum. The idea of serene beauty and sexual frankness that Keats and many others took from Greek and pseudo-Greek sculpture does seep through to *Crotchet Castle*. But despite some of his own poems Peacock was severe on that thread of popular taste that led from *Childe Harold* to the ruins of Mrs Hemans's *Modern Greece* (1817) and included the 'amorous mythology' of the Greekish Cockneys and of Moore's *The epicurean*. Finally, although Peacock saw ancient Greece as the home of *intellectual* liberty, he did not share his age's idealisation of the *political* liberty of Athens and the related enthusiasm for modern Greek independence.

Not only was he immune, he vigorously attacked the shallow Hellenism of his age through his criticisms of Moore and Barry Cornwall. But we have to weigh this virtue of seeing through what was represented by Moore, against Peacock's unawareness of what was represented by Keats and Shelley in intention and by Goethe in achievement.

For Goethe represented to Nietzsche the ideal of a creative scholar. He did not superimpose modern ideals but recognised how much in antiquity was alien or repugnant. Nietzsche said that

If the world at large ever discovered how unmodern the classics really are, the classicists would lose their jobs as teachers.[2]

If it were not for the traditional glorification of the classics, modern men would shrink from them in horror.[3]

Our classicists lack a genuine pleasure in the violent and powerful aspects of the ancient world.[4]

---

[1] *Arion, a quarterly journal of classical culture* (University of Texas Press), II, no. 1 (1963), 5–18, and II, no. 2 (1963), 5–27.
[2] *Ibid.* II, no. 2, 15. [3] *Ibid.* II, no. 1, 11. [4] *Ibid.* II, no. 2, 19.

However, Goethe was concerned with relating to his own age whatever *could* be assimilated from antiquity; and he achieved this assimilation as a creative writer:

> Remember how much Goethe knew of the classical world; surely less than a classicist, but yet enough to grapple with it with significant results. One *should not* know more of a thing than he could create. Moreover, the only means of really *understanding* something is by trying to *create* it. Try to live classically... [1]

Peacock seems to have been 'immune' or 'impervious' to this kind of classicism: he neither recognised it in others nor followed it himself. Firstly he tames Greek literature. He justifies frequently his idea of the sophists and their 'clear dispassionate investigation of truth'. But most of the Greek seriousness was for him absorbed by the philosophers and historians, leaving the poetry and drama with 'beauty'. He lacked 'a genuine pleasure in the violent and powerful aspects of the ancient world'. He ignored, too, the alien elements of Greek ethics. When in *Headlong Hall* he generalises from the relation of Ulysses to his crew, one detects public-school ethics and disguised Christianity. [2]

A second question raised by Nietzsche's remarks on Goethe, how far Peacock made creative use of the classics, goes outside the scope of this chapter. But the third question can be posed: how did Peacock relate his classicism to his own age? How did he balance classical and modern literature, in his critical assessment and more simply in his reading habits? 'Soyons de notre siècle', wrote Nietzsche, '—a standpoint which no-one forgets more easily than the classicist-to-be.' [3] To fix Peacock's stance we need some terms of comparison, especially tangible examples of the extremes of open and closed minds.

An unbelievably perfect case of one extreme—a mind closed like a vice—is provided in a digression in Hogg's *Life of Shelley*. It describes an acquaintance of Hogg's, a cleric of leisure:

> This excellent scholar and clergyman had no family; his clerical duties were none, or trifling; he was not a man to neglect any duty,

---

[1] *Arion*, ii, no. 2, 23.
[2] Halliford, i, 34–5 (chapter 4). Contrast Nietzsche's paragraph on *The Greek ideal. What did the Greeks admire in Odysseus?*, *Arion*, ii, no. 1, 12.
[3] *Ibid.* ii, no. 2, 6.

of superior, or inferior, obligation; and he had a competent or moderate income, derived from private sources, and independent of ecclesiastical stipends and benefices.[1]

He follows a regular and closed circuit of study:

I read nothing but Greek. I have a three-years' course of Greek authors, which I go over every three years...

Homer is an exception to my three-years' course—the only one. I read him every year.

I reside in a country town; and I go every year to the sea-side in the summer, during the long days, for a month. I read a book of the 'Iliad' every day before dinner, and a book of the 'Odyssey' daily after dinner. In a month there are twenty-four week-days; there being twenty-four books in each poem, it just does it.

The sea-side is the proper place to read Homer; he speaks so much of the sea. I throw in the 'Hymns'—there are commonly two or three rainy days in the four weeks, when I cannot take a walk; so I always contrive to throw in the 'Hymns' and the 'Frogs and Mice'.[2]

He has the self-conscious contempt for Roman literature typical of early nineteenth-century Hellenism:

I read a few pages of Virgil and of Cicero two or three times in the year, just to satisfy myself that although they are very clever, very good in their way certainly, they are not to be compared with the Greek writers, but are immeasurably inferior in all respects; that it is a waste of time for a man who can read Greek to read their writings.[3]

He hardly glances at modern works, and reads the papers on Sundays more to avoid reading pagan authors than to understand his own world.

On Sunday it is different. I do not read the classical authors; it would not be proper. I look over the newspapers very lightly...A newspaper once a week, and very little of it, is sufficient surely...since the publication of the last Greek author of acknowledged merit...there has been no event that we need trouble ourselves much about.[4]

He unites conventional Christianity ('our blessed religion') with eighteenth-century closet-scepticism—'When two or three scholars get together, we talk, you know, like heathens.'[5]

[1] T. J. Hogg, *The life of Shelley*, ed. H. Wolfe, 2 vols. (London, 1933), ii, 113.
[2] *Ibid.* pp. 112 and 113.   [3] *Ibid.*   [4] *Ibid.*
[5] *Ibid.* p. 113. This is exactly the safe library-scepticism that Leslie Stephen diagnoses in the eighteenth century. (*English literature and society in the eighteenth century*, London, 1904, p. 144.)

His Greek cannot be separated from tea, pedestrianism and dinner:

I rise early; I always did; and I take one mouthful of air before breakfast—no more. I begin to read immediately after breakfast, that I may get a walk and appetite before dinner, which is essential...

I have my tea pretty soon after dinner; it freshens me up. I cannot read again until I have had my tea. When I have finished my book, in the summer—in the winter it would be ridiculous—I take a turn round the garden, when I am at home; when I am by the sea-side, on the sands close to the sea. I am not much of a supper-man; I never was; but I love just to play with a crab before going to bed; or with something of the kind, and to swallow a spoonful or two of warm negus.[1]

Hogg considers this man 'to have actually and so admirably practised...the Tranquillity of life':[2] but it sounds more like the elaborate fending-off of boredom by imposing on oneself a routine as a duty. It exists not as intellectual activity but as a drug.[3] The whole passage describes one extreme, the worst kind of *tea, Greek and pedestrianism.*

Hogg also indicates the opposite extreme in contrasting that classicist with Shelley. He contrasts the poet's explorative mind with the classicist's closed circuit,

the regular orbit of an ordinary mind, although of a very high order, to whom the erratic course of a transcendent genius—of a comet that blazes across the zenith once in a century, would be perplexing and incomprehensible.[4]

Now Hogg's typically ambiguous tone here indicates his uncertain position. But clearly Hogg stood nearer the first extreme than the second. Evidence, confirmed everywhere else in his writings, is at hand in the immediate context of the passage just drawn on. Hogg usually spent his Law Vacations in classical and legal studies, but had recently been catechised by Godwin on his general reading. The conversation went like this:

'Do you never read English books?'
'Yes, sometimes.'
'Of what kind?'

---

[1] Hogg, *Life of Shelley*, p. 112.   [2] *Ibid.* p. 114.
[3] Cf. Nietzsche on 'learning as a drug', *Arion*, II, no. 2, 27.
[4] Scott, *Jefferson Hogg*, p. 114.

'Voyages and travels, history and biography.'
'All of them modern?'
'Almost entirely new publications.'
'Have you read none of our old English writers?'
'Very few. Shakespeare; little besides.'
I was strongly advised to take the old English writers in hand.[1]

Hogg therefore took home Chaucer and (prompted by another acquaintance) Richardson. He liked the *Canterbury Tales* but otherwise found little in these authors: 'it really seemed to me that these good people were dead, quite dead, fairly dead; they had died a natural death, and it was vain to try to resuscitate them'.[2] So he turned in relief to borrow a copy of Aristophanes from the cleric he describes. This complete episode is a faithful diagram of Hogg's reading habits.

The relative flexibility of Peacock's classicism can be fixed by showing that he is far from the Shelleyan extreme but not so far as Hogg. Thus Peacock, who was at first an intellectual leader for Shelley, was soon overtaken by Shelley, who became the intellectual leader in classical studies for all his friends: one can see this vividly in his study, acute appreciation, and translation of Plato, and the reactions to this in the letters of Peacock, Hogg and Leigh Hunt. It was as if Shelley saw the point and use of what for Peacock remained 'interests'. One reason for this overtaking lies in their different attitudes to study. Peacock, Hogg and Trelawny were all impressed by Shelley's eager, even greedy hunger for knowledge and his uncanny habit of complete and prolonged abstraction in a book. Hogg tells us how he and Shelley would begin reading a book together but that Shelley would race ahead—'his eagle glance, his comprehensive grasp, his inconceivable quickness, and miraculous powers and faculty of apprehension, enabled him to seize and to master in minutes what his less highly gifted fellow-learners acquired in hours, or days, or weeks'.[3] This description rightly links the two kinds of 'quickness'—mere swiftness of reading, and 'quickness... of apprehension'. The latter attributes to Shelley that aspect of genius which Johnson saw in Shakespeare as 'vigilance of observation and perspicacity,

---

[1] *Ibid.* p. 102.   [2] *Ibid.* p. 109.
[3] *Ibid.* p. 72.

in the highest degree curious and attentive',[1] and on which T. S. Eliot commented, 'Some can absorb knowledge, the more tardy must sweat for it. Shakespeare acquired more essential history from Plutarch than most men could from the whole British Museum.'[2] In contrast, Peacock studied for exercise and comfort, not exertion and expansion. He looked on his authors as companions and preferred old friends to new: 'I shall be very social with the Greek poets, and pass a day occasionally with Plato and Plutarch.'[3] By the time Shelley reversed their rôles and offered to broaden Peacock's reading—with contemporary poetry—Peacock's mind was set; he had no time for *Hyperion*: 'Hogg and I are now reading Demosthenes'.[4] Earlier his proud note on the winter of 1815–16—'Our studies were exclusively Greek'—chimes in exactly with Hogg's Scholar who boasted 'I read nothing but Greek'.

On the other hand, having entertained these worst suspicions, one must show that Peacock was more intelligent and free-minded than Hogg. As Mayoux says in a passage I shall return to later, 'le type Peacock', unlike 'le type Shelley' or 'le type Hogg', tends to hide his essential life, and in letters to act a rôle to please correspondents like Hogg. Hogg's facetious and long-worded letters to Peacock suggest that he saw Peacock as a dilettante and eccentric, and Peacock responded in similar style and character—but only to Hogg. (In confirmation one finds that Shelley and others felt obliged to adapt their style and narrow their topics when writing to Hogg—but not when writing to Peacock.) For example, the letter referring to tea, Greek and pedestrianism is a reply to one of Hogg's which shows *him* as the simple dilettante and *laudator temporis acti*. Hogg writes:

My enjoyments have consisted in taking down many books from the shelves and in replacing them, in changing my abode from this village to the Seashore and from the Seashore to the interior, in riding or

---

[1] Preface to Shakespeare: *Works* (1825), v, 122. The immediate subject is Shakespeare's experience of life, but the phrases are relevant to Johnson's adjoining discussion of his reading.

[2] 'Tradition and the individual talent', in *Selected essays* (London, 1932; reprinted 1951), p. 17.

[3] Letter to Hogg, 20 March 1818: *New Shelley letters*, p. 109.

[4] Letter to Shelley, 4 Dec. 1820: Halliford, viii, 219.

3

Peacock on the Regency

Largely because of the dogmatic finality of its style, and the prominence given it by Shelley's reply, 'The four ages of poetry' (1820) has fixed itself in most people's minds as Peacock's complete view of poetry. But it must be balanced by a better essay, written two years earlier but unpublished until this century: 'An essay on fashionable literature'.[1] It deserves emphasis and generous quotation because it is still rarely noticed, whereas 'The four ages' has been dwelt on for a century and a half. The 'Essay' should be used not as a replacement for 'The four ages' but as strongly conflicting evidence which will help upset generalisations about Peacock's mind and position. It gives a positive and coherent account of the spirit of the age, an account dramatised in *Nightmare Abbey*.

Peacock first describes the modern phenomenon of 'fashionable literature'. It aims only to amuse 'fashionable society', the growing company of the idle, bored and unthinking (I, II). It 'catches on' by striking superficial novelty and 'goes out' quickly for the same reason: 'as the soul of fashion is novelty, the books and dress of the season go out of date together; and to be amused this year by that which amused others twelve months ago would be to plead guilty to the heinous charge of having lived out of the world' (III). What is fashionable is *ipso facto* ephemeral and so demands an ever-increasing production, and ever larger and swifter 'stream of new books' (IV). Again like clothes, literary fashion is dictated by 'authority'— that is to say by the Reviews which, to complete the vicious circle, themselves 'form a very prominent feature in this transitory literature' (IX).

So far the idea remains general and little illustrated. But we

---

[1] First printed in full in *Works*, Halliford Edition, ed. H. F. B. Brett-Smith and C. E. Jones, 10 vols. (London, 1924–34), VIII, 263 ff. The Roman numerals in the account that follows refer to the numbered paragraphs of the *Essay*.

are impressed by Peacock's grasp of the mechanism behind the taste of an age—the reciprocal influence of manners and litera- ture, and the way popular literature is an index of the age.

The nature of this lighter literature, and the changes which it has undergone with the fashions of the last twenty years, deserve con- sideration for many reasons, and afford a subject of speculation which may be amusing, and I would add instinctive, were I not fearful of terrifying my readers in the outset. As every age has its own character, manners, and amusements, which are influenced even in their lightest forms by the fundamental features of the time, the moral and political character of the age or nation may be read by an attentive observer even in its lightest literature, how remote soever *prima facie* from morals and politics. (v)

He also points out the processes, more insidious than direct censorship, by which the force of real literature is deadened and prevented from stirring the mental inertia of the country. For instance:

In orthodox families that have the advantage of being acquainted with such a phænomenon as a reading parson (which is fortunately as rare as the Atropus Belladonna—a hunting parson, on the other hand, a much more innocent variety, being as common as the Solanum Nigrum—) or any tolerably literate variety of political or theological orthodoxy—the reading of the young ladies is very much influenced by his advice. He is careful not to prohibit, unless in extreme cases— Voltaire, for example...for prohibition is usually accompanied with longing for forbidden fruit—it is much more easy to exclude by silence, and pre-occupy by counter-recommendation. (xxiv)

For Peacock real literature is 'to awaken the mind, not en- chain it. Poetry precedes philosophy, but true poetry prepares its path...Cervantes—Rabelais—Swift—Voltaire—Fielding— have led fancy against opinion...Mr. Scott's successes have been attributed in a great measure to his keeping clear of opinion'. (xxv, xxvi)

The 'Essay' comes to focus on the Reviews. By the 1810s they have come to show more power but less honesty, generosity or knowledge (ix): each is blinkered by a political and literary faction into making inflated and insulated reputations—'All these have their own little exclusive circles of favor and faction, and it is very amusing to trace in any one of them half a dozen favoured names circling in the preeminence of glory in that little circle, and scarcely named or known out of it.' (xv) A writer's success depends on his contacts, the chain of influence between himself, a literary coterie, his bookseller and a reviewer. (xxi)

This stage in the argument, though again general, discerns an insular and exclusive spirit that was particularly strong in the Regency. Bulwer-Lytton in 1833 looked back on it as 'the day of literary jobbing; they created sinecures for the worthless',[1] when a typical group was the one around Murray the publisher: 'the Author's *clique* of Albemarle Street...they praised each other—were *the* literary class, and thought Stewart Rose a greater man than Wordsworth—peace be with them—they are no more—and fame no longer hangs from the nostrils of Samuel Rogers.'[2] The quality of Regency literature suffered from each group's wilful deafness to outside criticism. The age in fact encouraged even Peacock to shut himself off proudly from most intellectual society, and to avoid meeting or reading anyone who might have upset his insular tastes in modern thought— Horne Tooke, Knight, Forsyth and Drummond. He harks back nostalgically to the publication of 'one of the most admirable pieces of philosophical criticism that has appeared in any language: Knight's *Principles of taste*. One of the best metaphysical and one of the best moral treatises in the language appeared at the same time. The period seemed to promise the revival of philosophy.'

Exactly because of this taste, and his idea of the classics, we are uneasy at Peacock's claim that the Reviews have declined intellectually because they contain 'much less classicality and very much less philosophy'. (ix: cf. xix and xx) He is more convincing about the reviewer's methods.

Their basic method is to depend for spurious authority on the editorial *we*:

---

[1] Bulwer-Lytton, *England and the English* (London, 1834), i, 148 n.
[2] *Ibid.* pp. 147–8. Cf. Crabbe's experience in London in 1817: 'I daily met all our principal Rhymers [i.e. Rogers's circle] except Lord Biron who is not in England and the Poets of the Lakes, who form a Society by themselves; and, at once exclude and are excluded by our pride and theirs.' (A. M. Broadley and W. Jerrold, *The romance of an elderly poet*, London, 1931, p. 181.)

The *country gentlemen*[1] appear to be in the habit of considering reviews as the joint productions of a body of men who meet at a sort of green board, where all new literary productions are laid before them for impartial consideration, and the merits of each having been fairly canvassed, some aged and enlightened censor records the opinion of the council and promulgates its definitive judgment to the world. The solitary quack becomes a medical board. The solitary play-frequenter becomes a committee of amateurs of the drama. The elector of Old Sarum is a respectable body of constituents. This is an all-pervading quackery. (XII)

Another favourite method 'pronounces unintelligible whatever is in any degree obscure, more especially if it be really matter of deeper sense than the critic likes to be molested with. A critic is bound to study for an author's meaning, and not to make his own stupidity another's reproach.' (XVIII) Here Peacock specifies *The Edinburgh review* on *The excursion* and 'Christabel'.

The last part of the 'Essay' attacks the review of 'Christabel', which is probably by Moore,[2] as 'a tissue of ignorance, folly, and *fraud*'. (XXVIII) The fraud lies in misrepresenting Coleridge's statements on his metre; the ignorance is a matter of unimaginativeness put forward as a virtue by means of dull witticisms. Peacock traces some half-dozen 'standard jokes' repeated through the Reviews of the last thirty years and used several times in Moore's article: 'One...is the profundity of the Bathos...Another is that the work...is a narcotic, and sets the unfortunate critic to sleep. A third is that it is unintelligible... A fourth, that the author is insane...' (XXX) Peacock in fact understates this case against Moore, who, like Hazlitt in his reviews of 'Christabel' and of Coleridge's prose works,[3] displays no argument or attempt to understand but only a dull barrage of variations on the standard jokes.

But Peacock attacks Moore's destructive stupidity as part of the positive process of elucidating Coleridge. He gives for

[1] 'A generic term applied by courtesy to the profoundly ignorant of all classes.' (Peacock's footnote.)

[2] Convincing reasons for assigning this article to Moore, rather than Hazlitt or Jeffrey, are given by E. Schneider, 'The Unknown Critic of Christabel', *P.M.L.A.* LXX (June, 1955), 417–32. See also below, pp. 249–50.

[3] His review of 'Christabel' (*The examiner*, 2 June 1816, pp. 348–9) is no more creditable than Moore's. His other accounts of Coleridge will be discussed in chapter 8.

example (xxxii) a good account of the ballad-manner of 'Christabel' which may make the poem nearer a tame eighteenth-century mode than the 'wild and singularly original and beautiful poem' that Byron admired, but clears it from the cant, obscurity and mystification which was all Moore and Hazlitt could see. Most to Peacock's credit is his elucidation of the psychological meaning of the Conclusion to Part ii, on the relationship of a father and son—on this passage Moore, with that obtuse brand of 'common sense' often attributed to Peacock, calls down the insult Nonsense—'the third standard joke for the third time' (p. 287). It is worth pressing how common was Moore's reaction to these poems: no more intelligent review appeared until John Sterling's in 1828[1] and H. N. Coleridge's in 1834.[2] It may well be objected that, in common with other readers of the 1810s and with Hazlitt, who called it 'beneath criticism', Peacock ignored 'The pains of sleep' which was published in the same volume. No doubt the author of 'Palmyra' and 'Rhododaphne' found 'Christabel' superficially more accessible. But he obviously found more in it than medieval stage-décor. If appreciation of Coleridge were the crucial test of Peacock's intelligence, Peacock passes it here.

The 'Essay' breaks off uncompleted, unrevised and unpublished. Its value is as 'evidence' about Peacock's mind, not as a solid piece of criticism. Compared with *Nightmare Abbey*, which develops the same insights, the first part of the 'Essay' is a sketch: it wanders from epigrammatic assertions to leisurely paragraphs of facetious imagery that embroider rather than argue; it is more limited in scope and less specific in reference than the novel, and less forcible because not in dramatic form. But it shares with the novel a good working diagnosis of the characteristics of the age that are driven by cause and effect both ways round the vicious circle of education, criticism, literature and manners. The second part of the 'Essay' shows two things often denied Peacock: that he admired much of Wordsworth and Coleridge, and that he could read poetry imaginatively.

[1] 'An Appeal Apologetic from Philip Drunk to Peter Sober', *The Athenaeum* (2 July 1828).
[2] 'The poetical works of S. T. Coleridge', *Quarterly review*, ciii (August, 1834), 1 ff.

While I have used it as mitigating evidence, it could be argued that the 'Essay on fashionable literature' was *superseded* by 'The four ages of poetry' as Peacock's view of contemporary poetry. For immediately after the 'Essay' was written there begins a new attitude that leads directly to 'The four ages'. This new attitude is impatient rejection, and can be traced through the letters, reaching its worst in a letter of 1821 which brushes aside Shelley's request for a parcel of new books: 'the present state of literature is so thoroughly vile that there is scarcely any new publication worth looking at, much less buying'.[1]

This impatience comes out first in references to Byron:

I think it necessary to 'make a stand' against the 'encroachments' of black bile. The fourth canto of *Childe Harold* is really too bad. I cannot consent to be *auditor tantum* of this systematical 'poisoning' of the 'mind' of the 'reading public'.[2]

This is a justifiable reaction used in *Nightmare Abbey*. But in strong contrast to Shelley, Peacock seems mainly bored by Byron, and 'philosophically' remote from the actual man and poem. How much more lively is Shelley's reply in its concern and exasperation, and its acute attribution of Byron's 'sublime misanthropy' to mean self-disgust:

I entirely agree with what you say about *Childe Harold*. The spirit in which it is written is, if insane, the most wicked and mischievous insanity that ever was given forth. It is a kind of obstinate and self-willed folly in which he hardens himself...For its real root is very different from its apparent one, and nothing can be less sublime than the true source [i.e. his debauched life in Italy]. He...is heartily and deeply discontented with himself, and contemplating in the distorted mirror of his own thoughts, the nature and the destiny of man, what can he behold but objects of contempt and despair?[3]

He has no illusions about Byron's at once fashionable and vulgarising works:

He touched a chord to which a million hearts responded, and the coarse music which he produced to please them, disciplined him to the perfection to which he now approaches.[4]

[1] 3 June 1821: Halliford, VIII, 221.   [2] 30 May 1818: *ibid*. p. 193.
[3] 17 or 18 Dec. 1818: *Letters*, ed. F. L. Jones, 2 vols. (Oxford, 1964), II, 57–8.
[4] 18 June 1822: *ibid*. II, 436.

Equally lively is his account of Byron's changed life with Teresa Guiccioli, and of *Don Juan,*

which is astonishingly fine...I despair of rivalling Lord Byron, as well I may...there is not a word [in Canto v] which the most rigid assertor of the dignity of human nature could desire to be cancelled: it fulfils in a certain degree what I have long preached of producing something wholly new and relative to the age—and yet surpassingly beautiful. It may be vanity, but I think I see the trace of my earnest exhortations to him to create something wholly new.[1]

Peacock likewise praised *Don Juan*: '*Cain* is very fine; *Sardanapalus* I think finer[!] *Don Juan* is best of all.'[2] But what a difference of manner! Shelley is excited and involved, proud that he may have helped but envious that he has not written it; and enthusiastically exaggerating its merit, but striking and exact on the *kind* of merit ('something wholly new and relative to the age'); and forestalling the charge of inhumanity that had been widely made about the earlier cantos. In contrast Peacock says no more than the terse aphorism quoted above: it is difficult to tell whether he really admires those poems or whether he is merely humouring Shelley. In either case the effect is to say *That's my opinion* and to close the debate. His letters about contemporary literature never suggest excitement, sudden discovery, or growing knowledge and interest or even revulsion. They show no 'free play of mind', either toward the subject or toward Shelley in opening a discussion or inviting disagreement.

This manner, obvious even in Peacock's mixed reactions to Byron, is even more striking in his completely negative reaction to Keats. Here again Shelley was one of the first to recognise Keats's better poems, and to distinguish the authentic from the morass of false 'cockney poetry' in Keats and others:

the fragment called *Hyperion* promises for him that he is destined to become one of the first writers of the age.—His other things are imperfect enough, and what is worse written in the bad sort of style which is becoming fashionable among those who fancy that they are imitating Hunt and Wordsworth.—But of all these things nothing is worse than a volume by Barry Cornwall entitled the Sicilian Story.[3]

[1] 8 Aug. 1821: *ibid.* II, 323.   [2] 28 Feb. 1822: Halliford, VIII, 228.
[3] 29 Oct. 1820: *Letters*, ed. Jones, II, 239.

Again characteristic of Shelley is his eagerness to make personal contact and to help the genius he admired:

Where is Keats now? I am anxiously expecting him in Italy where I shall take care to bestow every possible attention on him. I consider his a most valuable life, and am deeply interested in his safety. I intend to be the physician both of his body and his soul, to keep the one warm and to teach the other Greek and Spanish. I am aware indeed in part that I am nourishing a rival who will far surpass me and this is an additional motive and will be an added pleasure.[1]

It must be recorded against Peacock that by 1820 Shelley was sending his more detailed letters on literature to other friends. The above outbursts were to Marianne Hunt; ten days later he sent a shortened and more hesitant recommendation to Peacock: 'I dare say you have not time to read it; but it is certainly an astonishing piece of writing'.[2] He guessed rightly; Peacock replied:

If I should live to the age of Methusalem, and have uninterrupted literary leisure, I should not find time to read Keats' Hyperion. Hogg and I are now reading Demosthenes...Considering poetical reputation as a prize to be obtained by a certain species of exertion, and that the sort of thing that obtains this prize is the drivelling doggrel published under the name of Barry Cornwall, I think but one conclusion possible, that to a rational ambition poetical reputation is not only not to be desired, but most earnestly to be deprecated. The truth, I am convinced, is that there is no longer a poetical audience among the higher class of minds, that moral, political, and physical science have entirely withdrawn from poetry the attention of all whose attention is worth having; and that the poetical reading public being composed of the mere dregs of the intellectual community, the most sufficing passport to their favour must rest on the mixture of a little easily-intelligible portion of mawkish sentiment with an absolute negation of reason and knowledge. These I take it to be the prime and sole elements of Mr. Barry Cornwall's *Madrigals*. Yours ever most faithfully, T. L. Peacock.[3]

The manner of this letter is as worth dwelling on as the opinions. The crushing opening rejection of Keats and the terse and abrupt ending suggest that Peacock wanted to be cutting to

[1] *Letters*, ed. Jones, II, 240. [2] *Ibid.* p. 244.
[3] 4 Dec. 1820: Halliford, VIII, 219–20.

Shelley. He implies scorn of Shelley's own poetic ambitions: to emulate Barry Cornwall is contemptible; to differ is futile. Admittedly he is taking up another part of Shelley's letter which had expressed hopelessness—'the reception the public have given me might [go] far enough to damp any man's enthusiasm'.[1] But Peacock's tone is not that of sympathy: even while correcting *Prometheus unbound* for the press he had lost real touch with Shelley's poetry. What else could explain the tactlessness and cynicism of a later letter?—

The poetry of your *Adonais* is very beautiful; but when you write you never think of your audience...If you would consider who and what the readers of poetry are, and adapt your compositions to the depth of their understandings and the current of their sympathies, you would attain the highest degree of poetical fame.[2]

That earlier letter of 4 December 1820 is undiscriminating in its opinions. Keats and Barry Cornwall are all one to Peacock, whereas Shelley, although himself spoilt by the influence of bad Regency verse, was nevertheless critical and interested enough to come to see the difference. And Peacock sweeps *all* intelligent readers suddenly away from poetry to 'useful literature'—as suddenly, significantly enough, as Peacock himself turned from poetry and boating to East India House. The main thread of the letter is in effect an outline of the contemporary 'Four ages of poetry'.

*

The sting of 'The four ages' is in its tail, its attack on contemporary poetry; but it is worth summarising the historical thesis intended to give the attack its body. Our summary will be fairest if we keep to Peacock's own words.

Poetry, like 'the world', may be said to have four ages, but in a different order: the first age of poetry being the age of iron; the second, of gold, the third of silver; and the fourth, of brass.
The first, or iron age of poetry, is that in which rude bards celebrate in rough numbers the exploits of ruder chiefs...The golden age of poetry finds its materials in the age of iron. This age begins when poetry begins to be retrospective, when something like a more

---

[1] *Letters*, ed. Jones, II, 245.   [2] 28 Feb. 1822: Halliford, VIII, 228.

extended system of civil polity is established...traditional national poetry is reconstructed and brought like chaos into order and form...

Then comes the silver age, or the poetry of civilized life. This poetry is of two kinds, imitative and original. The imitative consists in recasting, and giving an exquisite polish to, the poetry of the age of gold...The original is chiefly comic, didactic, or satiric...

Then comes the age of brass, which by rejecting the polish and the learning of the age of silver, and taking a retrograde stride to the barbarisms and crude traditions of the age of iron, professes to return to nature and revive the age of gold...

The iron age of classical poetry may be called the bardic; the golden, the Homeric; the silver, the Virgilian; and the brass, the Nonnic.[1]

The corresponding ages of modern poetry are the Dark Ages, the Renaissance, the Augustan Age and (to use our term) the Romantic Age.

The essay can best be evaluated by asking a number of questions. Is it serious? Is it original? Is it convincing?

Is it serious? It is important to take seriously as much as possible, for it has too often been dismissed by being called 'provocative'.[2] It is provocative, but none the less serious in that it demands answers.

Of course its manner *is* provocative, often outrageous. It is not a solemn 'cultural history' but more an exercise in close logic or the appearance of it. This logic and pattern of contrasts, although leading to a sting in the tail, is not simple: each age, while contrasting with Peacock's own, is incidentally damned —the monkish ignorance and superstition of the middle ages, the 'Venetian carnival' of Elizabethan drama, and so on. Again, much of the force of his account of the four ages of antiquity depends on our detecting disguised portraits of modern figures —as Mayoux says, 'pour le barde royal, lisez Southey—pour l'auteur de ballades guerrières, lisez Scott'.[3] On the ethics and poetry of the heroic age Peacock is more like Swift than Johnson in his universal destructiveness, and his winning and

[1] Halliford, VIII, 3, 6, 8, 10 and 13.
[2] E.g. 'The whole article is written in a vein of mocking wit which makes it a joy to read, but to take it as a serious attack on poetry would be absurd'— H. F. B. Brett-Smith, ed., *Peacock's four ages of poetry, Shelley's defence...* (Oxford, 1921), p. x.
[3] J.-J. Mayoux, *Un Epicuréen anglais: Thomas Love Peacock* (Paris, 1933), p. 326.

betrayal of the reader's confidence in his intentions as praise turns to satire. Our confidence is similarly seduced and betrayed when Peacock's bland reasonableness in the first half of the essay makes us assent to criticisms which in the second half become more scathing and extreme. Having agreed that the ancient age of brass, typified by Nonnus, 'professes to return to nature and to revive the age of gold. This is the second childhood of poetry',[1] we find outselves swept along by the pseudo-historical thesis to the pseudo-parallel of modern brass-age poets 'raking up the ashes of dead savages to find gewgaws and rattles for the grown babies of the age'.[2] Worse still, the charge is now fired not just at a modern Nonnus like Procter but at all modern poets. Above all, however, there is the particular provocation of all Shelley's views and poetic ambitions. His poetry too is damned, first with that of the age and then in a final direct hit:

As to that small portion of our contemporary poetry, which is neither descriptive, nor narrative, nor dramatic, and which, for want of a better name, may be called ethical, the most distinguished portion of it [consists] merely of querulous, egotistical rhapsodies, to express the writer's high dissatisfaction with the world and every thing in it...[3]

Is it original? Only in the provocativeness just described. The essay does not *sound* simple-minded or commonplace because the points are sharpened in terms of a particular opposition. Unlike Jeffrey or Hazlitt, Peacock is not confidently expounding to the passive minds of review-readers or lecture audience, handing out a ready-made guide to 'what's new'. But, if one examines the points and jokes themselves, and if one reads extensively the reviews and lectures of the 1800s and 1820s, then 'The four ages', far from being in defiance of the spirit of the age, sinks back into the age's commonplaces. It belongs to one strain of the age's taste, as expressed by those journalist-middlemen of ideas whom Peacock thought he scorned. He is here a 'sign of the times' despite himself.

Further, it belongs to a not very creditable side of the age's taste, a side at once obtuse and confident. As early as 1802 we find the urge to master and to sort away the new element in

---

[1] Halliford, viii, 13.   [2] *Ibid.* p. 19.   [3] *Ibid.* pp. 22-3.

poetry: Jeffrey, writing on Southey's 'Thalaba', in the very first article of the *Edinburgh review*, summarises the motives and sources of 'the new school'.[1] Again Jeffrey's general contrast of Crabbe with the new school builds on hopeless non-readings of individual poems.

> Mr. Wordsworth...has 'thought fit to compose a piece, illustrating this copious subject [love] by one single thought. A lover trots away to see his mistress one fine evening, staring all the way at the moon: when he comes to her door,
>
> > O mercy! to myself I cried,
> > If Lucy should be dead!
>
> And there the poem ends![2]

And there too the commentary ends! Such misfires make us recognise, with all the useful correctiveness of his incidental common-sense and the positive appreciation of Crabbe, how much in Jeffrey is 'trenchant ignorance'.[3] The ignorance or unimaginativeness is—to use Wordsworth's own distinction— 'sheer, honest insensibility, and stupidity' more than malice.[4] The trenchancy and confidence do the damage: it is the journalist's urge to appear master of the situation. It is the opposite of the common reader's impulse, which is to master outstanding poems, very tentatively build up from these impressions a coherent picture of one poet, then as tentatively to see his relation to other poets and eventually to other periods.

So far this shows only a general resemblance to 'The four ages of poetry'; and Jeffrey's ludicrous map of 1802 was soon superseded. But later maps are strikingly close to Peacock's. Hazlitt, like Peacock, saw the Romantics as a retrogression: 'They were for bringing poetry back to its primitive simplicity and state of nature, as [Rousseau] was for bringing society back to the "savage state".'[5] Macaulay, in 1828, saw the ages of poetry in terms of the seasons and the early nineteenth century as a St Martin's Summer: 'Pleasing and ingenious imitations...of the great masters appear...we look on [them]

---

[1] *Edinburgh review*, I (1802), 63 ff.   [2] *Ibid.* XII (1808), 136.

[3] George Eliot's phrase applied to Mr Vincey in *Middlemarch*.

[4] *The letters of William and Dorothy Wordsworth*, ed. E. de Selincourt (Oxford, 1937), I, 149.

[5] 'On the living poets', *Complete works*, ed. P. P. Howe, 21 vols. (London, 1930–4), V, 163.

with feelings similar to those with which we see flowers disposed in vases, to ornament the drawing-rooms of a capital.'[1] But as early as 1814 the *Quarterly review* asserted that this cyclical theory had been aired so much that the vicious circle of taste had already completed itself: the public were now inciting Byron and others 'to seek for subjects in the manner of these ruder ages'.[2]

Prominent among other parallels are sneers at the poets' 'characters':

Mr. Scott digs up the poachers and cattle-stealers of the ancient border. Lord Byron cruises for thieves and pirates... Mr. Wordsworth picks up village legends from old women and sextons. (Peacock)[3]

...a mixed rabble of idle apprentices and Botany Bay convicts, female vagrants, gipsies, meek daughters in the family of Christ, of idiot boys and mad mothers, and after them 'owls and night-ravens flew'. (Hazlitt)[4]

...hysterical schoolmasters and sententious leechgatherers. (Jeffrey)[5]

All use the same trick, too, of not talking about 'The Leech-Gatherer' or 'The Giaour', but multiplying them into leechgatherers and pirates and herding them together into a disreputable carnival-mob. As common is the accusation that Wordsworth and others do not represent these characters truly but

invent for themselves certain whimsical and unheard-of beings, to whom they impute some fantastical combination of feelings...

...fantastic and affected peculiarities in the mind or fancy of the author. (Jeffrey)[6]

Peacock echoes those phrases very closely:

Mr. Wordsworth...cannot describe a scene under his own eyes without putting into it the shadow of a Danish boy or the living ghost of Lucy Gray, or some similar phantastical parturition of the moods of his own mind.[7]

Peacock also echoes Jeffrey on Southey:

Every incident...every superstitious usage, or singular tradition,

[1] *Edinburgh review*, XLVII, 13.   [2] *Quarterly review*, XI, 456.
[3] Halliford, VIII, 19.   [4] *Complete works*, ed. Howe, V, 163.
[5] *Edinburgh review*, I, 79.   [6] *Ibid.* XII, 133 and 136.
[7] Halliford, VIII, 18–19.

that appeared to him susceptible of poetical embellishment, or capable of picturesque representation, he has set down for this purpose... When he had filled his commonplace book, he began to write; and his poem is little else than his commonplace book versified. (Jeffrey)[1]

...Mr. Southey wades through ponderous volumes of travels and old chronicles, from which he carefully selects all that is false, useless, and absurd, as being essentially poetical; and when he has a commonplace book full of monstrosities, strings them into an epic. (Peacock)[2]

Beyond this the resemblance is in the style, in the way 'ideas' melt into a standard jargon of insult. *Fantastical* has already been cited: other standard terms are *puling childishness, babyish...puling ..old nursery-maid's vocabulary* (Jeffrey); *drivel* (Hazlitt); *gewgaws and rattles, puling sentimentality, puling driveller, whining* (several times), and *driveller* (Peacock); *mysticisms* (all three writers, and three times in 'The four ages').

This demonstration of close parallels is not intended to show that Peacock borrowed from Jeffrey or Hazlitt. The point is in a way more damning: those ideas and even those very phrases (for cliché ideas circulate in cliché phrases) were 'in the air' and widely passed around as adequate, and Peacock unwittingly took them up without realising how far he was sinking back into a mere 'sign of the times'. That is, the stance of 'Peacock on the Regency' was precarious, and he often slipped back into being 'Peacock in the Regency'.

Is the essay convincing? This question, after the criticisms just made, depends upon the authority of the essay's positive criteria, upon how much weight Peacock can put behind his repeated terms *Reason* and *Utility*.

Amarasinghe thinks they have a double weight: Peacock joins the *Reason* of Johnson's reverence for *Reason, Truth and Nature* with the logical and utilitarian Reason of Bentham and his followers. Peacock also provides the meeting of disciplines looked for by Dr Cox: 'Had the intellectual seriousness of the Benthamites been accompanied by a more educated taste and sensibility, the *Westminster* might have proved an important check to the excesses of Romanticism.'[3]

[1] *Edinburgh review*, I, 77.   [2] Halliford, VIII, 19.
[3] R. G. Cox, 'Nineteenth-century periodical criticism', unpublished Cambridge Ph.D. Thesis (1935), p. 182.

Amarasinghe quotes:

Mr. Moore presents us with a Persian, and Mr. Campbell with a Pennsylvanian tale, both formed on the same principle as Mr. Southey's epics, by extracting from a perfunctory and desultory perusal of a collection of voyages and travels, all that useful investigation would not seek for and that common sense would reject.[1]

which 'has, in its concern for the common-sense realities of human experience and its weighty and antithetical style, a Johnsonian ring'.[2] This is true: the criticism, although not original, is just, and makes convincing use of a distinction Johnson often made and Peacock himself discussed in the 'Essay on fashionable literature'. The phrases and pattern, too, evoke Johnson. But is not the resemblance too uncannily close, verging on pastiche Johnson? Amarasinghe has picked a lucky and outstanding sentence. Does the climactic paragraph of the essay seem authentically Johnsonian?

Now when we consider that it is not to the thinking and studious, and scientific and philosophical part of the community, not to those whose minds are bent on the pursuit and promotion of permanently useful ends and aims, that poets must address their minstrelsy, but to that much larger portion of the reading public, whose minds are not awakened to the desire of valuable knowledge, and who are indifferent to anything beyond being charmed, moved, excited, affected, and exalted: charmed by harmony, moved by sentiment, excited by passion, affected by pathos, and exalted by sublimity: harmony, which is language on the rack of Procrustes; sentiment, which is canting egotism in the mask of refined feeling; passion, which is the commotion of a weak and selfish mind; pathos, which is the whining of an unmanly spirit; and sublimity, which is the inflation of an empty head: when we consider that the great and permanent interests of human society become more and more the main-spring of intellectual pursuit; that in proportion as they become so, the subordinacy of the ornamental to the useful will be more and more seen and acknowledged. . .[3]

—and so the same sentence rolls on for another thirty lines. Rabelais and Swift have contributed as much to this style as Johnson, and, if there is a Johnsonian influence, it is Johnson

[1] Halliford VIII, 20.
[2] U. Amarasinghe, *Dryden and Pope in the early nineteenth century* (Cambridge, 1962), p. 181.   [3] Halliford, VIII, 23–4.

distorted or parodied. It is what the Regency—including outstanding minds like Coleridge—*thought* Johnson was like, the Doctor's thundering knock-you-down manner that can be found in actuality more in the *We say so* of the Regency reviews than in Johnson. Again in conformity with the Regency idea of Johnson and in contrast to the real Johnson, this paragraph shows very little reasoning. The best of Johnson has the cumulative effect of an argument developing itself, with the force of a sequence of logic. Peacock here has only the crushing effect of a preconceived argument used as a steamroller, with the brute force of a steadily increasing and more striking set of assertions. And, as in much of the essay, there is an incongruity between the standard of *utility* and the style used. The style is grandiose and mock-epic, ornamental rather than useful. It is a style in which to push home a *parti pris* but not one in which to think.

If the style fails to give authority to Peacock's ideal of *utility*, so do his particular examples. Who are these minds who have built a pyramid 'into the upper air of intelligence'? We know Peacock had little respect for Bentham or Mill. If pressed, he would, as in the 'Essay on fashionable literature', have brought out people like Horne Tooke, Forsyth, and Drummond. More serious is that, whereas the novels are full of open discussions on the nature of real intellectual power and useful knowledge, in 'The four ages' Peacock's mind is closed. It is Shelley's mind, not Peacock's, that plays freely on the concept of utility:

We have more moral, political, and historical wisdom, than we know how to reduce into practice...we let '*I dare not* wait upon *I would*, like the poor cat in the adage'. We want the creative faculty to imagine that which we know; we want the generous impulse to act that which we imagine; we want the poetry of life: our calculations have outrun conception; we have eaten more than we can digest.[1]

Shelley thought Peacock's ideas of *utility* and *poetry* were equally hollow, and that he was knocking down the ghost of the one with the shadow of the other.[2]

[1] *Peacock's four ages of poetry, Shelley's defence...* ed. Brett-Smith, 52.
[2] These terms are close to those Shelley uses in his first draft for the 'Defence' when struggling to reply in the same spirit and with the same wit as Peacock's

What then happened to Peacock between 1818 and 1820 that lies behind the change from 'An essay on fashionable literature' to 'The four ages of poetry'? It is necessary to return to more biographical terms.

*

So far this chapter has tried to show that it is wrong to present Peacock's ideas as static. In the same way it is wrong to think him static as a person. His 'views' were unstable because the Peacock of the 1810s was searching for his identity and for his appropriate way of life. In 1820 he thought he had found them and shaken off his false starts. For one thing, he had shaken off the rôle of elegant Regency versifier which was too close to the Barry Cornwall he despised.

The description in chapter 2 of Peacock the poet and reader in the 1800s and early 1810s showed that one can barely discern Peacock in that sentimental tourist's costume from the background of the age. In fact as poet he scarcely stands out more boldly against the changed background of the later 1810s.

It is true that after meeting Shelley and his friends in 1812 Peacock 'found himself' as the satirical novelist. Yet the discovery did not take command of all his energies: throughout the 1810s he combined or rather jumbled several rôles and literary forms—he was in turn satirical novelist, Greek scholar, satirical versifier, burlesque medievalist, literary sociologist and pseudo-mythological poet. When other Regency *littérateurs* wandered from style to style they were largely adapting themselves consciously to supply the market. Peacock seems to have

provocation. Addressing the editor of *Ollier's literary miscellany*, he begins: 'The ingenious author of a paper which lately appeared in your Miscellany, entitled The Four Ages of Poetry, has directed the light of a mind replete with taste and learning to the illustration of a paradox...to prove that poetry is a bad thing. (I hope soon to see a Treatise against the light of the Sun adorn your columns.)' It is amusing to hear Shelley's voice grow high-pitched despite himself: 'It is an impious daring attempt to extinguish Imagination, which is the Sun of life, Impious attempt, parricidal and self-murdering attempt...', Just as characteristically, the final version of the opening moves far away from the particular provocation into the lofty world of abstraction: 'According to one mode of regarding those two classes of mental action, which are called reason and imagination, the former may be considered as mind contemplating the relations borne by one thought to another...' (See Brett-Smith's edition, pp. 108–9 and 23.)

been more unconscious of inconsistency and confusion. He might as well write in one form as another. *The genius of the Thames* happened to be in the travelogue/panegyric genre, but it could just as well be done, Peacock says, as a satire.[1] If you felt amused at J. F. Newton's ideas they were just the thing for a satirical novel (*Headlong Hall*); at the same time you could if you felt like it take them seriously and work them up into a mythological poem ('Ahrimanes', contemporary with *Headlong Hall*).

In 1814 came 'Sir Proteus: a satirical ballad', attacking and parodying Byron and Coleridge and making in lengthy footnotes comments on fashionable taste later developed in the 'Essay on fashionable literature' and *Nightmare Abbey* of 1818. But 1818 was also the year of his solemn mythological poem 'Rhododaphne'. Peacock was unconscious of his 'double life' and unconscious of how often he was floundering in the swamp of fashion.

It has been suggested earlier that, when we start collecting examples of, say, 'the Hellenic current' or the 'Medieval current' in the literature of a period, the examples present themselves to our imagination as stratified from mere abject conventionality upwards. The relation of 'Rhododaphne' to other Hellenic poems of the 1810s—the influences on it, and its influences on others—illustrates the related point, that there is a constant two-way commerce between the levels. A Keats can make something original and lasting out of what in lesser writers is trivial and ephemeral. But there is also a downward movement. For example, Shelley came to know Peacock through admiring his poems,[2] which influenced Shelley's own: but this does not pull Peacock above the level of the *Zeitgeist*; it drags Shelley down, and underlines the limiting Regency affiliations of his verse. The same is true of Peacock's influence on Keats.[3] Again Peacock himself, so scornful of the age's Greekish-Cockney verse, was like Keats influenced by it.

It is, then, worth outlining that group which F. E. Pierce

[1] See letter to E. T. Hookham, 6 June 1809: Halliford, VIII, 172.
[2] See especially Shelley's letter to T. Hookham, 18 Aug. 1812: *Letters*, ed. Jones, I, 32–5.
[3] See D. Bush, *Mythology and the romantic tradition* (Oxford, 1937), pp. 180 ff.

called 'the Eddy around Leigh Hunt'.[1] Mr Pierce is invoked because later scholars have provided more information about the group but less sense of what held the group together. As one of his attempts to relate *Zeitgeist* and individual talent, the image of an *eddy* is suggestive. Unlike the conventional image of a circle, it suggests the group's vital cohesion and attraction and changing pattern. It suggests the strong pull of the central figure—strong enough to draw even Keats and Shelley into the vortex. The geographical suggestion of the suburban peri-meter of London is appropriate too: Leigh Hunt drew together from the suburbs people of similar tastes, just as earlier Rogers was 'the magnet' of the Metropolitan poets, Scott the Northern group and even earlier Coleridge was the centre of 'the eddy around Bristol'.[2] The geographical point is important: Byron's description *the suburban school* fits their sentimental interest in the country and 'beauty', and in a snobbish way fits their dabbling in music and art. Its poetry too reduces everything to surburban tastes and proportions, vulgar in the sense of being at once pretentious but tame. It is decorated with souvenirs and gew-gaws of Elizabethan verse. A favourite genre is emasculated myth and tame magic, decorative 'Greekery' in the manner of Theocritus or at best of Ovid.

Once more one sees the reciprocal influence of the original and the imitative and conventional. Barry Cornwall (B. W. Procter), the worst of that group, imitated Hunt and other writers: many readers including Jeffrey were grateful for his digestible dilutions. But Keats himself was influenced and dragged down by Leigh Hunt and perhaps even by Procter.

Shelley too was pulled by that eddy and affected by its poetry, but he was critical of its cosiness and mutual flattery. Socially Peacock only touched it and withdrew: the following anecdote is told in *Fraser's magazine*:

Some years ago it entered the imagination of Hunt and Keats, and some others of that coterie, to crown themselves with laurels and take off their cravats. This was the jaunty thing, and quite poetical. While the coronetted and uncravatted company were sitting thus one

[1] *Currents and eddies in the English romantic generation* (Yale and Oxford, 1918), chapter 8.
[2] *Ibid.* especially p. 131.

day, 'with their singing robes about them', Peacock came in. 'Do,' said a lady, who officiated as coronet manufacturer, 'do, dear Mr. Peacock, let me weave you a chaplet, and put it on your head; then you will sit as poets altogether.'

'No, ma'am,' said Peacock, wiping his head, 'no, ma'am; you may make a fool of your own husband, but there is no need of your making a fool of me.'[1]

Yet shortly after this encounter he published 'Rhododaphne', which, although more simple and restrained in style, uses myth in basically the same way as Hunt and Procter.

The tale is of two lovers separated by the enchantress Rhododaphne and reunited when she is killed by Uranian Love. But anyone who read for the story would hang himself, for the idea is to spin out and smother the myth with scenic description. This is precisely the decorative mythologising of Nonnus and Theocritus, with the brass age's cosy nostalgia for the magic of Bygone Times. The poem itself acknowledges that

> great Pan is dead:
> The life, the intellectual soul
> Of vale, and grove, and stream, has fled.[2]

As 'The four ages of poetry' was to put it more witheringly, 'we know...that there are no Dryads in Hyde-park nor Naiads in the Regent's-canal'.[3] Hence the demand for the poetic substitute. The trouble is that Peacock's are exactly the sort of tame wizards and water-sprites a fanciful man might imagine as he crossed the Park or peered into the Canal on an after-dinner stroll.

'Rhododaphne' was poorly received: Peacock's letters became sour about popular taste. He rejected Cornwall's poems with 'Endymion', which is influenced by 'Rhododaphne'. Yet the violence of this rejection is surely the violent self-disgust of realising how close his own poetry was to the triviality of Cornwall's. Most of what he (and Shelley) say about fashionable

---

[1] IV (Aug. 1831), 19. Hunt of course had earlier been drawn by Peacock, Shelley and Hogg into their own circle of 'Athenians' (as they called themselves): but the ethos of the two circles were very distinct. Peacock, always suspicious of Hunt's influence on Shelley, Keats and Byron, attacked his cosy household in the review of Moore's *Byron*.

[2] Halliford, VII, 29–30.

[3] *Ibid.* VIII, 19.

poetry fits Peacock's own: and in writing 'The four ages of poetry' he was rejecting that particular rôle of the 1810s.

But with that essay's standpoint of utility Peacock was rejecting his whole way of life as 'Hermit of the Thames' in the name of his 'useful' occupation at East India House.

The change of life was abrupt, and took his friends by surprise. Biographers too, finding no introspective diaries or confessional letters, cynically reduce it to a need to find work as the financial allowances from Shelley dwindled. It is worth repeating that, whereas Shelley leaves long explicit accounts of all the crises of his life, to which we have only to add the necessary pinch of salt, we can only understand Peacock's emotional life by deducing from hints: 'tandis que le type Shelley s'exprime à fond à la moindre occasion, le type Peacock dissimule souvent avec soin, aux autres et au besoin à lui-même, un coin d'humanité que nous ne découvrons jamais'.[1]

We can deduce that 1817 and 1818, a climax of literary activity, and of quality at least in the novels, was also a time of obscure unease. The rôle of Hermit of the Thames wore thin once it actually became lonely; that is, once Shelley left for good and Hogg was usually away on his law-circuit. In a letter to Hogg just after Shelley's departure, loneliness and nostalgia alternate with bravado:

I have been here since Monday, as lonely as a cloud, and as melancholy as a gib-cat...Shelley left town on Wednesday, the 11th, at 5 in the morning. We had a farewell supper in Russell Street, with Mr. and Mrs. Hunt, on Tuesday night after the Opera. I stayed three or four days in pure dread of facing the associations of this scenery, and I did not venture abroad for two or three days more after my return... I have filled my shelves with a portion of Shelley's books...I shall be very social with the Greek poets, and shall pass a day occasionally with Plato and Plutarch. You have promised me a week in June.[2]

In subsequent letters one traces excited activity switching to a solitary boredom. Something insular and unadventurous made it impossible to follow Shelley to Italy: like Hogg Peacock 'deem[ed] it a moral impossibility that an Englishman, who is

[1] Mayoux, *Un Epicuréan anglais*, p. 297.
[2] 20 March 1818: *New Shelley letters*, ed. W. S. Scott (London, 1948), pp. 108–9.

not encrusted either with natural apathy or superinduced Giaourism, can live many years among such animals as the modern Italians'.[1] For some time he 'speculate[d] on your return within two years as a strong probability', snatching at any hints that Shelley was dissatisfied with Italy, trying pathetically to tempt him back: 'If the summer of last year had been like this, you would not I think be now in Italy.'[2]

This isolation merely hastened an inevitable change of life. Emotionally, it led him to get married once he had a job which would support a family: the reader hardly needs a commentary on what is involved in this decision. But intellectually too Peacock must have felt his way of life untenable once he realised, with "Rhododaphne', that he was no creative poet, and that being a general dealer in verse was not enough. And here again Peacock is representative of a point in literary social history: a point worth examining in some detail before comparing Peacock's personal solution with that of other contemporary figures.

For the problem of the intelligent mind with no strong creative pretensions was more acute than in the previous century. For those without private income or a church or university place (and thus unlike most of Johnson's circle) what profession was open to a gentleman that would allow him to continue the rôle of common reader and occasional writer? One could less easily settle into the Church: here the difference between Crabbe and Peacock is indicative of two ages. The Church itself suppressed non-residence and sinecures; and one was less likely to be even in passive agreement with Church doctrine —again representatively, Peacock's classicism, 'reason' and anti-clericalism went together. On the other hand, the age of 'Administration' and respectable 'Business' rather than 'Trade', which first blossomed fully in the era of Dickens, was hardly beginning: East India House, one of the first rare openings, was competed for by many more men like Lamb, Mill and Peacock. The great Reviews provided another new opening. A professional with no self-doubts, like Jeffrey, or an opportunist like Brougham seeing them as a way to power, would be at

[1] Letter to Shelley, 19 July 1818: Halliford, viii, 201.
[2] *Ibid.* p. 200.

ease in them. But the pressure towards omnicompetence and 'editorial consistency' would deter someone with more integrity and modesty from relying completely on the Reviews. This was the reaction of Hogg;[1] and Crabb Robinson felt similarly about his journalism for *The Times*.[2] Both men fell back on the legal profession.

The main point here is to judge Peacock's self-knowledge, his understanding and use both of the possibilities and of his own potential, compared with other men in a similar position in the early nineteenth century.

Hogg was always searching for 'something to do'. He claimed that Law was an idealistic choice: at Oxford 'the study of that highest department of ethics, which includes all the inferior branches, and is directed towards the noblest and most important ends, of jurisprudence, was always next to my heart.'[3] But on leaving Oxford he found himself involved not with jurisprudence—'the beautiful theory of the art of right'[4]—but with common law. Disillusioned by 'dull and unintellectual' work, in turn with a conveyancer in York, with a special pleader in the Middle Temple and on circuit in the North, Hogg tried at intervals to break out into reviewing, politics and university professorship.

If Hogg misjudged his chosen profession, De Quincey misjudged his own potential. Always confident that he could become the man to revolutionise English philosophy, he prepared himself for nothing better than literary odd-jobbing. Now Crabb Robinson's intelligence lay in not overestimating either his profession or himself. Unlike De Quincey, he did not believe himself the herald of the New Philosophy: 'Why did I come to Germany? Did I anticipate the German philosophy? ...Nothing of the sort. I came to Germany because I did not know what to do with myself in England.'[5] He came back more like a messenger who was not sure he understood the message.

---

[1] See Lady W. Scott, *Jefferson Hogg* (London, 1951), chapter xiv.
[2] See J. M. Baker, *Henry Crabb Robinson of Bury, Jena, The Times and Russell Square* (London, 1937), chapter iv.
[3] T. J. Hogg, *Life of Shelley*, ed. H. Wolfe, 12 vols. (London, 1933), i, 74.
[4] *Ibid.*
[5] Letter to his brother Thomas, 27 Nov. 1803; *Henry Crabb Robinson in Germany*, ed. E. J. Morley (Oxford 1929), p. 131.

His new life in England began with the odd-jobbing with which De Quincey's life ended: with war reports and arts reviews for *The Times*, articles on phrenology and the like, and a translation of *Egmont*. Realising that this was not a way of life and that he had not a creative mind, he decided in 1811 to go into the Law. The report of this decision, made in his diary, is worth quoting at length for use as a touchstone when we turn back to consider Peacock's similar decision.

This day I am willing to hope may prove one of the most important in my whole life; for it was then that my resolution was fixed to abandon the light various metaphysical–poetical reading in which I had for so many years unprofitably rioted, and to devote myself seriously to the acquisition of useful, more especially legal knowledge. I am now convinced I have no genius or taste whatever and therefore it is idle in me to waste my faculties in attempting to acquire what is not within my reach, viz., pre-eminence as a metaphysical philosopher or a critic. But I may still in humbler walks possess respectable attainments. I have no other faculties whatever than a moderately logical understanding and considerable facility in the expression of what I do understand...These are precisely the business talents of a lawyer and advocate. But I have still a vast deal to learn. Hitherto I have never read or studied or talked with any view to distant benefit of any kind. At the age of thirty-six it is time if ever to descend from such heights and enter into the business walks of life.[1]

It is a remarkable self-analysis of what he had in him, and remarkable realisation of what he had not. And, although he never patronised the law as at all 'below him', and knew it meant hard study, yet unlike Hogg he saw it as a means to a different end. 'My object...was to acquire a gentlemanly independence, such at least as would enable a bachelor of no luxurious or expensive habits, to enjoy good company with leisure.'[2] He would not work long hours and would retire at fifty. He underlined his rôle as 'common reader' and member of literary society by beginning his famous diary on that same day (3 March 1811).

[1] Quoted from unpublished entry in Journal, 3 March 1811, by F. Norman, *Henry Crabb Robinson and Goethe*, Publications of the English Goethe Society, new series VII (1930), p. 65 n. 2.

[2] Quoted from unpublished entry in Journal by E. J. Morley, *The life and times of Henry Crabb Robinson* (London, 1935), pp. 59–60.

With 'le type Peacock', not given to personal diaries, one has less evidence of what happened in his mind at the time of decision. He did however justify himself to Shelley:

It is not in the common routine of office, but is an employment of a very interesting and intellectual kind, connected with finance and legislation, in which it is possible to be of great service, not only to the company but to the millions under their dominion.[1]

This seems a true account of an activity in which Peacock distinguished himself and which Shelley envied. Here for a time was a union of the common reader and the useful member of society. But it is wrong to generalise with Amarasinghe that 'Peacock's peculiar merits are reflected in his friendship with Shelley on the one hand and with James Mill on the other'.[2] For by 'The four ages of poetry' he had become distant if not alienated from Shelley and detachedly superior about poetry. That essay ends with a vision of the 'useful' writers

who have built into the upper air of intelligence a pyramid, from the summit of which they see the modern Parnassus far beneath them, and, knowing how small a place it occupies in the comprehensiveness of their prospect, smile at the little ambition and the circumscribed perceptions with which the drivellers and the mountebanks upon it are contending for the poetical palm and the critical chair.[3]

The Peacock of 'The four ages' imagines himself looking down from that pyramid, jeering at those below in triumph at his escape. It was a false triumph, for it was soon clear that he did not stand with the political economists. He did not unite the friendship of Shelley and James Mill: he had become distant from the first and never grew intellectually close to the second.

In following Peacock's intellectual development we have as it were kept the lens fixed directly on him: but already the figure of Shelley has continually intruded into the camera-frame. And it is surely no coincidence that Peacock's mind was most positive and open during his friendship with Shelley up to 1818, the year of *Nightmare Abbey* and 'An essay on fashionable

---

[1] Letter to Shelley, 13 Jan. 1819: Halliford, VIII, 215.
[2] *Dryden and Pope in the early nineteenth century*, p. 179.
[3] Halliford, VIII, 24–5.

literature'. Conversely the hardening of Peacock's mind that leads to 'The four ages of poetry' in 1820 took place in the years after Shelley finally left England in 1818, when Peacock was losing touch with Shelley and rejecting the way of life they had shared. So that there is good reason to survey again the crucial decade 1810–20, this time focusing on that fruitful friendship.

4

Peacock and Shelley

The chief materials for a study of this friendship are their letters and Peacock's 'Memoirs of Shelley'. Although written in 1858–62 the 'Memoirs' draw on the insights of the 1810s.

'Insights' will seem an extravagant word to those who find that friendship only a source of curious anecdotes, or who think Peacock found in it only a source of detached satire, in which 'an author whose attitude is conservative and "eighteenth-century" satirises the excesses of modern literature' and 'avant-garde attitudes'.[1] That formula (to specify a contrast with Peacock) would fit very well *Edward Shore*, the poorest of Crabbe's *Tales, 1812*. Its subject—'freethinking' and free love, with Shore seducing his friend's wife—is curiously close to the atmosphere and events in Shelley's circle around 1812. But the tale offers no insights, for its 'conservative and "eighteenth-century" attitude' is too remote and predetermined even to see or respond to the age's new developments for what they are: it takes refuge in moral abstractions and dogmatism, whereas the only authentic kind of judgement is that which is implicit in the response itself. To draw on a modern *locus classicus* and apply what it says of the critic of literature to the critic of character, he 'is indeed concerned with evaluation, but to figure him as measuring with a norm which he brings up to the object and applies from the outside is to misrepresent the process. The critic's aim is, first, to realize as sensitively and completely as possible this or that which claims his attention; and a certain valuing is implicit in the realizing.'[2] The evaluation emerges 'as he matures in experience of the new thing'—that is, grows

---

[1] The common idea is conveniently summarised in these words from Ian Jack's *English literature 1815–32* (Oxford, 1963), pp. 213 and 218. He refers here to the results of the friendship in the novels.

[2] F. R. Leavis, 'Literary criticism and philosophy: a reply', *Scrutiny*, VI (1937), 61.

into a fuller understanding of the new thing, and also develops himself by 'taking in' the new thing. So the friendship did not just give Peacock a subject to which he applied a static attitude: it extended and developed him, as it also did Shelley.

Peacock tells us that Shelley

was particularly pleased with Wordsworth's stanzas written in a pocket copy of Thomson's Castle of Indolence. He said that the fifth of these stanzas always reminded him of me. I told him the first four stanzas were in many respects applicable to him.[1]

The stanzas themselves are not worth quoting here as their pair of contrasting friends resemble Wordsworth and Coleridge much more closely than Peacock and Shelley. But we get nearer the latter friendship with Shelley's comment:

He said: 'It was a remarkable instance of Wordsworth's insight into nature, that he should have made intimate friends of two imaginary characters so essentially dissimilar, and yet severally so true to the actual characters of two friends, in a poem written long before they were known to each other, and while they were both boys, and totally unknown to him.'[2]

The essence of friendship is to thrive on the sense of difference and, with all friendship's mutual influence, to preserve one's individuality and integrity and that of one's friends. The biographer too must respect that complex and balanced relationship. He must see that it cannot be formalised into contrasting attitudes, such as the cold reason of common sense against hot impetuousness, or Classicism against Romanticism.

First, let Peacock's Shelley introduce himself, in two letters written when he had particular reasons for attempting a full account of his life and mind. A punctilious biographer would correct some minor errors and exaggerations, most of which will be indicated in footnotes. But what the letters convey are not just biographical facts but the characteristically Shelleyan voice and idiom, temperament and tempo.

The first letter belongs to 1812, in the autumn of which Peacock and Shelley first met. Earlier that year Shelley and

---

[1] *Works*, Halliford Edition, ed. H. F. B. Brett-Smith and C. E. Jones, 10 vols. (London, 1924–34), VIII, 79.
[2] *Ibid.*

Harriet had gone north, on the run from Hogg's attempt to seduce Harriet. As a worshipper of *Political justice* Shelley was thrilled to hear that its author was still living and immediately wrote to Godwin:

You will be surprised at hearing from a stranger.—No introduction has, nor in all probability ever will authorise that which common thinkers would call a liberty; it is however a liberty which although not sanctioned by custom is so far from being reprobated by reason, that the dearest interests of mankind imperiously demand that a certain etiquette of fashion should no longer keep 'man at a distance from man' and impose its flimsy fancies between the free communication of intellect. I have but just entered on the scene of human operations, yet my feelings and my reasonings correspond with what yours were. My course has been short but eventful. I have seen much of human prejudice, suffered much from human persecution. The ill-treatment I have met with has more than ever impressed the truth of my principles on my judgement. I am young—I am ardent in the cause of philanthropy and truth; do not suppose that this is vanity. I am not conscious that it influences this portraiture. I imagine myself dispassionately describing the state of my mind.[1]

Godwin promptly replied: his curiosity was strongly aroused but Shelley's self-portrait was too 'generalising'. So, only a week after his initial letter, Shelley sent off the following:

Sir

It is not otherwise to be supposed than that I should appreciate your avocations far beyond the pleasure or benefit which *can* accrue to me from their sacrifice. The time however will be small which may be mis-spent in reading this letter, and much individual pleasure as an answer might give me, I have not the vanity to imagine that it will be greater than the happiness elsewhere diffused during the time which its creation will occupy.—You complain that the generalizing character of my letter, renders it deficient in interest; that I am not an individual to you: Yet, intimate as I am with your character and your writings, intimacy with *yourself* must in some degree precede this exposure of my peculiarities: It is scarcely possible, however pure may be the morality which he has endeavoured to diffuse, but that generalization must characterize the uninvited address of a stranger to a stranger.—I proceed to remedy the fault.—I am the Son of a man of fortune in Sussex.—The habits of thinking of my Father and

[1] 3 Jan. 1812: *Letters*, ed. F. L. Jones, 2 vols. (Oxford, 1964), I, 219–20.

myself never coincided. Passive obedience was inculcated and enforced in my childhood: I was required to love because it was *my duty* to love—it is scarcely necessary to remark that coercion obviated its own intention.—I was haunted with a passion for the wildest and most extravagant romances: ancient books of Chemistry and Magic were perused with an enthusiasm of wonder almost amounting to belief. My sentiments were unrestrained by anything within me: external impediments were numerous, and strongly applied—their effects were merely temporary.—

From a reader I became I [a] writer of Romances; before the age of seventeen[1] I had published two, 'St. Irvyne' and 'Zastrozzi', each of which, though quite uncharacteristic of me as now I am, yet serve to mark the state of my mind at the period of their composition. I shall desire them to be sent to you; do not however consider this as any obligation to yourself to misapply your valuable time.—It is now a period of more than two years since first I saw your inestimable book on 'Political Justice'; it opened to my mind fresh and more extensive views, it materially influenced my character, and I rose from its perusal a wiser and a better man.—I was no longer the votary of Romance; till then I had existed in an ideal world; now I found that in this universe of ours was enough to excite the interest of the heart, enough to employ the discussions of Reason. I beheld in short that I had duties to perform.—Conceive the effect which the Political Justice would have upon a mind before jealous of its independence, and participating somewhat singularly in a peculiar susceptibility.— My age is now *nineteen*; at the period to which I allude I was at Eton.— No sooner had I formed the principles which I now profess, than I was anxious to disseminate their benefits. This was done without the slightest caution.—I was twice expelled, but recalled by the inter- ference of my Father.[2] I went to Oxford.—Oxonian society was insipid to me, uncongenial with my habits of thinking.—I could not descend to common life. The sublime interest of poetry, lofty and exalted achievements, the proselytism of the world, the equalization of its inhabitants were to me the soul of my soul.—You can probably form some idea of the contrast exhibited to my character by those

---

[1] In fact he was seventeen when *Zastrozzi* (1810) was published, and eighteen when *St Irvyne* (1811) was published.

[2] F. L. Jones says: 'Though there is no evidence to support this statement, the general accuracy of Shelley's account of his life and character would lead one to dismiss the thought that the assertion is a pure fabrication. Nevertheless, it is hard to believe that he was twice actually expelled from Eton. Possibly his father had twice been advised to withdraw Shelley from Eton.' (*Letters*, I, 159n.)

with whom I was surrounded.—Classical reading and poetical writing employed me during my residence at Oxford.—In the meantime I became in the popular sense of the word 'God' an Atheist. I printed a pamphlet avowing my opinion, and its occasion. I distributed this anonymously to men of thought and learning wishing that Reason should decide on the case at issue. It was never my intention to deny it. Mr. Coplestone at Oxford among others had the pamphlet; he shewed it to the master and the fellows of University College, and *I* was sent for: I was informed that in case I denied the publication no more would be said.—I refused, and was expelled. It will be necessary in order to elucidate this part of my history to inform you that I am heir by entail to an estate of £6,000 per an.—My principles have induced me to regard the law of primogeniture an evil of primary magnitude. My father's notions of family honor are incoincident with my knowledge of public good. I will never sacrifice the latter to any consideration.—My father has ever regarded me as a blot and defilement of his honor. He wished to induce me by poverty to accept of some commission in a distant regiment, and in the interim of my absence to prosecute the pamphlet that a process of outlawry might make the estate on his death devolve to my younger brother. [??]— These are the leading points of the history of the man before you.

Others exist, but I have thought proper to make some selection, not that it is my design to conceal or extenuate any part, but that I should by their enumeration quite outstep the bounds of modesty.— Now it is for you to judge whether by permitting me to cultivate your friendship you are exhibiting yourself more really useful than by the pursuance of those avocations of which the time spent in allowing this cultivation would deprive you. I am now earnestly pursuing studious habits. I am writing 'an inquiry into the causes of the failure of the French revolution to benefit mankind'. My Plan is that of resolving to lose no opportunity to disseminate truth and happiness. I am married to a woman whose views are similar to my own.—To you as the regulator and former of my mind I must ever look with real respect and veneration.

Yours sincerely
P. B. Shelley.[1]

That was from the Lake District: in the next two years the Shelleys made a political and pamphleteering visit to Ireland; tramped around Wales, where they helped Maddocks build the Portmadoc Embankment, and settled at Tanyrallt until the notorious nocturnal attack; and took a cottage at Lynmouth

---

[1] 10 Jan. 1812: *Letters*, ed. Jones, I, 159–61.

in North Devon, where they were investigated by the police for launching seditious messages in bottles. Between these confused sallies and retreats belong the periods of rest and growth at London and Bracknell and the friendship with the Newtons and Boinvilles, in which circle Shelley saw a good deal of Peacock. After this (one cannot say as decisively as Shelley, '*because* of this') came the elopement abroad with Mary Godwin. The following letter, which takes up the autobiographical thread from roughly the time of the long 1812 letter to Godwin, was sent to Hogg shortly after Shelley and Mary's return to London in October 1814.

My dear Friend

After a silence of some months I hasten to communicate to you the events of the interval. They will surprise, and if any degree of our ancient affection is yet cherished by you for a being so apparently so inconsistent and indisciplinable as me, will probably delight you. You will rejoice that after struggles and privations which almost withered me to idiotism, I enjoy an happiness the most perfect and exalted that it is possible for my nature to participate. That I am restored to energy and enterprise, that I have become again what I once promised to become—that my friendship will no longer be an enigma to my friend, you will rejoice—if the causes that produced my errors have not made you indifferent to their reformation, and my restoration to peace liberty and virtue.

As soon as I returned from the Continent, (for I have travelled thro' France, Switzerland, Germany and Holland) I sought you to communicate what I will now detail.

In the beginning of spring, I spent two months at Mrs. Boinville's without my wife. If I except the succeeding period these two months were probably the happiest of my life: the calmest, the serenest, the most free from care. The contemplation of female excellence is the favourite food of my imagination. Here was ample scope for admiration: novelty added a peculiar charm to the intrinsic merit of the objects: I had been unaccustomed to the mildness, the intelligence, the delicacy of a cultivated female. The presence of Mrs. Boinville and her daughter afforded a strange contrast to my former friendless and deplorable condition. I suddenly perceived that the entire devotion with which I had resigned all prospects of utility or happiness to the single purpose of cultivating Harriet was a gross and despicable superstition. —Perhaps every degree of affectionate intimacy with a female, however slight, partakes of the nature of love. Love makes men quicksighted, and is only called blind by the multitude because he perceives the existence of relations invisible to grosser optics. I saw the full extent of the calamity which my rash and heartless union with Harriet: an union over whose entrance might justly be inscribed

Lasciate ogni speranza voi ch'entrate!

had produced. I felt as if a dead and living body had been linked together in loathsome and horrible communion. It was no longer possible to practise self-deception: I believed that one revolting duty yet remained, to continue to deceive my wife.—I wandered in the fields alone. The season was most beautiful. The evenings were so serene and mild.—I never had before felt so intensely the subduing voluptuousness of the impulses of spring. Manifestations of my approaching change tinged my waking thoughts, and afforded inexhaustible subject for the visions of my sleep. I recollect that one day I undertook to walk from Bracknell to my father's, (40 miles). A train of visionary events arranged themselves in my imagination until ideas almost acquired the intensity of sensations. Already I had met the female who was destined to be mine, already had she replied to my exulting recognition, already were the difficulties surmounted that opposed an entire union. I had even proceeded so far as to compose a letter to Harriet on the subject of my passion for another. Thus was my walk beguiled, at the conclusion of which I was hardly sensible of fatigue.—

In the month of June I came to London to accomplish some business with Godwin that had been long depending. The circumstances of the case required an almost constant residence at his house. Here I met his daughter Mary. The originality and loveliness of Mary's character was apparent to me from her very motions and tones of voice. The irresistible wildness and sublimity of her feelings shewed itself in her gestures and her looks—Her smile, how persuasive it was and how pathetic! She is gentle, to be convinced and tender; yet not incapable of ardent indignation and hatred. I do not think that there is an excellence at which human nature can arrive, that she does not indisputably possess, or of which her character does not afford manifest intimations.

I speak thus of Mary now—and so intimately are our natures now united, that I feel whilst I describe her excellencies as if I were an egoist expatiating upon his own perfections—*Then*, how deeply did I not feel my inferiority, how willingly confess myself far surpassed in originality, in genuine elevation and magnificence of the intellectual nature until she consented to share her capabilities with me.

I speedily conceived an ardent passion to possess this inestimable treasure. In my own mind this feeling assumed a variety of shapes. I disguised from myself the true nature of affection. I endeavoured also to conceal it from Mary: but without success. I was vacillating and infirm of purpose: I shuddered to transgress a real duty, and could not in this instance perceive the boundaries by which virtue was separated from madness, where self devotion becomes the very prodigality of idiotism. Her understanding was made clear by a spirit that sees into the truth of things, and affections preserved pure and sacred from the corrupting contamination of vulgar superstitions. No expressions can convey the remotest conception of the *manner* in which she dispelled my delusions. The sublime and rapturous moment when she confessed herself mine, who had so long been her's in secret cannot be painted to mortal imaginations—Let it suffice to you, who are my friend to know and to rejoice that she is mine: that at length I possess the inalienable treasure, that I sought and that I have found.—

Tho' strictly watched, and regarded with a suspicious eye, opportunities of frequent intercourse were not wanting.—When we meet, I will give you a more explicit detail of the progress of our intercourse: How in opposition to her father's will, to Harriet's exertions, we still continued to meet.—How Godwin's distress induced us to prolong the period of our departure. How the cruelty and injustice with which we were treated, impelled us to disregard, all consideration but that of the happiness of each other.

We left England and proceeded to Switzerland and returned thro' Germany and Holland. Two months have passed since this new state of being commenced. How wonderfully I am changed! Not a disembodied spirit can have undergone a stranger revolution! I never knew until now that contentment was any thing but a word denoting an unmeaning abstraction. I never before felt the integrity of my nature, its various dependencies, and learned to consider myself as an whole accurately united rather than an assemblage of inconsistent and discordant portions. Above all, most sensibly do I perceive the truth of my entire worthlessness but as depending on another. And I am deeply persuaded that thus ennobled, I shall become a more true and constant friend, a more useful lover of mankind, a more ardent asserter of truth and virtue—above all more consistent, more intelligible, more true.—

My dear friend I entreat you to write to me soon. Even in this pure and celestial felicity I am not contented until I hear from you.

Most affectionately yours
P B Shelley.[1]

[1] 4 Oct. 1814: *Letters*, ed. Jones, I, 401–3.

Through these letters comes a voice—an impression that matches exactly the one made by Shelley's headlong handwriting and the actual shrill and jarring voice Peacock described in the 'Memoirs'. It matches, too, the nervous, volatile eyes and lines of Shelley's face, as Peacock saw them in Leisman's self-portrait. As characteristically Shelleyan is the idiom, at once histrionic and pedantic, lurid and abstract. And through the voice and idiom emerge many of the qualities Peacock registered in Shelley. There is, for example, the impetuous directness and openness, the generous admiration and the eagerness to make contact with its subject. There is also the melodramatisation of the bleeding heart with its dizzy extremes of fortune ('after struggles and privations which almost withered me to idiotism, I enjoy an happiness the most perfect and exalted...'); the self-importance (for instance, 'my plan is that of resolving to lose no opportunity to disseminate truth and happiness'); the self-righteousness (particularly over Harriet); the mild perse-cution mania (especially from his father) that led to exaggeration and, the 'Memoirs' show, semi-hallucination; and the more pervasive hallucinatory tendency to confuse thought and desire with fact ('a train of visionary events arranged themselves in my imagination until ideas almost acquired the intensity of sensations'). But to dissect Shelley's personality and isolate the elements like this is quite against the spirit in which Peacock reports on his friend.

*

This is Peacock's account of the Newton–Boinville circle, in which he first got to know Shelley:

At Bracknell Shelley was surrounded by a numerous society, all in great measure of his own opinions in relation to religion and politics, and the larger portion of them in relation to vegetable diet. But they wore their rue with a difference. Every one of them adopted some of the articles of the faith of their general church, had each nevertheless some predominant crotchet of his or her own, which left a number of open questions for earnest and not always temperate discussion. I was sometimes irreverent enough to laugh at the fervour with which opinions utterly unconducive to any practical result were battled for as matters of the highest importance to the well-being of mankind.[1]

[1] Halliford, VIII, 70.

NVLA DI
SINE LI

Peacock's Shelley: the drawing of Antonio Leisman

'The various engraved portraits of Shelley appear to have been based on a posthumous portrait painted by Clint, which was composed from one or more water-colour sketches by amateurs. They are all, including the painting by Clint, feeble productions, inaccurate in drawing and sentimental in expression. As to their veracity, the most competent authority, Thomas Love Peacock, the intimate friend and executor of the poet, writing in 1858 remarked: 'These portraits do not impress themselves on me as likenesses. They seem to me to want the true outline of Shelley's features, and, above all, to want their true expression. There is a portrait in the

This description of 'predominant crotchets' and heated but unpractical discussions indicates that his visit to Bracknell was the point at which Peacock the satirist was born. That this was the main result is clear from the anecdotes that follow in the 'Memoirs', and from *Headlong Hall*. But the attitude is far from mere conservative intolerance. The quality of Peacock's response comes out in contrast with Hogg's attack on the same circle, which he met in London: Hogg enjoyed the charming ladies, the literary readings and the cups of tea, but found the meals unpunctual, the social ideas vulgar and the other guests disgusting:

I generally found there two or three sentimental young butchers, an eminently philosophical tinker, and several very unsophisticated medical practitioners, or medical students, all of low origin, and vulgar and offensive manners. They sighed, turned up their eyes, retailed philosophy, such as it was, and swore by William Godwin and *Political Justice*.[1]

Hogg's note here as always is picturesquely exaggerating, frivolous and snobbish: Peacock's is modest and precise, and his criticism is restrained in tone and serious in criteria. This contrast is not just between the two written accounts: it is also between what must have been Hogg's and Peacock's attitudes

[1] Hogg, *The life of Shelley*, ed. M. Wolfe, 2 vols. (London, 1933), II, 107.

Florence Gallery which represents him to me much more truthfully. It is that of Antonio Leisman, No. 155 of the *Ritratti de' Pittori*, in the Paris republication.' (See 'Memoirs of Percy Bysshe Shelley', *Fraser's magazine*, June, 1858.)

This is a reproduction of a facsimile by a zinco-line process of the engraving by Lasinio of Leisman's portrait, reproduced from Peacock's copy of the *Reale Galleria di Firenze Illustrata*, Paris edition. It will be observed that Peacock expressly states that the likeness to Shelley was in the Paris republication of the *Galleria di Firenze*—the 'Florence Gallery' of the excerpt. He had never been in Italy, and consequently had not seen the picture. But it doubtless occurred to him that, although he found this striking likeness to his friend in the engraved outline, it might not be present in the finished picture. Such happens to be the case. For whilst the engraving is spirited and brilliant, the painting is cold and dry.' (From Henry Wallis, *Peacock on the portraits of Shelley*, London, 1911.)

at the time, and their effect on Shelley. Hogg follows the passage just quoted with a typically self-congratulatory anecdote of how he laughed Shelley into joining in his abuse of the circle:

I bore with the rabble rout for a little while, on account of my friend, and because I could there enjoy his precious society; and they made him believe that their higgledy-piggle'y ways were very right and fine, and conducive to progress and perfectibility. However, a young English gentleman, of a liberal education, an Etonian and Oxonian, soon grew weary of persons so ill-suited to his aristocratical feelings and habits, and began to train off.

The last pilgrimage I made to the abode of the perfect republican equality, I met Bysshe near the door, towards which he was advancing with mighty strides and his wonted rapidity. I seized his arm, and said: 'Come along; let us take a walk together, let us leave the sentimentalists to ripen for the gallows by themselves!'

He laughed so long and so loud at a sally that strongly arrested his sympathies, and I joined him so heartily in the mirthful and contemptuous explosion, that several of the good people of the quiet street opened their windows, and looked out to discover the cause of the unusual disturbance. Whilst he was hesitating, I still kept hold of his arm, and finally I carried him off as a lawful prize. We had a long walk to the westward, through fields, and afterwards we enjoyed a cup of strong tea, or rather, to tell the truth, many cups, in a still coffee-room at Kensington.

'How I wish I could be as fastidious and exclusive as you are,' he sighed forth, as we walked; 'but I cannot—'...

We finished our tea at last, but not until we had sworn in our cups to cut the unprejudiced, levelling confraternity.[1]

Once more, Hogg's cure is tea and pedestrianism! There may have been such an incident, a passing mood of revulsion that responded to Hogg. But what follows in the *Life* puts Hogg in his place. First, Shelley moved house to Bracknell, close to the Newton circle—sufficient proof that Hogg's crude scorn could only have a passing effect on Shelley. Secondly, Shelley soon went from Bracknell to Edinburgh—not with Hogg but with his new friend Peacock.

Peacock in fact replaced Hogg as Shelley's closest friend. His tact and his wider interests made a greater impression on Shelley's mind and developed it away from—not just temporarily

[1] *Life of Shelley*, ed. Wolfe, ii, 108.

laughed him out of—his more eccentric ideas of vegetarianism[1]
and millenarianism, which he learned from Newton's circle
and expressed in the notes to 'Queen Mab'. And, while Peacock
and Hogg agreed, for different reasons, about those Newtonian
ideas, Hogg was rapidly losing interest in Shelley's fundamental
ideas and in political and social questions in general. The letters
between Hogg and Shelley show mutual irritation on that
subject and then, around 1813, a deliberate avoidance of it.
Hogg thus cut himself off from that important side of Shelley's
mind at about the time when Peacock began to make contact
with it. Outside Peacock's novels, political and social topics
recur in letters between Peacock and Shelley; and, while Shelley
was abroad, Peacock's letters and quarterly box of books and
magazines helped keep Shelley in touch with the state of England.
In 1813 Shelley wrote that Peacock's 'enthusiasm is not very
ardent, nor his views very comprehensive':[2] by 1816 he called
him 'an amiable man of great learning, considerable taste, an
enemy to every shape of tyranny and superstitious imposture'.[3]
The latter is an enthusiastic exaggeration of their common
ground, but it is clear from the letters that they agreed on
specific issues, such as taxation, parliamentary representation
and the relief of poverty. It is true that the evidence does not
let us decide other questions. How far did Shelley help form
Peacock's social ideas, and was it as much as Peacock modified
Shelley's? Were their arguments of the kind Shelley vividly
describes thus: 'I never met a man, by whom, in the short time
we exchanged ideas I felt myself excited to so much severe
and sustained mental competition, or from whom I derived so
much amusement and instruction.'[4]

The 'Memoirs' report no such arguments, although this and
the general lack of comment on Shelley's social ideas may be
the result of Peacock's fading interest in politics by the 1850s.
But we can judge from the other disputes in the 'Memoirs'

---

[1] Besides the incidents in the 'Memoirs of Shelley' and *Headlong Hall* see a skit
probably by Peacock: *Dinner by the amateurs of vegetable diet (extracted from an
old paper)*. This appeared in 1821 and is reprinted in N. I. White, *The unextinguished hearth* (Durham, N.C., 1938), pp. 267–8.
[2] *Letters*, ed. Jones, I, 380. [3] *Ibid.* p. 518.
[4] Letter to W. T. Baxter about a Mr David Booth, 30 Dec. 1817: *Letters*, ed.
Jones, I, 588.

that Peacock would have brought his criticism to bear with tact as well as tenacity. This criticism would have tried to limit Shelley's plans and ideas to the practical and the specific, and sober them with an understanding of the realities and expediencies of politics. The criticism of Shelley's poetry that closes the 'Memoirs' is equally a criticism of his ideas.

We can see Peacock's important position as a sympathetic critic, by contrasting it with that of Hunt and Southey. N. I. White says that 'except for Hogg during a brief year of youth, Leigh Hunt was the best and fittest friend that Shelley ever knew'.[1] The intention of the whole present chapter is to support the claim that Peacock was Shelley's best and fittest friend, but at the moment I confine the dispute to the relation of Shelley's friends to Shelley the political thinker. Certainly Hunt offered him more complete agreement. He also offered fuller knowledge, both in conversation in England and by letter and in *The examiner* when Shelley was abroad.[2] But Hunt's agreement was *too* complete for Shelley's good or for his own credit: he was an idoliser rather than a discerning friend. On Shelley's death Hunt wrote of him not as a young man but a spirit, 'so unearthly he always appeared to me, and so seraphical a king [thing ?] of the elements'.[3] In contrast, when Robert Southey met Shelley in 1811 he not only addressed him as a young man but himself assumed the rôle of a wise old man. This is Southey's own account:

Here is a man in Keswick, who acts upon me as my own ghost would do. He is just what I was in 1794. His name is Shelley...He is come to the fittest physician in the world. At present he has got to the Pantheistic stage of philosophy, and in the course of a week, I expect he will be a Berkeleyan, for I have put him on a course of Berkeley. It has surprised him a good deal to meet, for the first time in his life, with a man who perfectly understands him, and does him full justice.

[1] *The unextinguished hearth*, I, 502.
[2] Leigh Hunt was personally involved in politics and journalism: Peacock's knowledge depended on newspapers and reviews. In the election of 1818 Peacock wrote from Marlow that 'my distance from town renders my information tardy' (Halliford, VIII, 197) and that 'we have been very tranquil in our rotten borough amidst the bustle of the general election' (*ibid.*).
[3] *Morning chronicle* (12 Aug. 1822): 'king' is the plausible emendation in *A Shelley library*, ed. T. J. Wise (London, 1924), p. 107.

I tell him that all the difference between us is that he is nineteen and I am thirty-seven... [1]

This is conservatism at its worst. That Southey was as superior and paternal at the meetings themselves as in this letter, is clear from Shelley's own reports: 'he has a very happy knack when truth goes against him of saying, "Ah! when you are as old as I am you will think with me".'[2] Peacock clearly stood midway between Hunt and Southey.

The only important contemporary whom Shelley did not meet and who might have given Shelley help and criticism of a kind Peacock could not, was Coleridge. Shelley greatly admired Coleridge as a poet and a thinker; and Coleridge regretted that Shelley had met Southey and not himself. Here is part of a conversation John Frere had with Coleridge in 1830:

Frere: Did you ever see Shelley's translation of the Chorus in 'Faust' you were just mentioning?

Coleridge: I have, and I admire it very much. Shelley was a man of great power as a poet, and could he only have had some notion of order, could you only have given him some plane whereon to stand, and look down upon his own mind, he would have succeeded. There are flashes of true spirit to be met with in his works. Poor Shelley, it is a pity I often think that I never met with him. I could have done him good. He went to Keswick on purpose to see me and unfortunately fell in with Southey instead. There could have been nothing so unfortunate. Southey had no understanding for a toleration of such principles as Shelley's.

I should have laughed at his Atheism. I could have sympathised with him and shown that I did so, and he would have felt that I did so. I could have shown him that I had been in the same state myself, and I could have guided him through it. I have often bitterly regretted in my heart that I did never meet with Shelley.[3]

[1] Letter to G. C. Bedford, 4 Jan. 1812: *Life and correspondence of Robert Southey*, ed. C. C. Southey, 6 vols. (London 1849–50), III, 325–6.
[2] Letter to Elizabeth Hitchener, 7 Jan. 1812: *Letters*, ed. Jones, I, 223. Cf. letter to Godwin, 16 Jan. 1812: *ibid.* p. 231.
[3] From *Abstract of a discourse with Mr. Coleridge on the state of the country in December 1830, written at the time by John Frere*. This was first published in 1917 by E. M. Green, in 'A talk with Coleridge', *Cornhill magazine*, N.S. XLII, 402–9.

A variant of this speech is reported in Hogg's *Life of Shelley* (I, 300) where no source is given but 'Extract from a letter of Coleridge'. N. I. White confirms in his *The unextinguished hearth* (I, 186 and note on p. 620) that it

Much of Coleridge's and Shelley's thinking lay in the border-lands of many studies, such as philosophy, religion, anthropology, and psychology. Coleridge might have given Shelley's 'meta-physical reveries' more substance and direction. Peacock could toy with Lord Monboddo but in the main saw only confusion in those borderlands, about which he could give Shelley little more than the Johnsonian warning to clear his mind of cant.

On the other hand, the positive effect of Peacock, in encoura-ging Shelley to give a practical direction to his political energies and ideas, is underlined by an exchange of letters at the time of Peacock's appointment at East India House—an exchange from which critics have never drawn the full significance. Peacock (we saw earlier) wrote to Shelley: 'It is not in the common routine of office, but is an employment of a very interesting and intellectual kind, connected with finance and legislation, in which it is possible to be of great service, not only to the Company, but to the millions under their dominion.'[1] This self-justification refutes the critics who have looked on the post as at best a routine, at worst the time-serving of which Peacock accused Wordsworth and Southey. But he was uncertain how Shelley would receive the news; from his letter one guesses at what Leigh Hunt confirms, that friends teased Peacock about his post 'and his inevitable tendencies to be one of the corrupt, upon which he seems to apprehend Shelleian objurgation'.[2]

cannot be traced to any published letter. White appears not to know of Frere's *Abstract*.

    As the difference between the two versions has its critical interest, here is Hogg's: 'I *might* have been of use to him, and Southey could not; for I should have sympathised with his poetics, metaphysical reveries, and the very word metaphysics is an abomination to Southey, and Shelley would have felt that I understood him. His discussions—leading towards Atheism of a certain sort would not have scared *me*; for *me* it would have been a semi-transparent Larva, soon to be sloughed, and through which I should have seen the true *image*—the final metamorphosis.' It would be difficult to prove that Frere's version was the source for Hogg's, although in substance and in many phrases the two are strikingly close. Frere's is more valuable and more authentically Coleridgean in expression, especially in the words 'could you only have given him some plane whereon to stand, and look down upon his own mind...' Hogg's reads like a cruder version that has passed through his mind and become contaminated with his prejudices. The turn of phrase 'poetics [and] meta-physical reveries' is the authentic tone of Hogg patronising 'the Divine Poet'.

[1] 13 Jan. 1819: Halliford, VIII, 215.
[2] Leigh Hunt, *Correspondence*, ed. Thornton Hunt (London, 1862), I, 128.

Shelley's reaction was unexpected. He wrote to Hogg:

I have some thoughts, if I could get a respectable appointment, of going to India, or any place where I might be compelled to active exertion, and at the same time enter into an entirely new sphere of action.[1]

At about the same time he wrote to Peacock for help, who replied:

I should not like your Indian project (which I think would agree neither with your mind nor body), if it were practicable. But it is altogether impossible. The whole of the Civil Service of India is sealed against all but the Company's covenanted servants, who are inducted into it through established gradations, beginning at an early period in life. There is nothing that would give me so much pleasure (because I think there is nothing that would be more beneficial to you) than to see you following some scheme of flesh and blood—some interesting matter connected with the business of life, in the tangible shape of a practical man: and I shall make it a point of sedulous enquiry to discover if there be anything attainable of this nature that would be likely to please and suit you.[2]

Shelley's plan to become a maharaja's political adviser *was* impracticable, another of his 'many schemes of life' to which Peacock alludes in the 'Memoirs' when he reports 'the most singular that ever crossed his mind', 'that of entering the church'.[3] But the impulse behind the Indian plan was inspired by Peacock's own work at East India House, and is a tribute to what must have been the constant if imperfect effect of Peacock's criticism on Shelley the 'social thinker': to direct him to 'some scheme of flesh and blood—some interesting matter connected with the business of life, in the tangible shape of a practical man'.

Peacock's criticism of Shelley's poetry was suggestively related to this. Not that Shelley was so willing to accept it: on Peacock's doubts about *The Cenci*, which he was asked to edit and get produced, Shelley wrote,

I have just heard from Peacock saying he don't think my tragedy will do, and he don't much like it. But I ought to say, to blunt the edge of his criticism, that he is a nursling of the exact and superficial school of poetry.[4]

[1] 22 Oct. 1821; *Letters*, ed. Jones, ii, 361.   [2] ? Oct. 1821: Halliford, viii, 225–6.
[3] *Ibid.* pp. 75–6.   [4] 13 or 14 Oct. 1819: *Letters*, ed. Jones, ii, 126.

But there is nothing 'exact and superficial' about that criticism as expressed in the 'Memoirs': unlike the covert attack on Shelley in 'The four ages' it is constructive in tone and evokes the best of conservative or eighteenth-century criteria. Peacock rightly claims that 'Shelley's life in Italy is best traced in his letters' and that his poetry 'peopled Italian scenes with phantoms of virtue and beauty, such as never existed on earth. . . He only once descended into the arena of reality, and that was in the tragedy of the *Cenci*'[1] and there only imperfectly.

If the gorgeous scenery of his poems could have been peopled from actual life, if the deep thoughts and strong feelings which he was so capable of expressing, had been accommodated to characters such as have been and may be, however exceptional in the greatness of passion, he would have added his own name to those of the masters of the art of drama.[2]

The famous conclusion to the 'Memoirs' adds that 'he was advancing, I think, to the attainment of this reality. It would have given to his poetry the only element of truth which it wanted.'[3] And so Peacock made tactfully the essential criticism of Shelley which later writers have merely demonstrated in detail or rephrased more cruelly.

*

Peacock's most original insight into Shelley was into his temperament, and into the mutual influence of temperament and ideas. He was the first to discuss openly Shelley's 'imagination', and its straying into delusions and hallucinations, one of which is described as follows in the 'Memoirs':

I was alone at Bishopsgate, with him and Mrs. Shelley, when the visitation alluded to occurred. About the middle of the day, intending to take a walk, I went into the hall for my hat. His was there, and mine was not, I could not imagine what had become of it; but as I could not walk without it, I returned to the library. After some time had elapsed, Mrs. Shelley came in, and gave me an account which she had just received from himself, of the visitor and his communication. I expressed some scepticism on the subject, on which she left me, and Shelley came in, with my hat in his hand. He said, 'Mary tells me you do not believe that I have had a visit from Williams'. I said, 'I told her there were some improbabilities in the narration.'

---

[1] Halliford, viii, 118.   [2] *Ibid*. p. 119.   [3] *Ibid*. p. 131.

He said, 'You know Williams of Tremadoc?' I said, 'I do.' He said, 'It was he who was here today. He came to tell me of a plot laid by my father and uncle, to entrap me and lock me up. He was in great haste, and could not stop a minute, and I walked with him to Egham.' I said, 'What hat did you wear?'. He said, 'This, to be sure.' I said, 'I wish you would put it on.' He put it on, and it went over his face. I said, 'You could not have walked to Egham in that hat.' He said, 'I snatched it up hastily, and perhaps I kept it in my hand. I certainly walked with Williams to Egham, and he told me what I have said. You are very sceptical.' I said, 'If you are certain of what you say, my scepticism cannot affect your certainty.' He said, 'It is very hard for a man who has devoted his life to the pursuit of truth, and who has made great sacrifice and incurred great sufferings for it, to be treated as a visionary. If I do not know that I saw Williams, how do I know that I see you?' I said, 'An idea may have the force of a sensation; but the oftener a sensation is repeated, the greater is the probability of its origin in reality. You saw me yesterday, and will see me tomorrow.'[1]

The story continues with Shelley's hopeless attempts to produce proof. He retorts that he 'can see Williams tomorrow if I please' and the friends begin to walk to London to meet him; but on the way Shelley changes his mind. Later he produces a necklace which he claims Williams has sent as proof, but will not show the letter in which the necklace was enclosed. 'If you will not believe me, I must submit to your incredibility.' There the matter ended.[2]

This in itself is one of the most amusing stories in the biography. It reveals so many of Shelley's traits, especially his sense of persecution and his self-righteousness ('It is very hard for a man who has devoted his life to the pursuit of truth ...'). But by conveying them in a dramatic scene, by giving the individual voice and flesh and blood with which those traits are bound up, Peacock makes our contempt for those traits evaporate. Peacock, that is, confronts us not with a set of abstracted characteristics but with an autonomous complex personality to which he has responded. This underlying understanding of human nature makes Peacock's critical *manner* in this episode so distinctive and rare in quality. It is not Hogg's

---

[1] *Ibid.* pp. 101–2.   [2] *Ibid.* p. 103.

clumsy derision but a tactful, apparently diffident but immovable scepticism—a stone wall of reason against which Shelley's 'imagination' breaks itself.[1] Such was clearly Peacock's manner at the time, but the passage also stands out for the quality of its reporting, its exact recording of conversation. Neither at the time of the incident nor in this report did Peacock indulge in the sarcastic and self-congratulatory comments that Hogg added to his similar anecdotes.

There is in fact every difference between the way Hogg and Peacock applied their common sense to Shelley's 'imagination'. Hogg's impulse, as far as we can judge from his *Life of Shelley*, was always self-congratulation. He has no insights into Shelley's imagination and his general judgements are evasive or full of cruel innuendo:

Shelley had every qualification that a poet ought to possess, the highest qualifications in the most luxuriant and lavish abundance... He lived and moved under the absolute despotical empire of a vivid, fervid fancy, as his illusion respecting elephantiasis demonstrates.[2]

This linking of the poetry and the elephantiasis incident reminds one of Humbert Wolfe's complaint that throughout the *Life of Shelley* Hogg repeats the Homeric constant 'Divine Poet' as Mark Antony called Brutus 'an honourable man'.[3] In contrast Peacock's impulse is a penetrating curiosity about Shelley's mind, and his 'Memoirs' have several passages of analysis. The Williams episode is followed by this:

...I call them semi-delusions, because, for the most part, they had their basis in his firm belief that his father and uncle had designs on his liberty. On this basis, his imagination built a fabric of romance, and when he presented it as a substantive fact, and it was found to contain more or less of inconsistency, he felt his self-esteem interested in maintaining it by accumulated circumstances, which severally vanished under the touch of investigation, like Williams' location at the Turk's Head Coffee-house.[4]

---

[1] Mayoux comments that 'Tout le passage ressemble à un rapport judiciaire que Peacock représente, un brin narquoise, pivotant sur elle-même solidement pour faire face au névrosé dans ses positions successives et l'en expulser.' (*Un Epicuréan anglais*, p. 116.) I disagree however with Mayoux that we laugh, if not at Peacock's position, at his method: 'Il faut plus d'imagination pour combattre les excés d'imagination.' (*Ibid.*)

[2] Hogg, *Life of Shelley*, ed. Wolfe, II, 47.

[3] *Ibid.* I, ix.

[4] Halliford, VIII, 103–4.

Earlier Peacock suggests the partly physical and nervous cause of these delusions:

His vegetable diet entered for something in his restlessness . . . it made him weak and nervous, and exaggerated the sensitiveness of his imagination. Then arose those thick-coming fancies which almost invariably preceded his change of place.[1]

To this can be attached another amusing episode which reveals Peacock's manner towards Shelley. The friends went by boat up the Thames.

On our way up, at Oxford, he was so much out of order that he feared being obliged to return. He had been living chiefly on tea and bread and butter, drinking occasionally a sort of spurious lemonade, made of some powder in a box, which, as he was reading at the time the *Tale of a Tub*, he called 'the powder of pimperlimpimp'. He consulted a doctor, who may have done him some good, but it was not apparent. I told him, 'If he would allow me to prescribe for him, I would set him to rights.' He asked, 'What would be your prescription?'. I said, 'Three mutton chops, well peppered.' He said, 'Do you really think so?' I said, 'I am sure of it.' He took the prescription; the success was obvious and immediate. He lived in my way for the rest of our expedition, rowed vigorously, was cheerful, merry, overflowing with animal spirits, and had certainly one week of thorough enjoyment of life.[2]

Peacock detected another related aspect of Shelley that contributed to the delusions: the way in which worthless books could grip his imagination and even determine his actions—a fact treated solemnly in N. I. White's biography and comically in *Nightmare Abbey*. Peacock summarises the novels of Charles Brockden Brown and their appeal to Shelley, and comments:

he devotedly admired Wordsworth and Coleridge, and in a minor degree Southey: these had great influence on his style and Coleridge especially on his imagination; but admiration is one thing and assimilation is another; and nothing so blended itself with the structure of his interior mind as the creations of Brown.[3]

We can sum up Peacock's insight into Shelley's imagination with Mayoux's words:

S'il manque d'intuition de la dynamique psychologique on a vu qu'il était capable de donner une fort jolie description de la mécanique:

[1] *Ibid*. p. 80. [2] *Ibid*. p. 99. [3] *Ibid*. p. 78.

il est à peine possible de mieux analyser les processus des demi-illusions, ou demi-hallucinations.[1]

One can add that Peacock does reproduce Shelley's 'dynamique psychologique' and not just 'la mécanique', in the dramatic medium of *Nightmare Abbey*.

The Shelley of *Nightmare Abbey* is also the excitable and unstable Shelley of the earlier letters, breaking into 'metaphysical reveries' and rhapsodies that confuse real thought with emotional self-indulgence. Here is a typical snatch: 'Am I not mad? alas I am, but I pour my ravings in the ear of a friend who will pardon them—Stay! I have an idea; I think I can prove the existence of a Deity.'[2]—and the proof follows at length. Such letters to Hogg, and all those to Elizabeth Hitchener (to whom 'I pour out my soul',[3] which 'pants for communion with you'[4]) are very different from those written after Shelley met Peacock. He became more cautious about settling the nature of the universe, less ready to assume 'the presumptuous attitude of an instructor',[5] wiser about other people, and more aware of his egotism and critical of himself —'*self*, that burr that will stick to me. I can't get it off, yet'.[6] Many letters, like the one to Leigh Hunt that contains that phrase, have the phlegmatic and self-directed irony of Byron's. This change was obviously not just the result of Peacock's friendship, but Shelley was most wary of 'ascending in his balloon' when he wrote to Peacock:

I was very much amused by your laconic account of the affair [Peacock's marriage]. It is altogether extremely like the Dénouement of one of your own novels, and as such serves to a theory I once imagined, that in everything any man ever wrote, spoke, acted or imagined, is contained as it were, an allegorical idea of his own future state, as the acorn contains the oak. But not to ascend in my balloon...[7]

The curse of this life is that whatever is once known, can never be unknown...Time flows on, places are changed, friends who were with

[1] *Un Epicuréan anglais*, p. 117.
[2] To Hogg, 12 Jan. 1811: *Letters*, ed. Jones, I, 44.
[3] ?11 Nov. 1811: *ibid.* p. 134.   [4] 17 Nov. 1811: *ibid.* p. 141.
[5] See letter to Leigh Hunt, 29 May 1819: *ibid.* II, 96.
[6] 15 Aug. 1819: *ibid.* II, 109.   [7] ?2 May 1820: *Letters*, ed. Jones, II, 192.

us, are no longer with us; yet what has been, seems yet to be, but barren and stript of life. See, I have sent you a study for *Nightmare Abbey*.[1]

Peacock's 'Memoirs' mention the humour in Shelley's letters, and quote the description of Mr Gisborne's 'Slawkenburgian' nose:

It weighs on the imagination to look at it,—it is that sort of nose that transforms all the g's its wearer uses into k's. It is a nose once seen never forgotten and which requires the utmost stretch of Christian charity to forgive. I, you know, have a little turn up nose; Hogg has a large hook one; but add them together, square them, cube them, you would have but a faint idea of the nose to which I refer.[2]

The whole account of the Gisbornes in this letter shows a humour and a shrewdness about people which Peacock had helped to develop in Shelley.

The main test of Peacock's sympathetic understanding of Shelley is his reaction to Shelley's relations with Harriet and Mary. The quality of his understanding is suggested by the fact that Shelley turned to Peacock, not Hogg, for help in his dilemma, and is again illustrated by the 'Memoirs'.

The 'Memoirs' deal largely with the details and dates of the English marriage, the separation, the flight with Mary and Harriet's suicide, and with their exact sequence, so as to refute Lady Shelley's sentimental distortions. But Peacock also vividly describes the violence of feelings in Shelley's dilemma:

Nothing that I ever read in tale or history could present a more striking image of a sudden, violent, irresistible, uncontrollable passion, than that under which I found him labouring when, at his request, I went up from the country to call on him in London. Between his old feelings for Harriet, *from whom he was not then separated*, and his new passion for Mary, he showed in his looks, in his gestures, in his speech, the state of mind, 'suffering, like a little kingdom, the nature of an insurrection'. His eyes were bloodshot, his hair and dress disordered. He caught up a bottle of laudanum, and said 'I never part from this'.[3]

He could feel as tragedy, coloured with Shelleyan melodrama, what he interpreted in *Nightmare Abbey* as comedy.

Peacock took Harriet's side, and gives an appreciative

---

[1] 20 Apr. 1818: *ibid*. p. 6. [2] 24 Aug. 1820: *ibid*. p. 114.
[3] Halliford, VIII, 91.

portrait of her. But he also understood what lay behind the dilemma, Shelley's need of something more than was offered by Harriet. He deals cuttingly with Southey's claim that 'a man ought to be able to live with any woman. You see that I can, and so ought you...There is no great choice or difference.'[1] Peacock comments that '*Any woman*, I suspect, must have been said with some qualification',[2] and:

That Shelley's second wife was intellectually better suited to him than his first, no-one who knew them both will deny; and that a man, who lived so totally out of the ordinary world and in a world of ideas, needed such an everpresent sympathy more than the general run of men, must also be admitted; but Southey, who did not want an intellectual wife, and was contented with his own, may well have thought that Shelley had equal reason to seek no change.[3]

This judicious Johnsonian balance of evidence is reminiscent of passages in the *Lives of the poets*. If, quoted by itself, it seems too external, it is filled with meaning by a preceding description of Harriet.

When we turn to Peacock himself, we find that the little available evidence has been distorted to suggest that he was not a man likely to understand violent love. His letter of proposal to his future wife is often criticised as cool and business-like. But compared with Hogg's love-letters and given the situation (that Peacock and Jane Griffydh had been long separated) the letter is admirable, full of restrained respectful feeling. Here is the opening half:

It is more than eight years since I had the happiness of seeing you. I can scarcely hope that you have remembered me as I have remembered you: yet I feel confident that the simplicity and ingenuousness of your disposition will prompt you to answer me with the same candour with which I write to you. I long entertained the hope of returning to Merionethshire under better auspices than those under which I left it: but fortune always disappointed me, continually offering me prospects which receded as I approached them. Recently she has made me amends for her past unkindness, and has given me much present good, and much promise of progressive prosperity, which leaves me nothing to desire in worldly advantage but to

---

[1] Southey speaking to Shelley, as reported in Hogg, *Life of Shelley*, I, 246.
[2] Halliford, VIII, 93.   [3] *Ibid.* p. 95.

participate it with you. The greatest blessing this world could bestow on me would be to make you my wife: consider if your own feelings will allow you to constitute my happiness.[1]

If this letter raises any doubt or smile it is not at any suspicion of frigidity, but rather at the blandness with which Peacock conceals a good deal of his way of life in the previous eight or so years. He exaggerates both the prospects which fortune was 'continually offering me' and his own efforts to 'approach' them. But he suppresses all the affairs that caused Harriet Love to call him 'an universal lover' before his marriage. When engaged in 1815 to one girl he nearly rushed into marriage with another, an heiress: the details are obscure, but the result was a period in prison, and the whole affair, as N. I. White remarks, might have served just as well in *Nightmare Abbey* as the love-affairs of Shelley.[2]

Once more Hogg provides a contrast. There is no sign that he understood Shelley's dilemma or his needs. He echoed Southey in saying that 'any man who cannot make himself comfortable' in one house or with one wife is just fidgety by nature.[3] His idea of Shelley's relations with women is the Regency dandy's idea. although 'great as a poet—divine indeed; great as a philosopher, as a moralist, as a scholar, as a complete and finished gentleman',[4] etc., 'he was pre-eminently a lady's man',[5] 'cherished as the apple of beauty's eye...called Ariel ...the Elphin king'.[6] He was a rough pet and 'It was thought desirable to procure for him an introduction to the Countess of Oxford, in order that her wise and gentle influence might perchance make him less unlike other people.'[7] If he saw Shelley as a woman's pet, Hogg saw women as his own toys: the restraint and respect of Peacock contrasts with Hogg's arch and flowery love-letters, lacking any respect for the woman's intelligence or feelings. This is his style:

Was it then strange to attempt in every possible manner to procure the inestimable favour of an interview with the fair amiable? It was presumptuous; but yet, after having once presumed to love, what

---

[1] 20 Nov. 1819: *ibid.* p. 217.
[2] *The unextinguished hearth*, I, 387.
[3] *Life of Shelley*, I, 246.
[4] *Ibid.* I, 13.
[5] *Ibid.* I, 14.
[6] *Ibid.* II, 8.
[7] *Ibid.* II, 8.

can be additional presumption? Surely not to hope, when hope is essential to existence, when despair is death... [1]

As much to the point of the present argument is the list of fair amiables to whom Hogg sent his letters: Shelley's sister, Shelley's first wife, Shelley's second wife, and the widow of Shelley's Captain Williams.[2] The point of the list lies not only in the disgraceful two middle affairs but also in the extraordinary degree of emotional parasitism on Shelley revealed by all four.

Around the time of Shelley's marital crisis, Hogg wrote *The memoirs of Prince Alexy Haimatoff*.[3] This novel enforces our idea of Hogg (and enforced Shelley's) not only by its amorality, which Shelley attacked in his review,[4] but by the string of adolescent fantasies of sex and power that seem the only reason for the book. Shelley's analyses, in letters following Hogg's attempt on Harriet, of Hogg's lack of emotional self-knowledge were very perceptive and fully justified. By 1814 he knew Hogg, and in his crisis with Harriet and Mary turned away from Hogg to Peacock as the man able to understand his feelings and needs from the inside.

*

By frequently drawing on the 'Memoirs of Shelley', this chapter has probably made clear their quality as a memoir, not just their usefulness as a source. They contrast with Hogg's *Life of Shelley* in both usefulness and quality. Hogg is vivid, but his accuracy is more doubtful. He was at least once dishonest, suppressing Shelley's letters about his attempted seduction of Harriet but printing part of one disguised as a 'fragment of a novel' which he claimed Shelley wrote in imitation of *The sorrows of Werther*.[5] And he takes his revenge on Shelley's stinging attack on him, by appending a critical comment: 'This epistle from Albert to

---

[1] Letter to Elizabeth Shelley, 22 Aug. 1811: *New Shelley letters*, ed. W. S. Scott (London, 1948), p. 49. Cf. the whole of this letter and that on pp. 42 ff.

[2] For this last affair, see *After Shelley: the letters of Hogg to Jane Williams*, ed. Sylva Norman (London, 1934).

[3] Published under the pseudonym of John Brown and 'translated from the original latin MSS' (London, 1813). Few copies of this first edition exist, but the book is reprinted with Shelley's review by S. Scott, the Folio Society (London, 1952).

[4] *Critical review*, VI, no. 6 (Dec. 1814), ed. Wolfe.

[5] For Hogg's version, see *Life of Shelley*, ed. Wolfe, II, 123 ff. For the original, see *Letters*, ed. Jones, I, 178 ff. (?14 Nov. 1811).

Werther is forcibly written, with great power and energy; but it wants the warmth, the tenderness, of Goethe and Rousseau. The tone is rather that of the novels of William Godwin, or Holcroft; it is cold, bald, didactic, declamatory, frigid, rigid.'[1]

Hogg's interpretation of Shelley is always confused or evasive. For he attempted the hopeless task of combining Lady Shelley's reverence for 'the Divine Poet' with his own less solemn attitude. On the whole—as she and the family noted indignantly —Lady Shelley's attitude lost. Hogg said 'our book must be amusing';[2] it often is very funny, reading as a picaresque novel with a Regency wit that was a curious anachronism in 1858. But there is no respect for the subject, no sense of its size: Leigh Hunt saw the relation of Hogg and his subject by calling it 'Falstaff's biography of Hamlet, or Caliban's of Ariel'.[3]

The modern reader may complain that Hogg is a forgotten figure; may even suspect that he has been invented for the present book as an Aunt Sally. But the praise of Peacock's 'Memoirs' can be pressed home by a contrast with a major writer, Matthew Arnold. Arnold significantly praised Hogg's *Life of Shelley*,[4] and offers the same split interpretation although with more sincere motives. Compared with Peacock, Arnold's criticism of the *sale* and *bête* aspects of Shelley and his circle is morally ungenerous, the cold voice of rectitude judging the efforts of a man struggling with life. Yet Arnold tries to leave intact the Victorian idealisation of Shelley, 'the Shelley of marvellous gentleness, of feminine refinement, with gracious and considerate manners...the Shelley who was all this is the Shelley with whom I wish to end'.[5] To preserve this picture Arnold enlists the support of some of Hogg's false-ringing eulogies of Shelley 'the perfect gentleman'. There is no such strain or split in Peacock's interpretation. One might say that he does not 'interpret'. He does not manipulate the reality to fit terms that are applicable. He respects Shelley as someone unique and different from himself, even while he re-creates Shelley for us by means of all the inward knowledge of friendship.

[1] *Life of Shelley*, ed. Wolfe, II, 126.
[2] Unpublished letter quoted by W. Scott, *Jefferson Hogg*, p. 269.
[3] Letter to Mary Shelley, 2 July 1858: *Correspondence*, ed. Thornton Hunt, II, 368.
[4] 'Shelley', in *Essays in criticism*, 2nd series (London, 1888), p. 212.
[5] *Ibid*. pp. 245–6.

5

Headlong Hall

1815

This chapter will be deliberately as brief as *Headlong Hall* itself is thin. There is no reason to see it as the model for the later novels, simply because it is the first; rather it is a rickety prototype to be drastically modified. Nor is there point in dwelling too long on its indifferent handling of themes that can be discussed more positively when they reappear with more body in later novels.

It would be an even more thankless task to investigate the prehistory of the novels, the development of an original literary form, the form represented by the common phrase 'the Peacockian novel'. That very phrase suggests the difficulty. For Peacock is so individual, and the writers behind him form no tradition, have to him a much vaguer relation than sources or influences, and are as numerous and as miscellaneous as those behind Jane Austen. For example, it is possible to find interesting *parallels* with Lucian, Marmontel, Robert Bage or Isaac D'Israeli, but difficult to find tangible evidence of direct influence, or even of Peacock reading them or owning copies. The attempt has also been made to trace a dialogue tradition from Plato down to Peacock's contemporaries: but such a tradition will be a broken and circuitous path, or several criss-crossing ones; and we are still faced with the great leap from, say, the didactic dialogue form in Lord Monboddo and Horne Tooke to Peacock's mastery of the dialogue as the main element of a novel.

More is to be gained by acknowledging the heterogeneous influences on Peacock, including those outside literature: Miss P. J. Salz, for instance, concentrates usefully on the strong contribution made by opera.[1] This concentration, or modesty of

---

[1] 'Peacock's use of music in his novels', *Journal of English and Germanic philology*, LIV (June, 1955), 370–9.

scope, is a virtue, for a critic can usefully compare only those works of which he has first-hand understanding.[1]

This last point helps justify the following chapters in their focusing on 'the finished products', the novels themselves. Many critics (not only of Peacock) feel that a study of a novelist's relationship to his or her predecessors is a useful preliminary to a detailed critical study of his own finished products. Yet there is reason for arguing the opposite priority: the critical understanding of the objects of comparison must come first, or there will be nothing to compare but external labels.

The very phrase 'Peacockian novel' is an external label. It reduces the different Peacock novels to their lowest common denominator. Even Humphry House denies their individualities: for him the three Regency novels 'are all products of a single impulse and have very little separate artistic being—even those who know them well find it hard to remember exactly which characters come in which'.[2]

This claim is difficult to believe, even on superficial grounds. Given a few lines from *Nightmare Abbey*, no-one could mistake its exuberance of imagery and wit for the more pedestrian manner of *Headlong Hall*: given a sample of dialogue, no-one could mistake the quick and free-ranging exchanges of the later novel for the more lengthy and predictable set debates of the earlier.

Peacock's intention also varies within and between novels. Sometimes the intention is, in Lord Houghton's phrase, 'intellectual gaiety'. More often the purpose is satirical exposure. Sometimes however Peacock engages subjects in debates which he seems to take seriously. Although he implies too straight a line of development, Spedding was right in saying that, as novel follows novel, 'The humour seems to run deeper; the ridicule is informed with a juster appreciation of the meaning of the thing ridiculed; the disputants are more in earnest, and less like scoffers in disguise; there is more of natural warmth and life in the characters.'[3]

[1] Even Miss Salz relies more on dubious tags from Shaw and Tovey than on a first-hand appreciation of Mozart.
[2] 'The novels of Thomas Love Peacock', *The listener*, XLII (8 Dec. 1949), 998.
[3] *Edinburgh review*, LXVIII (Jan. 1839), 432.

Thirdly, each of the Regency novels engages with different contemporary subjects and different aspects of Shelley.

*

The 'form' of *Headlong Hall* is rather like that of a flexible holdall. It is a bag of samples of Peacock's various 'lines'. The first chapter, for instance, opens with an elaborately facetious pseudo-derivation, very mock-Tooke, of the names of Harry Headlong and other principal characters; and ends with a snatch of anti-clerical stage farce:

'Look at the rapid growth of corruption, luxury, selfishness—' [said Mr. Escot]

'Really, gentlemen,' said the Reverend Doctor Gaster, after clearing a husk in his throat with two or three hems, 'this is a very sceptical, and, I must say, atheistical conversation, and I should have thought, out of respect to my cloth—'

Here the coach stopped, and the coachman, opening the door, vociferated—'Breakfast, gentlemen;' a sound which so gladdened the ears of the divine, that the alacrity with which he sprang from the vehicle superinduced a distortion of his ankle.[1]

This looks forward to the more elaborate episode in chapter 8 where Cranium falls from the tower into the lake. We remember the two unpublished stage farces Peacock wrote around 1811–13 from which *Headlong Hall* and *Melincourt* borrow several characters and situations: the influence of these plays must also go far to explain the novels' mixture of dramatic speech and narrative.

Other materials bundled in which we recognise from the early Peacock are verses (comic and sentimental), comic Welsh characters and sublime Welsh scenery. But right from chapter 1 the holdall is given a shape by the Squire's invitation to various 'philosophers and dilettanti' to spend Christmas at Headlong Hall 'arguing, over his old Port and Burgundy, the various knotty points which had puzzled his pericranium'.

Headlong's house-party is based on a satirical reaction to the Newton circle and to the young, Godwinian Shelley whom Peacock found at Bracknell. What Bracknell had in common

[1] Chapter 1: Halliford, I, 11–12.

with *Headlong Hall* was a houseful of abstract philosophers discussing the destiny of man, 'voicing opinions utterly unconducive to any practical result'. Peacock uses the opinions of J. F. Newton, Shelley and Shelley's Godwin, as well as his own. But he detaches their ideas from their personalities; he shuffles them and deals them out to two speakers—Mr Foster the Perfectibilian and Mr Escot the Deteriorationist, between whom stands Mr Jenkinson the Statu-quo-ite. As a result of this shuffling and re-dealing there is no direct correspondence between these speakers and the 'originals' in life. Thus Foster is close to Shelley in his Godwinian optimism—'everything we look on attests the progress of mankind in all the arts of life, and demonstrates their gradual advancement towards a state of unlimited perfection'[1]—but not in his optimism at developments in travel and industry. Unlike Shelley again, Foster argues against vegetarianism. Similarly Escot's deteriorationism includes Newton's pet opinions, Peacock's own serious doubts about 'the march of mind', and the theories of Lord Monboddo that Peacock played with.

As a result, the general position of each extremist contains particular ideas that vary from the serious to the eccentric and the ridiculous: and so Peacock's attitude to the debates is also constantly changing. In chapter 4, 'The grounds', the discussion leads Mr Escot to say:

The sciences advance. True. A few years of study puts a modern mathematician in possession of more than Newton knew, and leads him at leisure to add new discoveries of his own. Agreed. But does this make him a Newton? Does it put him in possession of that range of intellect, that grasp of mind from which the discoveries of Newton sprang?[2]

This is Peacock's own serious idea, that recurs in his novels and essays. But when Escot goes on,

Give me the wild man of the woods...

Peacock is toying with Monboddo or laughing at Newton.

Once understood, this alternation of seriousness and playfulness is no drawback. The real drawback is that Peacock does

[1] Chapter 1: *ibid.* pp. 9–10. [2] Chapter 4: *ibid.* p. 35.

not exploit the opinions sufficiently for *any* purpose. The novel is not very fertile in serious thought, satirical analysis or 'intellectual gaiety'.

*

The passage on the progress of science and intellect, quoted above, is one of several in which Escot becomes Peacock's mouthpiece on serious subjects. In another he asks

What is the advantage of locomotion? The wild man is happy in one spot, and there he remains: the civilised man is wretched in every place he happens to be in, and then congratulates himself on being accommodated with a machine, that will whirl him to another, where he will be just as miserable as ever.[1]

This, says J. I. M. Stewart, 'looks back to Johnson's *Rasselas*, and forward to Matthew Arnold'.[2] It is, too, commonplace neither in thought nor expression. Yet such passages stand alone in speeches: they are not part of debates in which speakers fight for their views and develop them, or change one another's views. Escot's ideas are not sharpened by the changing challenge of a group of opponents. Foster's optimism is similarly unspecific, repetitive and simple; and Jenkinson is an inert compromise, without the active sophistry of (say) Seithenyn in *The misfortunes of Elphin*.

But the most would-be serious discussion in the book, that on industrialism in chapter 7 ('The walk'), is commonplace as well as undramatic. Its context, significantly, is a ramble through Snowdonia described in picturesque-tourist terms very close to those of Peacock's earlier letters.

The vale contracted as they advanced, and, when they had passed the termination of the lake, their road wound along a narrow and romantic pass, through the middle of which an impetuous torrent dashed over vast fragments of stone. The pass was bordered on both sides by perpendicular rocks, broken into the wildest forms of fantastic magnificence...

They now emerged, by a winding ascent, from the vale of Llanberris, and after some little time arrived at Bedd Gelert. Proceeding through the sublimely romantic pass at Aberglaslynn, their road led along

---

[1] Chapter 2: Halliford, I, 20–1.
[2] *Thomas Love Peacock*, British Council booklets, Writers and their work, no. 156 (London, 1963), p. 18.

the edge of Traeth Mawr, a vast arm of the sea, which they then beheld in all the magnificence of the flowing tide. Another five miles brought them to the embankment, which...excludes the sea from an extensive tract. [This is Madock's embankment for which Shelley helped raise money.][1]

The philosophers see the factories at Tremadoc, which was expanding from a village to an industrial town, 'a city, as it were, in its cradle'. Escot begins,

I confess, the sight of those manufactories, which have suddenly sprung up, like fungous excrescencies, in the bosom of these wild and desolate scenes, impressed me with as much horror and amazement as the sudden appearance of the stocking manufactory struck into the mind of Rousseau, when, in a lonely valley of the Alps, he had just congratulated himself on finding a spot where man had never been.[2]

This is still the picturesque tourist's view and is open to Macaulay's attack on Southey's 'way...in which the effects of manufactures and agriculture may be compared...To stand on a hill, to look at a cottage and a factory, and to see which is the prettier.'[3] This was the method of a good deal of Regency comment on industrialism.

Foster replies to Escot in terms very close to Macaulay's own praise of material prosperity. In response Escot turns from ugliness to human effects:

Profound researches, scientific inventions: to what end?...Complicated machinery: behold its blessings...contemplate the little human machines that keep play with the revolutions of the iron work, robbed at that hour of their natural rest, as of air and exercise by day; observe their pale and ghastly features, more ghastly in that baleful and malignant light, and tell me if you do not fancy yourself on the threshold of Virgil's hell...[4]

Peacock should be commended for noting this in 1815, and for incorporating it in a novel. Yet it is not ungrateful to ask the novelist to do more with the idea. No real debate follows and so no exploration of the subject. No one questions Escot's accompanying idea of pastoral life or produces any example from real life to balance the apparition that comes on stage, impeccably on cue, in support of Escot's case:

[1] Chapter 7: Halliford, I, p. 72–3. [2] *Ibid.* p. 77.
[3] *Edinburgh review*, L (Jan. 1830), 540. [4] Chapter 7: Halliford, I, 77–8.

As Mr. Escot said this, a little rose-cheeked girl, with a basket of heath on her head, came tripping down the side of one of the rocks on the left. The force of the contrast struck even on the phlegmatic spirit of Mr. Jenkinson, and he almost inclined for a moment to the doctrine of deterioration.[1]

Some other examples of Regency fiction on industrialism are needed, to judge what we can fairly expect from that standpoint and with that perspective. Whatever the justice of Macaulay's attack on the *Colloquies*, Southey gets nearer than Peacock to the subject in his earlier survey, *Letters from England by Don Espriella*. He sends his fictional narrator down into the streets of Birmingham and Manchester, close enough to the workers to reject Peacock's distant notion of 'pale faces':

Neither can I say that the people look sickly, having seen no other complexion on the place than what is composed of oil and dust smoke-dried. Every man whom I meet stinks of train-oil and emery. Some I have seen with red eyes and green hair; the eyes affected by the fires to which they are exposed, and the hair turned green by the brass works.[2]

He comes close enough to admire the toughness and ingenuity of Birmingham men as well as deplore their conditions. Most original of all, Espriella discusses child-labour with a cotton-manufacturer who prides himself on benevolence.[3]

It is surprising to find the subject explored by Wordsworth, whom many (including Peacock) thought incapable of objective description of ordinary people. In book 8 of *The excursion* (a year before *Headlong Hall*) the Pastor, Wanderer, Solitary and Narrator discuss like Peacock's philosophers 'changes in the Country from the manufacturing spirit'. The debate follows the same course as that in *Headlong Hall*, but adds a truth about rural life missing from Peacock: poverty and ignorance did not begin with factories. The Recluse describes beggars as degraded as Crabbe's, and a ploughboy

> Under whose shaggy canopy are set
> Two eyes, not dim, but of a healthy stare;

---

[1] Chapter 7: Halliford, I, 78.
[2] Robert Southey, *Letters from England by Don Espriella*, London, 1807: reprinted in Cresset Library, ed. Prof. J. Simmons (London, 1951), p. 197.
[3] *Ibid.* pp. 207–9.

Wide, sluggish, blank, and ignorant, and strange.
What penetrating power of sun or breeze,
Shall e'er dissolve the crust wherein his soul
Sleeps, like a caterpillar sheathed in ice?
This torpor is no pitiable work
Of modern ingenuity...
In brief, what liberty of *mind* is here?[1]

Peacock, then, shares the intelligent comment of his day on industrialism, but offers no startling new insights.

*

Of course most of the novel does not take the hill-top philosophers seriously. But there is little 'intellectual gaiety', either for its own sake or for satirical analysis.

The philosophers are above all monomaniacs. But monomaniacs soon become tedious. The pattern of each debate is the same: a pretext arises and each speaks in the same order; they repeat themselves in each chapter. 'The commonplaces...are not preserved from being tiresome by original humour or wit.'[2]

What could be done with Escot's deteriorationism? One thinks of the human generosity and intellectual high spirits with which Samuel Johnson could entertain and enjoy a mad theory, before defeating it with logic, analogy and imagery. This happens in the *Lives of the poets* as well as his conversations: here is one of Milton's ideas which is very close to Escot's deteriorationism.

There prevailed, in his time, an opinion that the world was in its decay, and that we have the misfortune to be produced in the decrepitude of Nature. It was suspected, that the whole creation languished, that neither trees nor animals had the height or bulk of their predecessors, and that everything was daily sinking by gradual diminution. Milton appears to suspect that souls partake of the general degeneracy, and is not without some fear that his book is to be written in 'an age too late' for heroick poesy...

His submission to the seasons was at least more reasonable than his dread of decaying nature, or a frigid zone; for general causes must operate uniformly in a general abatement of mental power; if

[1] William Wordsworth, *The excursion* (London, 1814), pp. 377–8.
[2] *Henry Crabb Robinson on books and their writers*, ed. E. J. Morley, 3 vols. (London, 1938), I, 226.

less could be performed by the writer, less, likewise, would content the judges of his work. Among this lagging race of frosty grovellers he might still have risen into eminence by producing something which 'they should not willingly let die'. However inferior to the heroes who were born in better ages, he might still be great among his contemporaries, with the hope of growing every day greater in the dwindle of posterity. He might still be a giant among the pygmies, the one-eyed monarch of the blind.[1]

That is intellectual gaiety *and* satirical analysis. Peacock sometimes gives touches of this to Escot's speeches, such as the claim that

In the course of ages, a boot of the present generation would form an ample chateau for a large family of our remote posterity.[2]

But his main idea of fun is to make Escot say in chapter 15 what he said in chapter 1.

Headlong Hall uses impressions of J. F. Newton and Shelley later reported in the 'Memoirs of Shelley': but they are more human and amusing in the 'Memoirs'. In the novel, the clash of vegetarian theory and practice is just a matter of Escot helping himself to a slice of beef as he declaims against meat. There is nothing like the tangle of habit, conviction and delusion we find in the stories of the 'Memoirs'—in Shelley giving up 'tea and bread and butter and a sort of spurious lemonade' for 'three mutton chops, well peppered',[3] or

While he was living from inn to inn he was obliged to live, as he said, 'on what he could get'; that is to say, like other people. When he got well under this process he gave all the credit to locomotion, and held himself to have thus benefited, not in consequence of his change of regimen, but in spite of it.[4]

On this topic it is the 'Memoirs' that read more like a novel or scenes from one, and *Headlong Hall* more like an expansion of notes to 'Queen Mab' or Newton's *Return to nature, or defence of vegetable regimen*. Again, to illustrate its motto

All philosophers, who find   Some favourite system to their mind,
In every point to make it fit,   Will force all nature to submit.

[1] Samuel Johnson, *Works*, Oxford English Classics (1825), VII, 102–4.
[2] Chapter 10: Halliford, I, 101.
[3] Halliford, VIII, 99.   [4] *Ibid.* p. 80.

the novel has nothing like the anecdotes in the 'Memoirs' of J. F. Newton finding the Zodiac in everything and rejecting obvious explanations in favour of the most *recherché*. Seeing four horseshoes on an inn-sign, and having 'immediately determined that this number had been handed down from remote antiquity as representative of the compartments of the Zodiac', he asked the landlord if he knew why there were four. '"Why, sir, I suppose because a horse has four legs." He bounced off in great indignation, and...said to me, "Did you ever see such a fool?"'[1] This *sounds* like a monomaniac's impatience with common sense, whereas in the novel we do not hear a particular voice or follow the movements of a particular mind or temperament.

The novel does not develop the human situation of the Newton–Boinville circle. The rivalry of Escot and Panscope over Cephalis does not do justice to the intrigues hinted at by Hogg. There is little feeling for the odd mixture of abstract philosophers, careerists, fashionable society and hangers-on that gathered at Bracknell and that Peacock brings out in *Nightmare Abbey*.

*

The novel has a full supporting chorus of English bards, Scotch reviewers, a craniologist and a landscape gardener; a dilettante painter; 'a compounder of novels, written for the express purpose of supporting every species of superstition and prejudice'; and 'Mr. Panscope, the chemical, botanical, geological, astronomical, mathematical, metaphysical, meteorological, anatomical, physiological, galvanistical, musical, pictorial, bibliographical, critical philosopher, who had run through the whole circle of the sciences, and understood them all equally well'.[2] But these are kept down to the level of minor crotcheteers who contribute little to the main stream of the book and are not brought fully into contact with the three 'philosophers'.

One of the few crotcheteers who steps forward as an individual figure from the chorus is Mr Cranium the craniologist. The claim to read character from the shape of the cranium now seems a fair-booth branch of nineteenth-century physiology and psychology, but it was taken seriously by many of Peacock's

---

[1] *Ibid.* p. 73.   [2] Chapter 3: *ibid.* I, 28.

contemporaries. The cult began with Gall's first published paper in 1798: after their meeting in 1804 Gall and Spurzheim gave a lecture-series in England, where their success can be judged from the fact that by 1832 there were twenty-nine phrenological societies and several journals. Even Coleridge was seriously interested and had his cranium examined by Spurzheim—who, ironically enough, found it lacked 'the organ of Ideality or Imagination'. Coleridge believed that 'If he had been content with stating certain remarkable coincidences between the moral qualities and the configuration of the skull, it would have been well; but when he began to map out the cranium dogmatically, he fell into infinite absurdities.'[1] He attacks as 'sheer quackery' the claim to identify specific lumps with specific qualities.

Peacock also ridicules this claim, but through Cranium's lecture he plays with the idea, develops it one step further into absurdity. As each animal embodies a certain faculty—'that of destruction in the tiger, that of architecture in the beaver'— so we may discover the salient qualities of any person by comparing his skull with those of animals. For instance: 'Here is the skull of a beaver, and that of Sir Christopher Wren. You observe in both these specimens, the prodigious developement of the organ of constructiveness.'[2] It thus follows that the best way for a parent to decide his son's career is to make a collection of animals' skulls, and 'compare with the utmost nicety their bumps and protuberances with those of the skull of their son'.[3] This development of an argument to the point where the plausible and the fantastic meet, is our first real glimpse of that playing with ideas which appears more in Peacock's later novels. It is the kind of wit that Johnson defined appreciatively when he wrote that Dryden 'delighted to tread upon the brink of meaning, where light and darkness begin to mingle; to approach the precipice of absurdity, and hover over the abyss of unideal vacancy'.[4]

Mr Cranium's lecture gives glimpses of other satirical techniques. Peacock serves two satirical purposes at once,

[1] *Specimens of the table-talk of the late Samuel Taylor Coleridge*, ed. H. N. Coleridge, 2 vols (London, 1835), I, 193.
[2] Chapter 12: Halliford, I, 114.   [3] *Ibid*. p. 116.   [4] *Works*, VII, 341.

against craniology and against the professions whose characters Cranium defines. There are also touches of Peacock's play with language in Cranium's professional pomposity and pseudo-scientific jargon, concerning the 'lumps and bumps, exuberances and protuberances, in the osseous campages of the occiput and the sinciput'. This (addressed to a Welsh-speaking audience who thought they were to hear a toast or see a conjurer) looks forward to Mr Flosky, and to Scythrop's Treatise on the Ear.

Here for a moment is the kind of intellectual gaiety for satirical purpose which we do not find in the main part of the book. Nor is that quality found in the treatment of Coleridge. The bare bones of Mr Panscope (and bare bones are all Peacock gives us) are: that he wakes from a reverie; joins the discussion by leaning on the *authority* of a long list of works he has read; and loses his temper on being told by Escot that he is unintelligible. The idea that Coleridge claimed to have read everything is unfair: in reading his notebooks or his table-talk one is struck by the range of subjects on which he could make acute comments without trying to pull them into any *system* of thought. The note on phrenology referred to above is representative. But what matters more is that Peacock cannot even bring his idea of Coleridge alive. Panscope merely *tells* us that he is weighed down with knowledge, but does not *sound* like a man stumbling under the weight. For a man who is encumbered with knowledge and who has just come from a 'deep reverie', he is remarkably brisk and quick-tempered in his exchanges with Escot. J. I. M. Stewart says that 'Coleridge, if we have at all studied him, comes to us, as does Henry James, pre-eminently as a voice—and here is not the voice we know as Coleridge's'.[1]

'The commonplaces of the literators of the day are not preserved from being tiresome by original humour and wit, so that the book is very dull'[2]—Crabb Robinson indicates well enough why *Headlong Hall* strikes us as so thin. Its materials are only the commonplaces and the eccentricities of the Regency, not the period's more advanced or distinguished ideas. If the ideas

[1] *Thomas Love Peacock*, p. 16.
[2] *On books and their writers*, I, p. 226.

as such do not sufficiently interest us, neither do the speakers amuse us for long, for they are not men, voices, temperaments, but the impersonal embodiments of extreme intellectual positions. Worse, throughout the book speakers and ideas alike remain tediously unalterable; for, by cutting the vital and fertile links between the two, Peacock has robbed both of the power of developing themselves. It was essential to dwell on those fertile links between ideas and personality if Peacock was to make any close imaginative approach to Shelley or Coleridge— an approach he does manage in *Nightmare Abbey*.

6

Melincourt

1817

In December 1816 Shelley wrote to Leigh Hunt:

Peacock is the author of *Headlong Hall*...He is now writing *Melincourt* in the same style, but, as I judge, far superior to *Headlong Hall*. He is an amiable man of great learning, considerable taste, an enemy to every shape of tyranny and superstitious imposture.[1]

That last phrase is truly Scythropian, the shrill note Peacock was to mock in *Nightmare Abbey*. But here it reminds us that the spirit of Shelley is indeed at the centre of *Melincourt*, not only in the hero Forester but in the subjects chosen and the judgements passed.[2] It is a later phase of Shelley than the one dealt with in *Headlong Hall*: the Shelley not of Bracknell but of 1817, the author of *The revolt of Islam* and its Preface, *A proposal for putting reform to the vote*, and (soon after) *A philosophical view of reform*.

This has an advantage and a disadvantage. On the one hand, the novel is fruitfully engaged with the wider world and newer ideas that this phase of Shelley was involved with. On the other hand the novel seems strained or constricted at the moments when the author's *attitude* is inseparable from Forester's: this is because there is something false and forced about Peacock's attempt at close intellectual sympathy with Shelley the 'enemy to every shape of tyranny and superstitious imposture'.

[1] *Letters*, ed. F. L. Jones (Oxford, 1964), I, 518.
[2] Forester often uses Scythropian jargon and imagery, and even echoes uncannily the very phrases of the letter just quoted: in chapter 37, for instance, he talks of 'nerving the arm of resistance to every variety of oppression and imposture, that winds the chains of power round the freeborn spirit of man' (Halliford, II, 388). But in *Melincourt* Peacock is not openly critical of this style.

While summarising the main strands of the novel, Spedding (in the *Edinburgh review* in 1839) suggested Peacock was unsure of the centre of interest as well as of the prevailing tone:

Anthelia Melincourt is an heiress endowed with all virtues of mind and body—not without an estate of ten thousand a year to make them manifest to the apprehension, and operative upon the happiness, of mankind. These combined attractions draw together a sufficient variety of suitors, and supply them with a fair opportunity for exhibiting their peculiarities. Aristocracy, landed propriety, established churchmanship, political economy, match-making maternity, barouche-driving baronetcy, and chivalry in modern attire—all gather round her as principals, or as seconds. They must disperse again as soon as her choice is made. In the mean-time, there is plenty of mutton to eat, of wine to drink, and of subjects to dispute about. Such circumstances would, in the common course of things, breed crosses and misunderstandings quite enough for all the author's purposes...But ...he has borrowed on this occasion the common-place book of a melodramatist...[Anthelia] is carried off by a noble suitor, and shut up in a solitary castle, nobody knows where. Her lover [Forester] sets off on foot to find her; accompanied by a political economist [Mr Fax] with whom he may hold dialogues by the way. He wanders about for some days, discussing in a very calm and philosophical spirit a variety of questions suggested by the scenes through which they pass—such as paper-money, surplus population, epitaphs, apparitions, the probable stature of the Patagonians, mountains, and the hopes of the world—but meets with no trace whatever of the heroine; till at length...he stumbles upon her, at that precise moment of time when, if he had not—the author must have found some difficulty in going on. The dialogues and conversations by which the weariness of this journey is beguiled...have so little to do with the heroine or the story, that they might be left out without diminishing the interest of the tale, and published as separate papers without losing any of their own.[1]

Spedding also found a split in the novel's tone. 'In *Melincourt* the same subject [modern corruption, as treated in *Headlong Hall*] is resumed, but in a graver strain. The motto, the opening, the purpose proposed, are all grave. The heroine is very grave.[2] Yet even this grave subject is entangled with buffoonery—

[1] *Edinburgh review*, LXVIII (Jan. 1839), 445–6.
[2] *Ibid*. p. 448.

in what other light can we view the introduction of Forester's friend, the dumb Baronet? His theory concerning the true and original man might have passed for the dreams of an enthusiast. But when coupled with the introduction in person of Sir Oran Haut-Ton, Bart. —that is to say, of a real orang-outang, caught young in the woods of Angola, brought up in society, and now mixing freely with his degenerate fellow-creatures, and wanting nothing of the civilized man except his vices and his powers of speech—what is it but buffoonery? And how are we to regard but as buffoonery, more or less Aristophanic —the election for the borough of One-vote—the description of Cimmerian Lodge, and the symposium at Mainchance Villa? All these are farce.[1]

He therefore advises Peacock to revise the novel:

Let him turn it into two distinct tales; the election of Sir Oran for the Borough of One-Vote being the subject of one, in which...he may introduce the humours of Mainchance Villa; the graver question concerning the realizations of the spirit of chivalry under the forms of modern society, being the argument of the other, with Forester and Anthelia for the central figures.[2]

This, and the accompanying detailed analysis (the best of *Melincourt* ever printed), oversimplifies in three ways. First, the distinction made is too clear-cut. Does not Sir Oran Haut-Ton, for instance, belong to *both* the novels Spedding would extract? With him, moreover, Peacock wavers between the serious and farcical, attempting irreconcilables: to ridicule Monboddo; yet also to entertain the idea of the noble savage so as to criticise modern manners; and to satirise an electoral system that could return an orang-outang to parliament. But Sir Oran, whose name forms the sub-title of the novel, has always had an over-generous share of comment. He is a clumsy way of introducing the qualities of the Natural Man, compared with Bage's *Hermsprong*,[3] or with Peacock's closer imitation of Hermsprong, the visitor from King Arthur's court in the unfinished novel *Calidore* (1817).[4]

Secondly, in his account of the 'serious' parts, it is Spedding's conventional deference to 'the heroine' that makes him suggest

---

[1] *Ibid.* pp. 450–1.   [2] *Ibid.* p. 451.
[3] W. Bage, *Hermsprong: or, man as he is not* (London, 1796).
[4] Halliford, VIII, 303 ff. *Calidore* also has in common with *Melincourt* a satirical attack on token currency.

that the novel's centre of gravity is or should be in Forester's relationship with Anthelia rather than his conversations with Fax. Even before Anthelia conveniently disappears, it is in the latter that the serious subjects come alive.

Thirdly, in so far as the two elements of the novel *can* be separated in the mind, Spedding simplifies their relative values by giving all the praise to the 'serious' parts and all the blame to the satirical. The latter seem on the contrary the most assured and effective, and the most safely within Peacock's natural scope. Peacock's touch is much less certain in the serious episodes. Yet, while saying this to Spedding, one needs to remember the modern reader who ignores those serious episodes, and to stress that they are at least the most ambitious and original part of the novel. For they bring together two apparent irreconcilables, a Malthusian and a Romantic, in fruitful dialogues on Regency society. 'Fruitful dialogue', now the bland phrase of modern diplomats, still has a meaning: unlike the immovable *opiniones* of *Headlong Hall*, Fax and Forester meet in mutual respect, through which one can influence the other and fresh thoughts can be developed. This ambitious experiment deserves first place in the following analysis of *Melincourt*.

*

Mr Fax is introduced ironically, as 'a tall, thin, pale, grave-looking personage':

'This is Mr. Fax,' said Mr. Forester, 'the champion of calm reason, the indefatigable explorer of the cold clear springs of knowledge, the bearer of the torch of dispassionate truth, that gives more light than warmth. He looks on the human world, the wild of mind, the conflict of interests, the collision of feelings, the infinitely diversified developments of energy and intelligence, as a mathematician looks on his diagrams, or a mechanist on his wheels and pulleys, as if they were foreign to his own nature, and were nothing more than subjects of curious speculation.'[1]

The irony is remarkably subtle in tone: the imagery conveys some awe at Fax's ruthless efficiency while showing that such efficiency depends on ignoring the complexities of human nature

[1] Halliford, II, 73.

and society. The passage holds in compressed form the balanced points and judgements we find later in Mill's essay on Bentham.

As Fax, Forester and Sir Telegraph Paxarett sit down to breakfast, they find themselves talking about marriage and celibacy. Their opening exchange of similes establishes not only the opinions but also the contrasting voices of the speakers:

Sir Telegraph Paxarett:...What is life without love? A rose-bush in winter, all thorns and no flowers.
Mr. Fax: And what is it with love? A double-blossomed cherry, flowers without fruit; if the blossoms last a month, it is as much as can be expected: they fall, and what comes in their place? Vanity, and vexation of spirit.
Sir Telegraph Paxarett: Better vexation than stagnation: marriage may often be a stormy lake, but celibacy is almost always a muddy horsepond.
Mr. Fax: Rather a clear calm river—
Mr. Forester: Flowing through a desert, where it moves in loneliness, and reflects no forms of beauty.[1]

Mr Fax then states his Malthusian position:

Feelings and poetical images are equally out of place in a calm philosophical view of human society...The cause of all the evils of human society is single, obvious, reducible to the most exact mathematical calculation...The cause is the tendency of population to increase beyond the means of subsistence. The remedy is in universal social compact, binding both sexes to equally rigid celibacy, till the prospect of maintaining the average number of six children be as clear as the arithmetic of futurity can make it.[2]

Forester replies that

The arithmetic of futurity has been found in a more than equal number of instances to baffle human skill. The rapid and sudden mutations of fortune are the inexhaustible theme of history, poetry, and romance...[3]

One of the few critics to comment at any length on Fax believes that 'Peacock does not treat Mr Fax's ideas satirically, but presents them as the product of reason and factual observation in reply to the idealism of the romantic attitude'.[4] Mr

---

[1] Chapter 7: *ibid.* pp. 75–6.   [2] *Ibid.* pp. 76–7.   [3] *Ibid.* p. 77.
[4] J. Hampson, 'The novels of Thomas Love Peacock', unpublished M.A. thesis, Bristol University, 1959, p. 119.

Hampson does not analyse the Malthusian chapters in detail so as to support this view, which certainly does not hold true of chapter 7. In the speeches already quoted, and in the debate that follows them, it is Fax who is inadequate. At only one point does Peacock make Forester speak as a vague idealist, and through him satirises a common Shelleyan rhetoric and confusion of imagery: 'We want no philosophical ice-rock, towed into the Dead Sea of modern society, to freeze that which is too cold already. We want rather the touch of Prometheus to revivify our frozen spirits...'[1] Otherwise, Forester's replies to Fax are all precise and convincing. It is Fax's calculations that are unrealistic: not until the end of the chapter does he show the positive side of his views, as he comments on Paxarett's carriage: 'Those four horses...consume the subsistence of eight human beings, for the foolish amusement of one.'[2]

The balance of Peacock's approval alters, however, in the next discussion between Fax and Forester, which extends through chapters 11 and 12. In chapter 11, 'Love and Marriage', Forester describes his ideal of a wife and, in doing so, gives his alternative to Malthusianism: 'a liberal discriminating practical philanthropy, that can select with justice the objects of its kindness...'.[3] Fax's replies to Forester in this chapter are not specifically Malthusian: his rôle here is to argue the dangers of forming 'a visionary model of female perfection, which has rendered you utterly insensible to the real attractions of every woman you have seen'.[4] But in chapter 12 the argument returns to Fax's home ground, 'Love and Poverty', and Peacock now balances speeches in a way that suggests he finds both speakers worthy of serious consideration: Forester in the consolations of marriage, and Fax's corrective picture of 'love and poverty'—

For the picture you must draw in your mind's eye is not that of a neatly-dressed young, healthy-looking couple, weeping in each other's arms in a clean, however homely cottage, in a fit of tender sympathy; but you must surround them with all the squalid accompaniments of poverty, rags and famine, the contempt of the world, the dereliction of friends, half a dozen hungry squalling children, all

---

[1] Chapter 7: Halliford, II, 78.   [2] *Ibid*. p. 79.
[3] *Ibid*. p. 117.   [4] *Ibid*. p. 115.

clothed perhaps in the cutting up of an old blanket, duns in presence, bailiffs in prospect, and the long perspective of hopelessness closed by the work-house or the gaol.[1]

This debate is followed, in a way characteristic of *Melincourt*, by an episode illustrating the subject and giving the general debate some engagement with real life. The story of Desmond (chapters 13 and 14) confirms Forester's idea of the heartlessness of modern society, and vindicates his ideal of 'a liberal discriminating practical philanthropy' which comes here in the shape of Anthelia's help to Desmond and his family. But the episode also shows that Fax is not heartless or unbenevolent in practice, and shares much of Forester's indignation at modern corruption.

Thereafter, Fax and Forester influence each other's ideas, and (except for Fax's lapse at the Rustic Wedding) react by later episodes. In chapter 24, 'The Barouche', they join forces in condemning Paxarett's wasteful luxury, his barouche and horses: Forester in himself blends the Utilitarian formula for justly shared happiness with the Christian notion of society as a family: 'Yet what is human society but one great family? What is moral duty, but that precise line of conduct which tends to promote the greatest degree of general happiness?'[2] Fax supports this by a combination of mathematical calculations with moral implications:

Let us suppose that ten thousand quarters of wheat will maintain ten thousand persons during any given time: if the ten thousand persons be increased to twenty, the consequence will be immediate and general distress: yet if the proportions be equally distributed, as in a ship on short allowance, the general perception of necessity and justice will preserve general patience and mutual goodwill; but let the first supposition remain unaltered, let there be ten thousand quarters of wheat, which shall be full allowance for ten thousand people; then, if four thousand persons take to themselves the portion of eight thousand, and leave to the remaining six thousand the portion of two (and this I fear is even an inadequate picture of the common practice of the world), these latter will be in a much worse condition on the last than on the first supposition; while the habit of selfish prodigality deadening all good feelings and extinguishing all sympathy on the one hand, and the habit of debasement and suffering combining with

---

[1] *Ibid.* p. 124.   [2] *Ibid.* p. 266.

the inevitable sense of oppression and injustice on the other, will produce an action and reaction of open, unblushing, cold-hearted resentment, which no philanthropist can contemplate without dismay.[1]

By this combined attack, the upper-class *homme moyen sensuel* Paxarett is (at least in principle) converted.

This first account of the Fax–Forester scenes has established Peacock's subject, and his ambitious intention: to satirise the worst and combine the best aspects of two violently opposed camps of Regency social thinkers. These scenes must be re-examined to decide the quality of his treatment of Malthus. To do this, we need first to examine how Malthus mattered to Peacock's contemporaries, and compare the ways in which other writers dealt with him.

The year of *Melincourt*, 1817, was in many ways the climax of Malthus's influence. The many pro-Malthusian writings of 1815–17 include a Christian defence of Malthus and Curwen's book on the Poor Laws. Between 1816 and 1817 the *Quarterly review* changed its point of view and joined the *Edinburgh review* in support of Malthus. In 1817 the fifth edition of Malthus's *Essay on population* appeared, containing a new preface, a new character on the Poor Laws and an answer to recent attacks, which all show that his case had received much abuse but no authoritative challenge. It was also the year of David Ricardo's *Principles of political economy*, which, despite initial disagreements between Malthus and Ricardo, was in its effect on later thought an interpretation of Adam Smith's economic writings in the light of Malthus. It was largely through Ricardo that Malthus was assimilated into Utilitarian thought and accepted by such democrats as Bentham and James Mill.[2]

The practical effects of Malthus's work were suffused through the whole national life. If his attackers often misrepresented the spirit or the arguments of the *Essay*, it is because they were aroused less by the *Essay* itself than by those who seized on and distorted Malthus for their own purposes.

[1] Halliford, ii, 267–8.
[2] See especially E. Halévy, *The growth of philosophical radicalism*, trans. M. Morris (reprinted London, 1952), pp. 225–48.

The effective political economy of this period that guided the action of Parliament, of the Justices of the Peace, of the new millowners, and of the enclosing landlords, was a selection and an exaggeration of those parts of Adam Smith, Malthus and Ricardo which suited the acquisition of wealth by the wealthy, and a quiet ignoring of the other doctrines of those eminent philosophers.[1]

At first the government used Malthus's theory as an excuse: Nature, not Westminster, was constantly held responsible for the state of the poor. But 1817 marks a change towards the more active use of Malthus: parliament appointed a committee to investigate the Poor Laws, and the proposers clearly wanted the committee to vindicate Malthus's case for abolishing poor relief.

Malthus's *Essay* was conceived as a reply to the optimism of Godwin's *Political justice*; and it is Godwin, in his reply of 1820, who describes most convincingly the effect of Malthus on the spirits of the nation. Before Malthus, he says, we faced hardship with a basic optimism and desire to live: we now respond with gloomy hopelessness.[2] Shelley too held Malthus largely responsible for the fact that 'gloom and misanthropy have become the characteristics of the age in which we live'.[3]

1817, H. A. Boner shows, opened the period of Malthusian triumph (1817–34) and was marked in Malthus's enemies by 'not gloom, but redoubled rage'[4] typical of which is the attack in Shelley's Preface to *The revolt of Islam*. As remarkable as the violence of hatred is the variety of thinkers who, from 1798 onwards, joined the attack. The range stretches from Coleridge[5] to Cobbett, and includes Byron, Shelley, Wordsworth, Southey and Hazlitt. Their typical note of impotent rage—impotent because it shouts down but does not refute Malthus—can be heard in one of Cobbett's many outbursts:

[1] G. M. Trevelyan, *British history in the nineteenth century and after, 1782–1919* (London, 1937), p. 143.
[2] *Of population* (London, 1820), book VI, chapter 8 ('Conclusion').
[3] Preface to *The revolt of Islam*.
[4] *Hungry generations: the nineteenth-century case against Malthusianism* (New York, 1955), p. 87.
[5] Coleridge wrote copious marginal notes that influenced Southey's attack on Malthus. See also *Specimens of the table-talk of the late Samuel Taylor Coleridge*, ed. H. N. Coleridge, 2 vols. (London, 1953), II, 880.

I have, during my life, detested many men; but never any one so much as you. Your book on *Population* contains matter more offensive to my feelings even than that of the Dungeon-Bill... Your principles are almost all false; and your reasoning... is the same. But, it is not my intention to waste any time on your abstract matter. I shall come, at once, to your practical result; to your recommendation to the Borough-mongers to pass laws to *punish the poor for marrying*.[1]

In this strictly contemporary atmosphere of gloom and rage, Peacock, who in *Melincourt* shares Shelley's rage at other aspects of England, is amazingly mild in his reaction to Malthus, even when he satirises him. Fax is at worst an eccentric who makes a scene at a wedding but who usually practices more generously than he preaches. He is harmless: unlike Malthus, he has no evil influence on society or politics, and no bond with perse-cuting landlords or the politics of Mainchance Villa. Linked with Peacock's mildness is the mildness of Forester's reaction to Fax, compared with Shelley's reactions to Malthus. Compare Forester's introduction of Fax and his arguments with him, with a passage Shelley wrote not long after *Melincourt*:

A writer of the present day (a priest of course, for his doctrines are those of a eunuch and of a tyrant) has stated that the evils of the poor arise from an excess of population, and after they have been stript naked by the tax-gatherer and reduced to bread and tea and fourteen hours of hard labour by their masters, and after the frost has bitten their defenceless limbs, and the cramp has wrung like a disease within their bones, and hunger and the suppressed revenge of hunger has stamped the ferocity of want like the mark of Cain upon their countenance, that the last tie by which Nature holds them to the benignant earth whose plenty is garnered up in the strongholds of their tyrants, is to be divided; that the single alleviation of their sufferings and their scorns, the one thing which made it impossible to degrade them below the beasts, which amid all their crimes and miseries yet separated a cynical and unmanly contamination, an anti-social cruelty, from all the soothing, elevating and harmonious gentleness of the sexual intercourse and the humanizing charities of domestic life which are its appendages—that this is to be obliterated. They are required to abstain from marrying under penalty of starvation.[2]

[1] 'Letter to Parson Malthus', *Cobbett's weekly political register*, 8 May 1819: xxxiv, col. 1019.
[2] *A philosophical view of reform*, in *Political tracts of Wordsworth, Coleridge and Shelley*, ed. R. J. White (London, 1953), p. 239.

How does *Melincourt* compare with contemporary treatments of Malthus, other than those of blind rage? Valid comparisons can only be found for the element of satire in Peacock's treatment.

Godwin in 1820 saw the weakness of most earlier attacks on Malthus:

> It is not a little extraordinary, that Mr. Malthus' book should now have been twenty years before the public, without any one, so far as I know, having attempted a refutation of his main principle. It was easy for men of a generous temper to vent their horror at the revolting nature of the conclusions he drew from this principle; and this is nearly all that has been done...They seem with one consent to have shrunk from a topic, which required so much patient investigation.[1]

Godwin therefore set out, in his 1820 book *Of population*, to refute Malthus on the latter's chosen ground—*facts*. This factual retaliation is unsatisfactory, however, and the book's distinction lies elsewhere. Firstly, Godwin attacks Malthus's belief that he had behind his case 'the laws of Nature, which are the laws of God'. Counter-appealing to 'what has been the creed of all ages and nations',[2] and in several eloquently persuasive passages describing the full meaning of marriage, Godwin argues that the laws of Nature and of God demand that people should marry: 'neither man nor woman has fulfilled the ends of their being, nor had a real experience of the privileges of human existence, without having entered into the ties, and participated in the delights, of domestic life'.[3] Godwin's second telling method can be described as 'ridicule in the shape of reasoning' (to reverse Coleridge's phrase), and can best be illustrated by book VI, chapter VI: 'Of marriage, and the persons who may justifiably enter into that state'. The aim here is to expose Malthus's attempts to make calculations about aspects and prospects of human life that cannot be calculated, and to show how 'the misery of all our author's reasonings upon human affairs is that they are pictureless, and dwell entirely in abstractions and generalities'.[4] He quotes a passage from Malthus to the effect that anyone who marries without a fair 'prospect of being able to support a family' has 'erred in the face of a

[1] *Of population*, pp. vii–viii.
[2] *Ibid*. p. 105.
[3] *Ibid*. p. 585.
[4] *Ibid*. p. 572.

most clear and precise warning': 'To the punishment of Nature therefore he should be left.'[1] Godwin gives particular instances of the chance ill-fortunes 'that await us in the darkness of the future', and with each instance he repeats with more and more ridiculous effect the key phrases from Malthus. What, for example, if a husband dies?

The Essay on Population makes no provision for this. 'They should not have families, without being able to support them.' And, as to his children, 'a fair, distinct and precise notice' was given, two years or upwards before they were born, and therefore, though perishing with hunger, they 'have no right to complain'.[2]

The method of this chapter could certainly be developed in a novel, particularly in a novel of dialogue and episode such as Peacock's.

In 1832 Coleridge said that Malthus's abominable tenet 'should be exposed by reasoning in the shape of ridicule. Asgill and Swift would have done much.'[3] It is suprising that, before Dickens, *Melincourt* was the only sustained work answering to Coleridge's description. Even *Melincourt* does not develop very fully the possibilities which Malthus offered a novelist.

'The weapon of Thomas Love Peacock', says H. A. Boner, 'was ridicule and the *reductio ad absurdum*.'[4] But, even when Peacock's intention is clearly to ridicule, the debates do not develop far enough to reach the *reductio ad absurdum*. Fax and Forester keep too close to the commonplace points that had always been made in the Malthusian debate: they argue on an intellectual level that Godwin, as quoted above, was to see as too low to produce real thought. Admittedly it would not be in place in a novel, even a dialogue novel, to argue about Fax's facts. What *would* be in place is something like the destructive reasoning of Godwin's book VI, chapter VI. Peacock, in an exchange I have quoted before, touches on the subject of that chapter:

Mr. Fax:...The remedy is an universal human compact, binding both sexes to equally rigid celibacy, till the prospect of maintaining the average number of six children be as clear as the arithmetic of futurity can make it.

[1] *Of population*, p. 573.   [2] *Ibid.* p. 579.
[3] *Table-talk*, II, 88.   [4] *Hungry generations*, pp. 78–9.

Mr. Forester: The arithmetic of futurity has been found in a more than equal number of instances to baffle human skill. The rapid and sudden mutations of fortune are the inexhaustible theme of history, poetry and romance.[1]

The point is forcefully made: but, once made, the subject is left, and not argued out.

The illustrative episode seems a promising method of developing the debates. For instance, the abstractions and generalities of Fax and Forester's first exchanges are put to the test of real and particular life by the episode of Desmond. Peacock intends this to show the corruption of society, to refute Fax by an example of love surviving poverty, and to support Forester by an example of the effect of 'discriminating practical philanthropy'. But the test-case is not convincing. Desmond is not a man born and always living in poverty, with narrow experience and views: he is a sensitive unemployed intellectual. The episode reads like an *exemplum* life-history from *The rambler* or *Joseph Andrews* or its imitations. A sign of this is the uncertainty of style. Fax claims to relate the story in Desmond's own words, and the chapter is written in the first person, as if by Desmond. As he begins his story he sounds like the conventional Man of Integrity ingenuously encountering the Corrupt World and being righteously shocked by it. This style is soon overtaken by a cynical and epigrammatical wit that is obviously Peacock's:

They seemed not to be aware that a corrupt administration estimates conscience and Stilton cheese by the same criterion, that its rottenness was its recommendation.[2]

She was...proficient in French grammar, though she had read no book in that language but *Télémaque*, and hated the names of Rousseau and Voltaire, because she had heard them called rascals by her father who had taken his opinion on trust from the Reverend Mr. Simony, who had never read a page of either of them.[3]

Into this merges a Foresterian self-righteous rhetoric: 'To what end could a pupil of the ancient Romans mingle with such a multitude? To cringe, to lie, to flatter? To bow to the insolence of wealth, the superciliousness of rank, the contumely of

[1] Chapter 7: Halliford, ii, 76–7.   [2] Chapter 13: *ibid.* p. 138.
[3] Chapter 13: *ibid.* p. 140.

patronage...'[1] The only life of the chapter lies in Peacock's comments on fashionable society and the literary world. There is no feeling for Desmond's own experience, for the miseries of poverty and of searching for work, such as we get from a contemporary book from real life like Samuel Bamford's *Passages in the life of a radical* or from Mark Rutherford's *Revolution in Tanner's Lane*, which is based on Bamford's autobiography.

A more convincing episode is 'The rustic wedding' (chapter 35), in which Fax interrupts the ceremony with his theories and is met with the bridegroom's real feelings and common sense. The scene is a good satirical idea which was to be used with variations by Cobbett[2] and Dickens.[3] The bride and groom are stage rustics, and speak stage 'dialect' but visually they are authentic:

The bridegroom, with a pair of chubby cheeks, which in colour precisely rivalled his new scarlet waistcoat, and his mouth expanded into a broad grin, that exhibited the total range of his teeth, advanced in a sort of step that was half a walk and half a dance, as if the pre-conceived notion of the requisite solemnity of demeanour were struggling with the natural impulses of the overflowing joy of his heart.[4]

They are not used to Fax's abstractions:

I stand here as the representative of general reason, to ask if you have duly weighed the consequences of your present proceeding...
The Bridegroom (scratching his head): There be a mort o' voine words, but I zuppose you means to zay as how this General Reason be a Methody preacher; but I be's true earthy-ducks church, and zo be Zukey.[5]

They cannot argue, or follow arguments: Fax mystifies and alarms them: but the bridegroom's reason is final:

Lord love you, that be all mighty voine rigmarol; but the short and the long be this: I can't live without Zukey, nor Zukey without I, can you, Zukey?[6]

[1] Chapter 13: Halliford, II, 147.
[2] *Surplus population, and the Poor-Law Bill. A comedy...by the late William Cobbett...published at Cobbett's Register Office* [no date].
[3] *The Chimes* (London, 1844): first quarter.
[4] Chapter 35: Halliford, II, 364.
[5] *Ibid.* pp. 364–5. [6] *Ibid.* p. 371.

The drawback of this episode lies not in these rustics but in Fax. He here becomes a simple figure, a crank possessed by an idea, who would do very well in *Headlong Hall* but who contradicts the sense of Fax we have by this late point in the book—our sense of a man and a temperament being behind the 'frosty philosophy'.

By this point in the novel, Peacock has in fact brought out a positive side to this 'frosty philosophy' that can unite with the solid part of Forester's ideas. But this in itself has a weakness. The more Fax comes to be taken seriously, the less is he clearly related to Malthus. The focus is always changing: sometimes he is like Malthus, sometimes like any social economist or scientist, and often in his reasoning and his realism about politics he is more like Peacock himself. He has Peacock's approval only by having views uncharacteristic of Malthus: for instance, he emphasises the effect on the poor of the luxuries of the rich, the very point that most writers accused Malthus of ignoring. Fairly early in the novel, Fax is led away from his own Malthusian ground, on to Forester's more emotional and moral preoccupations, with the ideas of Chivalry and Modern Heartlessness.

Malthusianism, with its related strands of nineteenth-century thought, is the theme of *Hard times*. A comparison of this novel with *Melincourt* has so far been kept at bay because it would engulf Peacock's individuality: in any case, Dickens had the advantage of a further thirty-seven years of history, with all the change in perspectives they brought. Yet some reference to the later novel will serve to draw together what we have already independently seen on the Malthusian part of *Melincourt*.

Firstly as to method: the principles ruling Coketown are seen not as 'pictureless ideas', as is often the case with *Melincourt*, but in terms of their effect on the lives of their exponents and those under their power. The course of the story, through three books called 'Sowing', 'Reaping' and 'Garnering', is the inevitable working out of human logic. That is, it traces what would happen, because of the laws of human nature, to those who like Bounderby and Gradgrind adopt those principles. Whatever the modern disagreements over the success of the

novel, and whatever its frequent false notes, it will be agreed
that its *medium* is not ideas but human needs and feelings, the
life of various Victorian social classes. The medium of *Melincourt*,
on the other hand, is most often the discussion of ideas *qua*
ideas. The debaters *talk* about human needs and feelings, and
the effects of ideas on individual lives: but these lives and
feelings are *seen* only in illustrative stories like that of Desmond.
While Peacock's method has its fruits, the disadvantage is a
less compelling relation to contemporary and particular life.

The second general point of contrast is that Dickens sees the
close link of Malthusianism with other influential ideas in
Victorian life—individualism, materialism, philistinism, and
Benthamite education. This sense of how these different threads
are related and strengthen one another gives a unity to Dickens's
pictures of the many aspects of Coketown. There is no such
perception, and therefore no such unity, in *Melincourt*: it remains
a medley of episodes and discussions on aspects of society only
loosely related in Peacock's mind. What may be called the glue
that holds this medley together is a diffuse and vague Foresterian
lament at the Corruption of Modern Life—the lament Forester
makes in many of the discussions, and into the spirit of which
Fax is often assimilated.

*

The medley of social topics includes the episodes of dramatic
satire such as 'The election' and 'Mainchance Villa'. It is
worth examining first, however, the other topics that go with
the Malthusian theme in being seriously treated. They arise
mainly in solemn speeches by Forester and discussions with
Fax and others, which Peacock believes will develop our
thoughts on the topics.

Representative is the recurring theme of Country and Agriculture versus Town and Industry. Here the same criticism
applies to *Melincourt* that was made of the corresponding part
of *Headlong Hall*. Forester is so vague on the subject that what
he says is scarcely distinguishable from the glue of the medley,
the Foresterian lament at Modern Corruption. His case for
country life is bound up with some of the sillier ideas we first
met in Escot in *Headlong Hall*, such as the gradual 'diminution
of the species', intellectually and physically, owing to meat and

drink, clothes and city life.[1] For this idea Peacock's footnotes refer us to Lord Monboddo's *Ancient metaphysics*, but the link is equally with J. F. Newton and so with an earlier stage of Shelley than is represented by other of Forester's ideas.

No effective dramatic episode illustrates this theme, which the following brief encounter hardly brings alive:

Anthelia...was more and more delighted with the neatness and comfort of the dwellings, the exquisite order of the gardens, the ingenuous air of happiness and liberty that characterised the simple inhabitants, and the health and beauty of the little rosy children that were sporting in the fields. Mr. Forester had been recognised from a distance. The cottagers ran out in all directions to welcome him: the valley and the hills seemed starting into life, as men, women, and children poured down, as with one impulse, on the path of his approach...[2]

This is interesting as Peacock's tribute to Shelley as a noble person, who had the disinterested and instinctive generosity that modern society lacked. But Forester is here an ethereal ideal, too near the Victorian picture of Shelley as an angel. Forester here reminds us of the idealised, serene benevolence of M. de Wolmar in *La Nouvelle Héloïse*, rather than the impetuous and exhausting help Shelley gave to (for instance) the poor people in Marlow in 1817. The peasants, too, are from Rousseau, not the desperate and often starving poor of the years between Waterloo and Peterloo, of whom there is no sign in *Melincourt*. A feeling of the real Shelley and the real poor of 1817 is given by Mrs Shelley in a note on *The revolt of Islam*:

During the year 1817, we were established at Marlow, in Buckinghamshire...Marlow was inhabited (I hope it is altered now) by a very poor population. The women are lace-makers, and lose their health by sedentary labour, for which they were very ill paid. The poor-laws ground to the dust not only the paupers but those who had risen just above that state, and were obliged to pay poor-rates. The changes produced by peace following a long war, and a bad harvest, brought with them the most heart-rending evils to the poor. Shelley

[1] In the very first scene in which we meet Forester (chapter 4) he is engaged in research on skulls and bones. For the larger theme of Country *v.* Town, see especially chapters 25, 26, 36 and 37.

[2] Chapter 26: Halliford, ii, 284–5.

afforded what alleviation he could. In the winter, while bringing out his poem, he had a severe attack of ophthalmia, caught while visiting the poor cottages. I mention these things—for this minute and active sympathy with his fellow-creatures gives a thousandfold interest to his speculations, and stamps with reality his pleadings for the human race.[1]

This contrast of Forester and Shelley, like that of Fax and Malthus, is not made in order to complain that Peacock is 'untrue to his sources' and fails to 'transcribe his originals'. If one were presented with the passages without knowledge of their authorship or context, Mrs Shelley's would (even without the documentary details and dates) impress as authentic, as having 'the stamp of reality', and Peacock's as idyllic and remote from reality.

It is unnecessary to show in detail that the weaknesses of the theme of country life are shared by the related serious themes, such as the idea of modern chivalry and the qualities and duties of an ideal woman. Forester's ideas on these subjects (which amalgamate Peacock's and Shelley's ideas) were not the commonplaces of the age: Anthelia's intellectual interests and philanthropic activities are intended as a criticism of the Regency idea of womanhood. But she does not come alive for most readers—who really worries about her when she is kidnapped? She is less a character than an ideal figure produced to fit Forester's abstract requirements. The whole theme of womanhood exists mainly in Forester's speeches—as do the other serious themes.

The author has, therefore, too often surrendered his independence of mind to Forester. A rough analogy may be made with Aldous Huxley's *Point Counter Point*, which attempts among other things a conversation-novel on the intellectual world of the 1920s similar to *Melincourt*'s treatment of the intellectual world of the 1810s. *Melincourt* stands in the same relation to Shelley as *Point Counter Point* does to D. H. Lawrence (this is in no way to compare the writers themselves). Huxley includes a half-critical, half-appreciative portrait of Lawrence as Rampion: but the influence appears also in long stretches of second-hand

---

[1] *Poetical works of Shelley*, ed. Mary Shelley, 4 vols. (London, 1839), I, 376.

Lawrentianism in the words of the novelist himself or those of Rampion who is usually the novelist's mouthpiece. In the process of transfer from Lawrence to Huxley, the ideas become stale, wordy and sermon-like. Lawrence resented this taming process and wrote to Huxley that 'Your Rampion is the most boring character in the book—a gas-bag. Your attempt at intellectual sympathy!—It's all rather disgusting, and I feel like a badger that has its hole on Wimbledon Common and trying not to be caught.'[1] Shelley was less sensible and self-critical than Lawrence, and was pleased by Forester. But Peacock's 'attempt at intellectual sympathy' is forced. *Melincourt's* Shelleyanism is as stale as Huxley's Lawrentianism, and Forester often 'the most boring character in the book—a gas-bag'.

*

If the subject of the whole medley of *Melincourt* is 'modern corruption', it becomes precise and vivid when focused on political corruption. Mr Fax says that 'All the arts and eloquence of corruption may be overthrown by the enumeration of these simple words: boroughs, taxes, and paper-money'[2] and each of these has its dramatic episode.[3] Many episodes however are important not in what happens but in what is said: representative speakers reveal their political attitudes, sophistry and cant. They are damned out of their own mouths, not Forester's. One such representative figure is Mr Feathernest, the radical turned reactionary and Poet-Laureate, who is modelled on Robert Southey. 'The symposium' (chapter 16) is dramatic in the way it follows the natural development of an after-dinner conversation, which (with the accompanying tongue-loosening drinks) leads Feathernest to give himself away. The subject of drinks leads by way of allusions to the Poet-Laureate's claret, to Feathernest's acknowledgement that he gets his wine 'for a song'. By now he is jovially drunk enough to give a brazen self-justification.

The scene stands out, too, for its lively language and quick exchanges. Peacock does not (until the end) rely on long tirades

---

[1] *Letters*, ed. Aldous Huxley (London, 1932), p. 758.
[2] Chapter 39: Halliford, ii, 414.
[3] For taxes, see chapter 32, 'The deserted mansion', which does not merit extended discussion.

by Forester to make his point. Forester's part is at first quiet disapproval:

I am unfortunately one of those, Sir, who very much admired your Odes to Truth and Liberty, and read your royal lyrics with very different sensations.[1]

He becomes more violent in attacking radicals turned courtiers:

for there is in these cases no criterion by which the world can distinguish the baying of a noble dog that will defend his trust till death, from the yelping of a political cur, that only infests the heels of power to be silenced with the offals of corruption.[2]

Feathernest has heard it all before and is 'quite callous to it, I assure you'. He laughs it off with the condescension of worldly wise age to the earnestness of naïve youth, and with the hint that it is at best priggish cant, and at worst malice and envy.

While I was out, Sir, I made a great noise till I was let in. There was a pack of us, Sir, to keep up your canine metaphor: two or three others got in at the same time: we knew very well that those who were shut out would raise a hue and cry after us: it was perfectly natural: we should have done the same in their place: mere envy and malice, nothing more.[3]

Truth and liberty, Sir, are pretty words, very pretty words—a few years ago they were the gods of the day...I acted accordingly the part of a prudent man: I took my station, became my own crier, and vociferated truth and liberty, till the noise I made brought people about me, to bid for me: and to the best bidder I knocked myself down.[4]

This interpretation of Southey's motives has by most critics been called funny but unfair. That is true: its value is as a general picture of self-interest for which one can find models less respectable than Southey from any period. But, if Peacock misses Southey's motives, he catches other aspects of the man. This encounter of Forester and Feathernest (and Paperstamp) is vividly reminiscent of the meeting of Shelley and Southey in 1811. There is the same infuriating condescension towards youthful liberalism. Southey had said that Shelley acted on him uncomfortably 'as my own ghost would do. He is just what I

[1] Chapter 16: Halliford, II, 177.   [2] *Ibid.* p. 178.
[3] *Ibid.* p. 179.   [4] *Ibid.* p. 182.

was in 1798'.[1] Similarly 'Mr Paperstamp did not much like Mr Forester's modes of thinking; indeed he disliked them the more, from their having once been his own'.[2] And Anthelia's Foresterian question about chivalry 'burst upon [Feathernest] like the spectre of his youthful integrity, and he mumbled a half-intelligible reply, about truth and liberty—disinterested benevolence....'.[3] Southey sneered at Shelley's philosophy as 'a phase' just as Feathernest calls truth and liberty out-of-date fashions. Both Southey and Feathernest end with the advice, 'When you are my age...'.

This is more than a personal grudge of Shelley avenged by Peacock: it represents a common and justifiable resentment felt by many of their contemporaries at the need Southey, Wordsworth and others felt to apologise for their earlier radical views. Shelley's general account of this can be found in the Preface to *The revolt of Islam*, where he describes the mistaken pessimism produced by the later bad developments of the French Revolution. That this was not a purely Shelleyan resentment can be seen from a passage (of the same date) in the diary of Henry Crabb Robinson, who belonged not to Shelley's but to Wordsworth's and Southey's generation. Reviewing his reactions to the history of the previous twenty years, he concludes:

Most intensely did I rejoice at the Counter Revolution. I had also rejoiced when a boy at the Revolution, and I am ashamed of neither sentiment...The immediate alone is within our scope of action and observation. But now that the old system is restored, with it the old cares and apprehensions revive also, and I am sorry that Wordsworth cannot change with the times. He ought, I think, now to exhort our Government to economy, and to represent the dangers of a thoughtless return to all that was in existence twenty-five years ago.[4]

This is the feeling that Peacock interprets in 'The symposium'.

The corruption of parliamentary representation is illustrated by an episode that makes its point largely by what *happens*. In his

[1] See above, p. 70.   [2] Chapter 39: Halliford, II, 398.
[3] Chapter 8: *ibid*. p. 85.
[4] *On books and their writers*, I, p. 183. The year when this comment was written is, appropriately enough, 1816—the year of the Preface to *The revolt of Islam* and of the commencement of *Melincourt*.

England in 1815, Halévy shows that it was common for an election to begin like a fair or race-meeting—a 'great political carnival which the common people regarded as their right'— and lead through the 'wretched farce' of the election itself to a final riot.[1] This is exactly what happens at the Borough of Onevote. This constituency 'stood in the middle of a heath, and consisted of a solitary farm'. By the time the 'motley cavalcade' of spectators arrive from Novote (the nearby industrial town without representation), 'The heath had very much the appearance of a race-ground; with booths and stalls, the voices of pie-men and apple-women, the grinding of barrel-organs'.[2] Then comes the farcical election by one voter of two members of parliament, one of whom is an orang-outang. Finally Sir Oran Haut-ton, not liking being chaired, causes the riot.

The main critical effect of the episode, however, lies as usual not in what happens but in what is said. Mr Sarcastic's speeches justifying the electoral system in terms of virtual and actual representation, belong with the speeches at Mainchance Villa. Peacock keeps very close to the actual arguments used by conservatives, altering their words and changing the force of their images just enough to bring out their real motives and evil implications. The power of this technique can be shown by parallel quotations, from the *Quarterly review* article on parliamentary reform to which Peacock explicitly refers, and from the novel itself. Thus the *Quarterly* says:

Others there are who have made a direct purchase of their seats, and these may thus far be said to be the most independent men in the House, as the mob-representatives are undoubtedly the least so. [Thus] the House obtains some of its most useful, most distinguished, and most intelligent members.

The Ultra Whigs differ widely in the means of reform they propose, the object however in which they generally agree, is that of rendering all elections popular. The principle that the representative must obey the instructions of his constituents, which many of the reformers profess, would follow as a necessary consequence; and the moment that principle is established, 'chaos is come again', anarchy begins, or

[1] *A History of the English people in the nineteenth century,* trans. E. I. Watkin and D. A. Barker, 2 vols., 2nd ed. (London, 1961), i, *England in 1815,* 150–2.
[2] Chapter 22: Halliford, ii, 241.

more truly an ochlarchy, a mob-government, which is as much worse than anarchy, as the vilest ruffians of a civilized country are more wicked than rude savages.[1]

Mr Sarcastic argues on similar lines:

The duty of a representative of the people, whether actual or virtual, is simply *to tax*. Now this important branch of public business is much more easily and expeditiously transacted by the means of virtual, than it possibly could be by that of actual representation... which might, perhaps, look black on some of [the minister's] favourite projects, thereby greatly impeding the distribution of secret service money at home, and placing foreign legitimacy in a very awkward predicament. The carriage of the state would then be like a chariot in a forest, turning to the left for a troublesome thorn, and then to the right for a sturdy oak; whereas it now rolls forward like the car of Juggernaut over the plain, crushing whatever offers to impede its way.[2]

At Mainchance Villa:

Mr. Killthedead: The members for rotten boroughs are the most independent members in the Honourable House, and the representatives of most constituents least so.
Mr. Fax: How will you prove that?
Mr. Killthedead: By calling the former gentlemen, and the latter mob-representatives.
Mr. Vamp: Nothing can be more logical.
Mr. Fax: Do you call that logic?
Mr. Vamp: Excellent logic. At least it will pass for such with our readers.[3]

At Mainchance Villa the parody is intensified by direct quotations from, and footnote references to, the *Quarterly review* article, and by the variety of Canning's arguments that Peacock satirises. The dramatic point of the episode is to take us behind the scenes, and behind the hypocrisy, to hear the conservatives planning the tactics of their article. For example:

Mr. Feathernest Mr. Killthedead, and Mr. Paperstamp: The Church is in danger! The Church is in danger!
Mr. Vamp: Keep up that. It is an infallible tocsin for rallying all the old women about us when everything else fails.

---

[1] *Quarterly review*, XVI (Oct. 1816), 258.
[2] Chapter 39: Halliford, II, 412–13.   [3] *Ibid.* p. 402.

Mr. Paperstamp: We shall make out a very good case; but you must not forget to call the present public distress an awful dispensation: a little pious cant goes a great way towards taming the thoughts of men from the dangerous and jacobinical propensity of looking into moral and political causes for moral and political effects.[1]

It is in reply to that speech of Paperstamp's that Fax lists the facts of modern corruption:

Mr. Fax: But the moral and political causes are now too obvious, and too universally known, to be obscured by any such means. All the arts and eloquence of corruption may be overthrown by the enumeration if these simple words: boroughs, taxes, and paper-money.
Mr. Anyside Antijack: Paper-money! What, is the ghost of bullion abroad?[2]

Antijack's retort is echoed by most readers, who feel that Peacock's hatred of paper-money is merely one of his own crotchets or obsessions. But it was not an irrational dislike of token currency as such, for in the financial state of England after Waterloo the paper-money issued did not correspond to the actual wealth of the country, and its value was therefore precarious. Peacock attacks not only the suspension of specie payments that continued after the war, but the failure of provincial banks. In this he was no alarmist: between 1798 and 1818, two hundred and thirty banks failed.[3]

The episode of 'The paper-mill' (chapter 30) presents, in the words of the victims, the effect of a bank-failure on the variety of individual lives in a town. A farmer loses all his savings. A lady has been cheated twice but cannot connect this with the system itself:

'Indeed,' she said, 'she had something better to do than to trouble herself about politics, and wondered he [Fax] should insult her in her distress by talking of such stuff to her.'[4]

The vicar was forewarned: Fax asks

'Why did not you warn your flock of the impending danger?
'Sir,' said the reverend gentleman, 'I dined every week with one of the partners.'[5]

---

[1] Chapter 39: Halliford, II, 413–14.   [2] *Ibid.* p. 414.
[3] See J. H. Clapham, *An economic history of modern Britain; the early railway age* (London, 1930), p. 270.
[4] Chapter 30: Halliford, II, 324.   [5] *Ibid.* p. 321.

He calls Mr Lookout, who did warn them, 'the libellous, seditious, factious, levelling, revolutionary, republican, demo-cratical, atheistical villain'.[1]

*

Of the novel's incidental literary satire, the best known is unfortunately the ponderous parody of Coleridge in 'Cimmerian Lodge' (chapter 31). Peacock shoots very wide of Coleridge, who is seen as a mere parrot of Kant. Moreover he shoots just as wide of Kant himself. Relying on garbled hearsay, Peacock— to adapt what Desmond says of clergymen condemning Voltaire —took his opinion on trust from Sir William Drummond, who had never read a page of Kant.

Drummond's attack, in chapter IX of *Academical questions*, provided the whole idea of 'Cimmerian Lodge'. He translates Professor Born's Latin version:

This region [of pure intelligence] is an island, shut in by nature herself in immoveable prisons. This is the region of truth (the beautiful name), surrounded by a vast and stormy ocean, the proper seat of deceitful form.[2]

Drummond leaves Kantian 'mystagogues' to 'measure their island of pure intelligence'.[3] And so Peacock takes up the description of their voyage:

Mr. Mystic invited Mr. Fax and his friends to step with him into the boat, and cross over his lake, which he called the *Ocean of Deceitful Form*, to the *Island of Pure Intelligence*, on which Cimmerian Lodge was situated.[4]

Peacock copies exactly Drummond's words of abuse:

The young and ignorant disputant...may be gratified in over-whelming his astonished adversaries with a pedantic and cumbrous jargon...But the philosopher, who merits the name...will say that mysticism is not congenial with philosophy, nor is bombast diction.[5]

So in *Melincourt*,

The reader who is deficient in *taste for the bombast*, and is no *admirer of the obscure*, may well wait on the shore till they return [from] the regions of mystery.[6]

[1] *Ibid*. p. 327.
[2] *Academical questions* (London, 1805), I [no more published], 380.
[3] *Ibid*. p. 381.   [4] Halliford, II, 329–30.
[5] Drummond, *Academical questions*, p. 353.
[6] Halliford, II, 331.

Once in those regions, Mystic exclaims

Ha! in that cylindrical mirror I see three shadowy forms:—dimly I see them through the smoked glass of my spectacles. Who art thou? —MYSTERY!—I hail thee! Who art thou?—JARGON—I love thee! Who art thou?—SUPERSTITION!—I worship thee![1]

Drummond also provides cylindrical mirrors, pure anticipated cognitions and all the other props Peacock needs.

A bland footnote to 'Cimmerian Lodge' announces that

The reader who is desirous of elucidating the mysteries of the words and phrases marked in italics in this chapter may consult the German works of Professor Kant, or Professor Born's Latin translation of them, or M. Villar's [sic] *Philosophie de Kant, ou Principes fondamentaux de la Philosophie Transcendentale*; or the first article of the second number of the *Edinburgh Review*, or the article 'Kant' in the *Encyclopaedia Londiniensis*, or Sir William Drummond's *Academical Questions*, book ii [sic] chap. 9.[2]

But Drummond, with *his* brief quotations from Villers and Born, accounts for everything at Cimmerian Lodge. There is absolutely no evidence that Peacock had himself looked into the Latin or French works, never mind Kant's German. (Drummond, too, did not read the original German.) Nor does Peacock make use of Thomas Brown's *Edinburgh review* article—which would have confronted him with a fairer and *reasoned* disagreement with Kant, but not brought him nearer the original, for Brown admits quite cheerfully 'that we are unacquainted with [Kant's] original works'.[3]

We are clearly up against an intellectual laziness and insularity which Peacock shared complacently with his period. Conservatism is too imposing a term for this response to Kant: we are reminded more of a child who covers his ears and shouts so as to drown what he *will* not hear.

A lesser-known chapter of literary satire deserves more credit: the confrontation of Derrydown and Feathernest in 'The philosophy of ballads' (chapter 9).

[1] Halliford, II, 339.   [2] *Academical questions*, p. 330 n.
[3] *Edinburgh review*, VI (Jan. 1803), 256–7.

Derrydown the ballad-monger, who reminds us partly of Scott, partly of Coleridge, is introduced by one of the outrageously simplified life-histories that are used extensively in *Nightmare Abbey*:

Mr. Derrydown had received a laborious education, and had consumed a great quantity of midnight oil over ponderous tomes of ancient and modern learning, particularly of moral, political and metaphysical philosophy, ancient and modern. His lucubrations in the latter branch of science having conducted him, as he conceived, into the central opacity of utter darkness, he formed a hasty conclusion 'that all human learning is vanity'; and one day, in a listless mood, taking down a volume of the *Reliques of Ancient Poetry*, he found, or fancied he found, in the plain language of the old English ballad, glimpses of the truth of things, which he had vainly sought in the vast volumes of philosophical disquisition. In consequence of this luminous discovery, he locked up his library, purchased a travelling chariot, with a shelf in the back, which he filled with collections of ballads and popular songs; and passed the greater part of every year posting about the country, for the purpose, as he expressed it, of studying together poetry and the peasantry, unsophisticated nature and the truth of things.[1]

A discussion develops between Derrydown and the conservative Feathernest:

'Surely,' said Mr. Feathernest one evening, 'you will not maintain that Chevy Chase is a finer poem than Paradise Lost?'
Mr. Derrydown: I do not know what you mean by a fine poem; but I will maintain that it gives a much deeper insight into the truth of things.
Mr. Feathernest: I do not know what you mean by the truth of things.
The Reverend Mr. Grovelgrub: Define, gentlemen, define; let the one define what he means by a fine poem, and the other what he means by the truth of things.
Mr. Feathernest: A fine poem is a luminous development of the complicated machinery of action and passion, exalted by sublimity, softened by pathos, irradiated by scenes of magnificence, figures of loveliness, and characters of energy, and harmonised with infinite variety of melodious combination...
Mr. Derrydown: The truth of things is nothing more than an exact view

[1] Halliford, II, 83–4.

of the necessary relations between object and subject, in all the modes of reflection and sentiment which constitute the reciprocities of human association.[1]

Derrydown illustrates it by a lengthy gloss on the ballad of Old Robin Gray as 'a more profound view than the deepest metaphysical treatise or the most elaborate history can give you of the counteracting power of opposite affections, the conflict of duties and inclinations, the omnipotence of interest, tried by the test of extremity, and the supreme and irresistible dominion of universal moral necessity'.[2] The demonstration that follows forms a classic of satire on preposterous inflationary 'interpretation'.

The whole scene brings home the split in critical taste and criteria in the Regency. Feathernest's bland and mechanical neo-classical definition means nothing to Derrydown, whose modish psychological-cum-philosophical formula baffles Feathernest. The other guests are puzzled by both.

This split in taste is described by Mr Crotchet in *Crotchet Castle*:

> The sentimental against the rational, the intuitive against the inductive, the ornamental against the useful, the intense against the tranquil, the romantic against the classical; these are great and interesting controversies, which I should like, before I die, to see satisfactorily settled.[3]

Quoting this speech, Mr G. D. Klingopulos comments:

> There is some penetration in this; we think of similar perceptions in Hazlitt and, later, in John Stuart Mill. But there is no feeling of the importance of what has been perceived. The 'settling' desired by Mr. Crotchet is far removed from the constant striving of Hazlitt to think beyond this opposition of the 'rational' and 'inductive' to the 'sentimental' and 'intuitive'.[4]

The point might be made against the *social* debates in *Melincourt* and *Crotchet Castle*—does Peacock underestimate the difference between the Romantic and the social or political scientist? But

---

[1] Halliford, ii, 90–2.   [2] *Ibid.* pp. 93–4.
[3] Chapter 2: Halliford, iv, 22.
[4] 'The spirit of the age in prose', in *From Blake to Byron*, ed. B. Ford (London, 1957), p. 136.

the criticism misses the point of a *literary* episode like 'The philosophy of ballads'. It is conceived as a comic social scene, and the split is made to produce embarrassment, irritation and pomposity (reporters of Regency literary society, like Haydon or Crabb Robinson, remind us how frequently such scenes occurred). An essential comic figure is the promoter rubbing his hands at having arranged a good fight:

The Reverend Mr. Grovelgrub: Define, gentlemen, define; let the one explain what he means by a fine poem, and the other what he means by the truth of things.[1]

Similarly the key figure of *Crotchet Castle* is Mr Crotchet, the dilettante hungry for after-dinner and journalistic 'controversy'. Not finding the duties and pleasures of a country gentleman sufficient 'modes of filling up his time that accorded with his Caledonian instinct',

The inborn love of disputation...burst forth through the calmer surface of rural life. He grew as fain as Captain Jamy, 'to hear some airgument betwixt ony tway;' and being very hospitable in his establishment, and liberal in his invitations, a numerous detachment from the advanced guard of the 'march of intellect', often marched down to Crotchet Castle.[2]

Having gathered and entertained his experts he is keen to have his money's worth: at breakfast (chapter 2) he speaks only once, as quoted above, and his son once to propose a river-excursion on which 'we will try to settle all the questions over which a shadow of doubt yet hangs in the world of philosophy'.[3] His interest in the split in taste is first to dramatise and exaggerate it, and then paradoxically to 'settle' it. Peacock's interest, here and in 'The philosophy of ballads', is in this popular and journalistic exploitation of the split, and not, as with Fax and Forester, investigating and healing the split itself.

*

The object of *Melincourt* was (in the words Peacock used of *Nightmare Abbey*)[4] 'to bring to a sort of philosophical focus' the

---

[1] Halliford, II, 91.   [2] Chapter 1: Halliford, IV, p. 6.
[3] *Ibid.* pp. 24–5.
[4] See letter to Shelley, 15 Sept. 1818: Halliford, VIII, 204.

England of 1817. How full is Peacock's knowledge of that England, how firm his grasp of it?

Such questions are unavoidably clumsy, and to answer them must be an essay in tact and a search for valid methods of comparison. For we have no definitive picture of, no 'absolute historical truth' about, the Regency, by which to check the novel. Ultimately all 'sources' have to be submitted to a critical appraisal, to decide which is most reliable, and commands most authority, which convinces and gives us most.

Yet there is some use in trying first the crude check of the history book for the events of that year *as* events—as, simply, 'what happened'.

In the sphere of social theory and legislation, it has been seen that 1817 was a year of climax for Malthusian influence and anti-Malthusian fury. Similarly in the sphere of social conditions and protest, it was the crest of the first wave of rebellion and suppression to follow the Peace of 1815. By late 1816 the moderate Burdett, backed by Major Cartwright, had lost control of the London Movement to the hotheaded ultra-radical Henry Hunt, backed by Cobbett. In November Hunt held the first London open-air meeting in support of the petition to the Regent for reform: on display was the tricolour flag of the future British Republic. By December even Hunt was too moderate for the London mob, who broke away from a meeting to murder a gunsmith, arm themselves with his stock, and terrorise the City. On his way to open parliament in January 1817 the Prince Regent was hissed; a bullet or a stone went through the carriage window. Investigations brought to light other plots of assassination and rebellion. Parliament quickly passed a Habeas Corpus Suspension Bill, and a Seditious Meetings Bill which stopped all public meetings and societies including the Hampden Clubs. Cobbett fled to America. Protest now took desperate and hopeless forms: the Blanketeers' March set out 'to take London', and in July the plotters of another northern uprising were arrested.

Behind these events were not only political principles but also the plain facts of hardship and hunger. Arrested with the other plotters of July, Samuel Bamford told the Cabinet that 'if ministers were thoroughly acquainted with the distress of the people, they would be almost surprised that the country was not a scene of confusion and horror, instead of being as it was, peacable, though discontented'.[1] The distress was not confined to the north and the areas of uprising: I have quoted earlier in this chapter Mrs Shelley's account of the state of the poor in Marlow in 1817, where Peacock and the Shelleys were living at the time.

Now we have no right to demand that all novels should engage closely with contemporary society and politics. But the earlier sections of this chapter have, I think, shown that *Melincourt* itself constantly invites us to relate it closely to the world of 1817. Even so, we cannot expect a novel to embody contemporary facts *as* facts. But we can expect to feel their particular pressures behind the general social discussions in the book, affecting its tone and tempo. *Melincourt* rarely betrays any such pressure: on the contrary, its manner is remarkably calm and general.

This in itself does not establish a criticism, for a philosophical detachment might be fruitful, lifting the work above the hot practical confusions of the moment-to-moment battle, and so taking in wider perspectives and ultimate issues. Such a claim is made by Mr R. J. White for comparable works, the political essays of Wordsworth, Coleridge and Shelley:

Their authors were rather 'recluse men of genius' than working politicians or men of the market-place. Their very detachment from the necessary disciplines of parliamentary life and from the detailed exigencies of administration enabled them to see more clearly and to feel more deeply the great movements which ebb and flow in the minds and emotions of ordinary men and women...The strength and value of the work here presented may indeed be said to spring chiefly from the philosophic detachment of the poets, and from the consequent freshness and profundity of their vision.[2]

In this sweeping claim, the possible combination of 'detachment' and 'profundity' is represented as inevitable cause and effect. Matthew Arnold can both convincingly define and fill such a rôle of social critic who is above the practicalities of the

[1] Samuel Bamford, *Passages in the life of a radical*, 2nd ed. (Heywood, Lancs., 1842), I, 144.
[2] *Political tracts of Wordsworth, Coleridge and Shelley*, ed. White, p. viii.

moment.[1] But in Shelley's *Philosophical view of reform* there is a good deal of the generality of ignorance and distance.[2]

As for *Melincourt*, it can be criticised in Mr White's own terms: it is aloof not only from political facts and exigencies but the movement of the times as registered in 'the minds and emotions of ordinary men and women'. This lack of close engagement makes scenes like 'The cottage' (of Desmond) and 'The cottagers' (who welcome Forester) a little unreal, and the characters too near literary 'rustics'. It also weakens the Malthusian discussions: no writer could develop a subject like Malthus very far and avoid a cul-de-sac of generality without turning to the human effects of an influential theory.

The phrases 'human effects', 'the life of the English people', 'ordinary men and women', are vague, even when used as a general contrast with contemporary events, theories and arguments. If the question is asked, 'Where then *can* we feel the life of at least one stratum of the English people in the Regency?', I would point to a specific and outstanding example: Samuel Bamford's autobiography *Passages in the life of a radical*. All the events of 1817 I have listed above as raw facts, Bamford conveys as his own lived experience.

The opening paragraph indicates his scope: he will record the 'events which took place in the manufacturing districts of Lancashire, and other parts of England, during the years 1816, to 1821', with the activities of 'the parliamentary reformers and their opponents'. He then gives his personal credentials: 'The writer was a partaker in most of the scenes he will describe. They are vividly impressed on his memory, some of them are also interwoven with the feelings of his heart.'[3] A summary

[1] See especially *The function of criticism at the present time*: 'There is the world of ideas and the world of practice', and the critic (in this wide sense) must be '*disinterested*', 'must keep out of the region of immediate practice in the political, social, humanitarian sphere, if he wants to make a beginning for that more free speculative treatment of things, which may perhaps one day make its benefits felt even in this sphere.' (*Essays in criticism*, series I, London, 1865, pp. 12 and 26.)

[2] This is confirmed by a detailed study of letters to and from Shelley during his last period in Italy. His information on the state of England was vague, he thought reports of unrest were exaggerated, and was as much surprised as shocked by Peterloo.

[3] Bamford, *Passages in the life of a radical*, I, 3.

with several quotations will indicate the variety and first-handedness of his presentation.

Bamford, a Lancashire silk weaver, knows personally the effect of industrialism and national economics on the material conditions of life. He shows the workers' growing urge to read, understand and act. We see the involvement of radicalism with noncomformism, and the feeling for reform as a moral crusade. Bamford and his friends constantly see themselves in terms of characters and situations from *Pilgrim's progress* and adapt Bunyan's hymn as follows:

> Nor lions can him fright,
> He'll with the giants (tyrants) fight,
> And he shall have his right,
> To be a pilgrim.[1]

He is aware however of the different temperaments and lesser intelligences of other radical leaders, such as the traditional rebel Jeremiah Brandreth, and the Blanketeer marcher who was asked what they would have done had they reached London: '"Done?" he replied, in surprise at the question; "Why iv wee'd nobbo gett'n to Lunnun, we shud ha' tan' th' nation, an sattl't o' th' dett."'[2] Another element is the power and vanity of the London leaders like Hunt: here is his part in the day that the Prince Regent was hissed and shot at:

Now it was that I beheld Hunt in his element. He unrolled the petition, which was many yards in length, and it was carried on the heads of the crowd, perfectly unharmed. He seemed to know almost every man of them, and his confidence in, and entire mastery over them, made him quite at ease. A louder huzza than common was music to him; and when the questions were asked eagerly, 'Who is he?' 'What are they about?' and the reply was, 'Hunt! Hunt! huzza!' his gratification was expressed by a stern smile.[3]

Finally, because of the oddly direct relation of rulers and people, by which suspects like Bamford were questioned by the Cabinet itself, we have sketches of the ministers of the day.

Bamford helped found his local Hampden Club. He conveys what the restrictive Bills of 1817 meant to his community:

[1] *Ibid.* ii, 234.
[2] *Ibid.* i, 34.
[3] *Ibid.* i, 19–20.

Our Society, thus houseless [through the chapel-keepers' fear] became divided and dismayed; hundreds slunk home to their looms, nor dared to come out, save like owls at nightfall, when they would perhaps steal through bye-paths or behind hedges, or down some clough, to hear the news at the next cottage...

Personal liberty not being now secure from one hour to another, many of the leading reformers were induced to quit their homes, and seek concealment where they could obtain it.[1]

Yet he was involved in all the major demonstrations of that and succeeding years. The experiences reported range from the dispirited futility of the Blanketeers, to the good-natured fun on the occasion of Hunt's famous visit to the Manchester Theatre, and the religious solemnity of the march to St Peter's Field followed by the horror of the massacre:

'Stand fast,' I said, 'they are riding upon us, Stand fast.' And there was a general cry in our quarter of 'Stand fast'. The cavalry were in confusion: they evidently could not, with all the weight of man and horse, penetrate that compact mass of human beings; and their sabres were plied to hew a way through naked held up hands, and defenceless heads; and then chopped limbs, and wound-gaping skulls were seen...

In ten minutes from the commencement of the havock, the field was an open and almost deserted space. The sun looked down through a sultry and motionless air. The curtains and blinds of the windows within were all closed...several mounds of human beings still remained where they had fallen, crushed down, and smothered. Some of these were still groaning,—others with staring eyes, were gasping for breath, and others would never breathe more. All was silent save those low sounds, and the occasional snorting and pawing of steeds. Persons might sometimes be noticed peeping from attics and over the tall ridgings of houses, but they quickly withdrew, as if fearful of being observed, or unable to sustain the full gaze, of a scene so hideous and abhorrent.[2]

So often in Bamford one feels an urge to point to a passage and say, '*That* is what it felt like to live then', '*There* is Regency society, or one part of it'.[3] *Melincourt*, in contrast, rarely

[1] Bamford, *Passages in the life of a radical*, I, 44–5.
[2] *Ibid.* I, 207–8.
[3] In this and similar attempts to apprehend the life of the time, and to relate it to *Melincourt* and other contemporary works, I am very indebted to the example

conveys this feeling of the specific and the experienced, to 'stamp with reality its pleadings for the human race'.[1] Even without independent evidence Bamford, like ourselves, would have placed the author in one of those groups of general social theorists whom Bamford contrasted with those who acted and suffered.

With exactly *which* group of general social theorists are *Melincourt*'s affiliations strongest? Those affiliations divide, I think, roughly in line with the division between the successful satirical episodes and the over-ambitious serious debates.

The satirical episodes can rely happily on Peacock's particular kind of knowledge of contemporary England. It was not Bamford's, but that of an observer with sharp intelligence who read and deduced from the newspapers and reviews. He studied them not only for information and the leading topics of the day, but also with a keen eye for sophistry and hypocrisy. He is intellectually detached almost to the point of enjoying sophistry and hypocrisy as a pure intellectual challenge, to be attacked for itself rather than for its social effects; his concern often seems to be reason and intellectual clarity rather than honesty

of Dr David Craig's discussion of 'The age of Scott', in his book *Scottish literature and the Scottish people, 1680–1830* (London, 1961). The spirit of his chapter 'The age of Scott' may be evoked here in my support, at least as a witness to what he rightly calls the 'delicacy' of the critical task.

Asking of the Scottish novelists 'how far their work was charged with the life lived in their place and time', and with due acknowledgement of the different ways a writer may engage with his time, Dr Craig complains that they were 'uncertain, for one thing, in their sense of what was essential in the life then going forward. To formulate such a lack is delicate. Yet surely, faced with a literature so bitty as the Scottish, we find ourselves, willy-nilly, compelled to keep referring to the sense of history we have accumulated from sources outside the literature. We wonder, "Did no novelist see anything in *that*, or *that*?"' (p. 140). Dr Craig's 'sources outside the literature' (that is, outside imaginative literature), include histories as records of social 'facts', but also letters and memoirs which register those 'facts' as specific experiences and perceptions. Quoting Cockburn's report of the 'Radical war' (which was roughly contemporary with Peterloo), Dr Craig points: '*There* is contemporary life' (p. 155).

A similar insistence on the specific and the experienced, leading to a use of Bamford and interest in Peterloo not different in kind from my own, will be found in a good historical work like E. P. Thompson's *The making of the English working class* (London, 1963).

[1] See quotation from Mrs Shelley above, pp. 113–14.

and justice. This is far from the spirit of Bamford, and in fact from the main current of Reformism in the 1810s.[1] But, if we move the comparison from Bamford to Shelley and then to Southey, we see that the satirical rationalism of scenes like *Mainchance Villa* has two linked advantages. It confirms Shelley, but does not rely on Shelley's frequently blind rage. It avoids, too, the emotional bias that led Southey's thoughts in a contrary direction. The main reaction of the timid recluse of Keswick to reformers and the working class is pure panic:

Think for a moment what London,...nay, what the whole kingdom would be, were your Catilines to succeed in exciting as general an insurrection, as that which was raised by one madman in your own childhood! Imagine the infatuated and infuriated wretches...a frightful population, whose multitudes, when gathered together, might almost exceed belief! The streets of London would appear to teem with them, like the land of Egypt with its plague of frogs; and the lava floods from a volcano would be less destructive than the hordes whom your great cities and manufacturing districts would vomit forth![2]

This selfish fear, toward the end of a discussion of the sufferings of the London poor, appears the reason for worrying about those sufferings.[3] In contrast Peacock's case for reform and the poor is quite disinterested and fearless.

There is every difference, then, between the detached rationalism of Peacock's satire and the recluse's conservatism of Southey's *Colloquies on society*. Yet there are many similarities in the mode of the *Colloquies* and of the 'serious' sections of *Melincourt*. That mode was a common one in the Regency, and Wordsworth's *Excursion* provides a third notable example.

[1] Bamford in particular frequently illustrates what Halévy argues on more general evidence: the eighteenth-century French anti-clerical rationalism of the London clubs, like that of the poets of rebellion and the early philosophical radicals, 'was out of harmony with the national temper'. (E. Halévy, *A history of the English people*, ii, *The Liberal awakening (1815–1830)*, p. 30.)

[2] *Colloquies on society* (London, 1829), i, 114–15. Although not published until 1829, the book was begun in 1817 (the year of *Melincourt*) and the first conversation is set just after Princess Charlotte's death that year.

[3] Compare Southey's reasons for supporting 'schemes for general education': 'the rapid increase of the labouring classes renders education *as a corrective and conservative*, not merely desirable for the well-being of society, but absolutely needful for the existence of our institutions and of social order itself' (*ibid.* ii, 78: my italics).

In all three works, several *philosophes* pace the mountains of the Lake District holding leisurely 'Colloquies on the progress and prospects of society' and 'The hopes of the world'.[1] They are aloof from the world of immediate problems. Wordsworth's characters are the Solitary, the Pastor and the Wanderer, while Southey's are the ghost of Sir Thomas More and his own persona, the Keswick country-lover and bibliophile. Their historical perspective is always broad—back to the Middle Ages or even Ancient Greece—and their approach tends to the abstract.[2] Here and there they come across some rural figure, or look down on some settlement, that serves to illustrate their arguments. It is particularly this that prompts Macaulay's attack on the mode as ineffectual and irrelevant. Southey and More look down from the mountains on a manufacturing settlement: Macaulay's gibe (which I have already quoted à propos *Headlong Hall*) is that 'Mr. Southey has found out a way, he tells us, in which the effects of manufactures and agriculture may be compared. And what is this way? To stand on a hill, and to see which is the prettier.'[3] It is a telling instance of the division which cuts through the whole period of the Regency; the lack of contact between what may for brevity be called the practical and theoretical thinkers. Another instance of this division is even more telling, for it shows both sides straining in vain to bridge the gulf. Coleridge, eager to remind 'unprincipled' statesmen of first principles, sent to Lord Liverpool a long letter dealing with the ideas of his Lay Sermons. The only visible result was Liverpool's note:

From Mr. Coleridge, stating that the great object of his writings has been to rescue speculative philosophy from false principles of reasoning and to place it on that basis, or give it that tendency, which would make it best suited to the interests of religion as well as of the

---

[1] The second phrase is the title of chapter 40 of *Melincourt*, in which Fax and Forester hold their last discussion.

[2] Hazlitt in fact thought that the illustrative episodes in *The excursion* did not fit in with the basic form of the poem: 'We could have wished that our author had given to his work the form of a didactic poem altogether, with only incidental digressions or allusions to particular instances. But he has chosen to encumber himself with a load of narrative and description, which sometimes hinders the progress and affect of the general reasoning.' (Review of *The excursion*.)

[3] *Edinburgh review*, L (Jan. 1830), 540.

state; at least, I believe this is Mr. Coleridge's meaning, but I cannot well understand him.[1]

At least Coleridge and Liverpool made the desperate attempt at contact. But the *Colloquies* pushed Southey and Macaulay even further away from each other: reading the work hardened Macaulay's blind confidence in practicality and materialism, and the reception consigned Southey deeper and deeper into the rôle of an out-of-touch Jeremiah. *Melincourt* makes a more creditable attempt than the *Colloquies* to bridge that Regency division. But, while it sees past the practicalities of 1817 to just principles and ultimate issues, it seldom refers tellingly back to the practical world. It would not challenge and change the 1817 equivalent of Macaulay.

As Peacock looked over the mixed successes and weaknesses of *Melincourt*, what guidance could they give him for the planning of his next novel? First that, even when drawing on Shelley and Shelley's interests, he could be most natural and most forceful by guarding his independence of manner and judgement. Secondly, that when surveying the age he should choose aspects on which a 'Hermit of the Thames' could be well informed. He relied, that is, less on wide direct experience like Bamford's or Byron's and more on reading and deductions from reading. These directions, taken together, suggest that Peacock would be in his element and within his depth with a satire on Regency literature and taste, combined with—even centring on—an ironical case-history of Shelley.

The way was now open, that is, for the success of *Nightmare Abbey*.

[1] See C. D. Yonge, *Life and administration of Lord Liverpool* (London, 1867), II, 300–7.

7

Nightmare Abbey

1818

'The object of *Nightmare Abbey*', Peacock wrote to Shelley, was 'to bring to a sort of philosophical focus a few of the morbidities of modern literature.'[1] And in May 1818 he told him:

I have almost finished *Nightmare Abbey*. I think it necessary to 'make a stand' against the 'encroachments' of black bile. The fourth canto of *Childe Harold* is really too bad. I cannot consent to be *auditor tantum* of this systematical 'poisoning' of the 'mind' of the 'reading public'.[2]

Shelley characteristically leapt to the conclusion that Peacock was fighting the same battle he had fought in *The revolt of Islam* and its Preface, against what he termed the 'gloom and misanthropy' caused largely by the disappointment of the French Revolution. He wrote back: 'You tell me that you have finished *Nightmare Abbey*. I hope that you have given the enemy no quarter. Remember, it is a sacred war.'[3] But the centre of the novel turned out to be Scythrop, a character satirically based on Shelley himself.

Shelley reacted to the book with generous praise but with a significant qualification:

I am delighted with *Nightmare Abbey*. I think Scythrop a character admirably conceived and executed, and I know not how to praise sufficiently the lightness, chastity and strength of the language as a whole. It perhaps exceeds all your works in this. I suppose the moral is contained in what Falstaff says—'For God's sake talk like

[1] 15 Sept. 1818: Halliford, VIII, 204.
[2] 30 May 1818: *ibid.* p. 193.
[3] 25 July 1818: *Letters*, ed. F. L. Jones, 2 vols. (Oxford, 1964), II, 27.

a man of this world;' and yet looking deeper into it, is not the misdirected enthusiasm of Scythrop what J.C. calls the salt of the earth?[1]

This balance of admiration and dissent perfectly conveys the response of genuine friendship—the response that was suppressed or distorted on both sides over *Melincourt*. Shelley here shows towards Peacock what Peacock (through Scythrop) shows towards Shelley: appreciation with an awareness of difference—perhaps we can simply say appreciation of difference.

Shelley defended Scythrop's 'misdirected enthusiasm'. But he found nothing offensive or cruel in the parody of himself, and enjoyed the art and wit of the whole novel. The two qualities go together. Whereas *Melincourt* moves only fitfully, tied down by too close reference to its various 'sources' in the life of 1817, *Nightmare Abbey* is a self-propelled and fully airborne construction. Scythrop and Flosky get off the ground with a life independent of control by sources. While they offer by analogy and implication many insights into Shelley and Byron (which this chapter will largely treat in the notes rather than the text), they are not slavish transcriptions. As Humphry House puts it, Peacock 'took elements from the Shelley situation and explored the thoughts that accrued around them'.[2]

*

The accepted account of the novel, and its difference from (say) a comparable one by Jane Austen, is that 'In *Northanger Abbey* the characters are individuals, whereas in *Nightmare Abbey* the characters are abstractions and it is their opinions which form "the main matter of the work". Unlike Jane Austen, Peacock is more interested in ideas than in people.'[3] On the relation of Peacock's characters to his 'originals' it is, therefore, usually considered enough to say that 'The views of Mr. Flosky the Kantian satirize those of Coleridge: the views of Mr. Toobad, the manichaean Millenarian, satirize those of J. F. Newton:

[1] *Letters*, ed. Jones, ii, 98.
[2] *The listener*, xlii (8 Dec. 1949), 997.
[3] This conveniently succinct version of the widespread view is from Ian Jack's *English literature 1815–32* (Oxford, 1963), p. 213.

while those of Mr. Cypress satirize Byron...Scythrop's opinions caricature those of Shelley at a certain point in his life.'[1]

Nightmare Abbey is the shakiest of grounds on which to base a generalisation that Peacock is 'more interested in ideas than in people'. In the earlier two novels he uses the *views, opinions* or *ideas* of Shelley and others, either satirically or seriously: the characters opinionate at length. One rarely catches Scythrop passing an opinion. In the discussion-scenes he keeps quiet, except for the occasional aside to Marionetta and the brief exchange with Mr Cypress. He makes occasional speeches to his father and his girls, but more often to himself. He much prefers the silence of mystery, brooding and inward fantasy.

When Scythrop does burst into speech, Peacock dwells on the underground connections of opinions with character. Such an outburst comes at the climax of chapter 3. He is chasing Marionetta, whom he has frightened by proposing a blood-drinking pact, 'when, at an ill-omened corner, where two corridors ended in an angle, at the head of a staircase, he came into sudden and violent contact with Mr. Toobad, and they both plunged together to the foot of the stairs, like two billiard-balls into one pocket'.[2] To Mr Toobad this is 'one of the innumerable proofs of the temporary supremacy of the devil'. He is a survival from *Headlong Hall*, a crotchet who opinionates, and is always of the same opinion. But there is more to Scythrop's reply:

...you are perfectly in the right, Mr. Toobad. Evil and mischief, and misery, and confusion, and vanity, and vexation of spirit, and death, and disease, and assassination, and war, and poverty, and pestilence, and famine, and avarice, and selfishness, and rancour, and jealousy, and spleen, and malevolence, and the disappointments of philanthropy, and the faithlessness of friendship, and the crosses of love—all prove the accuracy of your views...[3]

There is nothing here worth considering as an *idea*. What matter are the particular and personal motives behind the generalisations about the Triumph of Evil: the list leads from the universal (death, war) to Scythrop's own grudges in the background of his mind ('the disappointments of philanthropy') to 'the crosses

[1] *Ibid.* p. 217.   [2] Halliford, III, 25.   [3] *Ibid.*

of love' in the immediate foreground. The whole breathless paragraph conveys to us Scythrop's temperament and nervous system, with his overflowing pity and self-pity, that are inseparable from his emotional fluctuations and violence in the preceding scene with Marionetta, and his physical volatility in the headlong chase. The words that come to mind about Scythrop are 'headlong', 'erratic', 'impetuous', 'self-preoccupied'. They are terms that characterise the individual centre of personality from which radiate all the particular facets of voice, movements, physical appearance, actions—and ideas.[1]

The outburst on the stairs is a rarity, for Scythrop usually retreats into his inner world where his emotionalism and violence gnaw away in silence.

How this character developed is told in an ironical case-history in chapter 2:

He had some taste for romance reading before he went to the university, where, we must confess, in justice to his college, he was cured of the love of reading in all its shapes; and the cure would have been radical, if disappointment in love, and total solitude, had not conspired to bring on a relapse. He began to devour romances and German tragedies, and, by the recommendation of Mr. Flosky, to pore over ponderous tomes of transcendental philosophy, which reconciled him to the labour of studying them by their mystical jargon and necromantic imagery. In the congenial solitude of Nightmare Abbey, the distempered ideas of metaphysical romance and romantic metaphysics had ample time and space to germinate into a fertile crop of chimeras, which rapidly shot up into vigorous and abundant vegetation.[2]

In so far as this is true of Shelley's youth, it is (so far) a criticism which Shelley himself could make. It will be recalled that in his second letter to Godwin he wrote:

[1] It would be necessary to apologise for making so much use of that accident on the stairs, had not other readers made so much fuss about Peacock making (they claim) so little of it. 'This is splendidly funny,' says Mr Dyson, 'and entirely in keeping with all that has led up to it, but do we even begin to wonder whether Scythrop or Mr. Toobad has been hurt? The precipitation of each into his gloomiest philosophising strikes us, rather, as a festive comic release. Everything depends upon the timing, as in a Laurel and Hardy film. Peacock sets out to entertain us, and any moral lessions are very much on the way.' (*The crazy fabric; essays in irony*, London, 1965, p. 61.)

[2] Halliford, III, 13–14.

I was haunted with a passion for the wildest and most extravagant romances: ancient books of Chemistry and Magic were perused with an enthusiasim of wonder, almost amounting to belief...From a reader, I became a writer of romances; before the age of seventeen I had published two, 'St. Irvyne' and 'Zastrozzi'...[1]

Shelley, however, claimed that reading *Political justice* made him

a wiser and better man. I was no longer a votary of Romance; till then I had existed in an ideal world—now I found that in this universe of ours was enough to excite the interest of the heart...I beheld, in short, that I had duties to perform...My plan is that of resolving to lose no opportunity to disseminate truth and happiness.[2]

But Scythrop's *passion for reforming the world* only extends his private fantasy-world. 'He built many castles in the air, and peopled them with secret tribunals, and bands of illuminati, who were always the imaginary instruments of his projected re-generation of the human species.'[3] The world of Godwin is submerged in that of Schiller's *Robbers*.[4] In this fantasy he has a flattering rôle: 'As he intended to institute a perfect republic, he invested himself with absolute sovereignty over these mystical dispensers of liberty.'[5] His self-importance grows: he 'foresaw that a great leader of human regeneration would be involved in fearful dilemmas, and determined, for the benefit of mankind in general, to adopt all possible precautions for the preservation of himself'.[6] His only practical act is to publish a treatise called *Philosophical gas; or, a project for a general illumination of the human mind*, which he expects to 'set the whole nation in a ferment' but which sells only seven copies. The validity of this portrait does not depend on its fitting Shelley: but in fact all these characteristics of Scythrop's *passion for*

---

[1] 10 Jan. 1812: *Letters*, ed. Jones, I, 227. [2] Halliford, III, 14.
[3] *Ibid*. pp. 227–9.
[4] In the 'Memoirs of Shelley', Peacock notes that 'Brown's four novels, Schiller's *Robbers*, and Goethe's *Faust*, were, of all the works with which he was familiar, those which took the deepest root in his mind, and had the strongest influence in the formation of his character' (Halliford, VIII, 78). For the sketch of Scythrop's political fantasy, Peacock owed something to the eleutherarchs of Hogg's *Prince Alexy Haimatoff*.
[5] Halliford, III, 14. [6] *Ibid*. p. 17.

reforming the world can be detected either in Shelley's first letters to Godwin or in his subsequent writings and actions.[1]

Into this same fantasy-world Scythrop tries to assimilate the two girls.

Marionetta is a poor choice for this purpose:

Being a compound of the *Allegro Vivace* of the O'Carrolls, and of the *Andante Doloroso* of the Glowries, she exhibited in her own character all the diversities of an April sky. Her hair was light-brown; her eyes hazel, and sparkling with mild but fluctuating light; her features regular; her lips full, and of equal size; and her person surpassingly graceful. She was a proficient in music. Her conversation was sprightly, but always on subjects light in their nature and limited in their interest: for moral sympathies, in any general sense, had no place in her mind. She had some coquetry, and more caprice, liking and disliking almost in the same moment; pursuing an object with earnestness while it seemed unattainable, and rejecting it when in her power as not worth the trouble of possession.[2]

For several reasons this should be compared with the description of Harriet in the 'Memoirs of Shelley':

She had a good figure, light, active, and graceful. Her features were regular and well-proportioned. Her hair was light brown, and dressed with taste and simplicity. In her dress she was truly *simplex munditiis*. Her complexion was beautifully transparent; the tint of the blush rose shining through the lily. The tone of her voice was pleasant; her speech the essence of frankness and cordiality; her spirits always cheerful; her laugh spontaneous, hearty, and joyous. She was well educated. She read agreeably and intelligently. She wrote only letters, but she wrote them well. Her manners were good, and her

---

[1] For self-importance, cf. Scythrop's determination, 'for the benefit of mankind in general, to adopt all possible precautions for the preservation of himself', with Shelley at the end of his second letter to Godwin: 'My plan is that of resolving to lose no opportunity to disseminate truth and happiness' (10 Jan. 1812: *Letters*, ed. Jones, I, 229), or his invitation to Elizabeth Hitchener to join his pamphlet campaign in Ireland: 'you would share with me the high delight of awakening a whole nation from the lethargy of its bondage' (27 Feb. 1812: *ibid.* p. 263).

K. N. Cameron complains that the reception of the Irish pamphlets, and even of those launched by balloon and bottle in Devon, is not fairly represented by the reception of Scythrop's pamphlet. But Peacock's main target is the self-importance and visionary optimism of both ventures.

[2] Chapter 3: Halliford, III, 20–1.

whole aspect and demeanour such manifest emanations of pure and truthful nature, that to be once in her company was to know her thoroughly. She was fond of her husband, and accommodated herself in every way to his tastes. If they mixed in society, she adorned it; if they lived in retirement, she was satisfied; if they travelled, she enjoyed the change of scene.[1]

There are resemblances between Marionetta and Harriet, with great differences. But the main resemblance is that both passages are real and serious descriptions of character. The passage from the novel is not a skit or caricature: if anything, the livelier style makes it a less conventional reading of character than that of Harriet. In fact the temperament read through Marionetta's appearance and manner is more complicated and interesting than Harriet's. Here and through the novel she is perverse and capricious, both *allegra vivace* and *andante dolorosa*. The description, as different from a skit as from the conventional admirabilities of Anthelia Melincourt, is something new in the novels.

Scythrop falls in love with Marionetta, although she does not realise his '*pure anticipated cognitions* of combinations of beauty and intelligence'.[2] When she suddenly turns cold, he does not argue or plead with her but, characteristically, retreats into his tower and his fantasy, 'muffled himself in his nightcap, seated himself in the president's chair of his imaginary secret tribunal, summoned Marionetta with all terrible formalities, frightened her out of her wits, disclosed himself, and clasped the beautiful penitent to his bosom'.[3] Caught in the act by the real Marionetta, he tries to co-opt her to the council as 'the auxiliary of my great designs for the emancipation of mankind'—and manages to frighten her too out of her wits. The pattern of cross-purposes in this scene—his fantasy, breast-beating violence and 'passionate language of romance' against her archness, puzzlement and alarm—continues through the novel.

Marionetta cannot fit into the fantasy-world, but Stella seems to spring from it. She appears like a ghost in the tower, a mysterious fugitive from 'atrocious persecution' and, as a reader of *Philosophical gas*, emphatically an enemy to every shape of tyranny and superstitious imposture.

[1] *Ibid.* VIII, 95.   [2] Chapter 3: *ibid.* III, 21.   [3] *Ibid.* p. 22.

141

Stella, in her conversations with Scythrop displayed a highly cultivated and energetic mind, full of impassioned schemes of liberty, and impatience of masculine usurpation. She had a lively sense of all the oppressions that are done under the sun; and the vivid pictures which her imagination presented to her of the numberless scenes of injustice and misery which are being acted at every moment in every part of the inhabited world, gave an habitual seriousness to her physiognomy, that made it seem as if a smile had never once hovered on her lips.[1]

It is usual to compare this with the description of Mary Shelley given in Peacock's 'Memoirs of Shelley', or to speculate whether Claire Clairmont, rather than Mary, was the model.[2] But the critic is concerned not with Peacock's historical model but with his human subject. A more useful comparison will therefore be with a character from another novelist whom nobody would suggest was 'more interested in ideas than in people'.

a smile of exceeding faintness played about her lips—it was just perceptible enough to light up the native gravity of her face. It might have been likened to a thin ray of moonlight resting upon the wall of a prison...

The unhappiness of women! The voice of their silent suffering was always in her ears, the ocean of tears that they had shed from the beginning of time seemed to pour through her own eyes. Ages of oppression had rolled over them...[3]

Admittedly the description of Stella is brief, and little is subsequently shown of her, whereas the description of Olive Chancellor merely indicates what is to be fully conveyed in the drama of the novel. But Peacock and James are here interested in the same thing: not in ideas, but in the emotional nature that makes both women take on the burden of the world's evils—'ages of oppression', 'all the oppressions...under the sun'—and the way this burden is registered in their faces.

Scythrop's ensuing dilemma is comic:

Passing and repassing several times a day from the company of the one to that of the other, he was like a shuttlecock between two

[1] Chapter 10: Halliford, III, 93–4.
[2] Among several critics, N. I. White (*Shelley*, 2 vols., London, 1947, I, 705 n. 47) argues for Claire Clairmont, who first presented herself to Byron as Stella presents herself to Scythrop. J.-J. Mayoux (*Un Epicuréan anglais: Thomas Love Peacock*, Paris, 1933, p. 269) gives further evidence in favour of Claire.
[3] Henry James, *The Bostonians* (London, 1886), I, 10–11 and 55.

battledores, changing its direction as rapidly as the oscillations of a pendulum, receiving many a hard knock on the cork of a sensitive heart, and flying from point to point on the feathers of a super-sublimated head...The old proverb concerning two strings to a bow gave him some gleams of comfort; but that concerning two stools occurred to him more frequently, and covered his forehead with a cold perspiration.[1]

But he is not the deflated figure of fun that Dr Jack suggests in saying that his situation 'recalls that of a hypocritical rake in Goldsmith or Sheridan'.[2] The dilemma is serious in the sense that we understand it as we understand Shelley's dilemma in the 'Memoirs' and the corresponding letters: the novel has created the *données*, Scythrop's temperament and the qualities of the two girls that fit his various needs.

For a solution he first turns to Romance, hoping that Stella approves the ideal of Goethe's play which bears her name, and will agree to set up a *ménage à trois*. Failing this, he adopts the ultimate Romantic role from *The sorrows of Werther* and orders for dinner

> A pint of port and a pistol.
> [*Raven the butler:*] A pistol!
> [*Scythrop:*] And a pint of port.[3]

All of Scythrop's words and attitudes reek of second-rate fashionable literature which has 'blended itself with the interior structure of his mind'.[4]

*

'The views of Mr. Flosky', runs the common account, 'satirize those of Coleridge.'[5] On the basis of this common account stands the commonest criticism of Peacock, that he fails to do justice to Coleridge's ideas. 'It is a serious failure,' says Humphry House, 'and points plainly to Peacock's limitations. He did not really understand or care about philosophy; he never dealt with the deeper and more exacting struggles of thought but only with thought as it emerged into opinion or emotional attitude.'[6]

[1] Chapter 10: Halliford, III, 95–6. [2] *English literature, 1815–32.*
[3] Chapter 14: Halliford, III, 137.
[4] The phrase is from the 'Memoirs of Shelley': Halliford, VIII, 78.
[5] Ian Jack, *English literature, 1815–32*, p. 217.
[6] *The listener*, XLII (8 Dec. 1949), 998.

This sweeping account and charge can be undermined by a number of general caveats to be supported by close illustration. First, Peacock has no one view of Coleridge. We must balance against his caricatures his appreciation of the poet in the *Essay on fashionable literature*. Among the caricatures, Panscope in *Headlong Hall* and Mystic in *Melincourt* never spring to life as persons as Flosky does. There is nothing more to them than their intellectual labels imply—Panscope the Polymath, Mystic the Kantian. No such label attaches itself to Flosky. He reminds us of many sides of Coleridge's mind. More important, whereas Panscope and Mystic are eager to expound their views, the only common factor in Flosky's ideas is his almost pathological difficulty in communicating them. A second reply to Humphry House is that a study of 'thought as it emerged into [or *from*] . . . emotional attitude' need not be trivial. The underground connections between temperament and ideas which Peacock also studies in Scythrop, Coleridge was himself ready to dwell on in his notebook introspections.

Unlike Panscope and Mystic, Flosky grows through the novel. Different scenes focus on different aspects.

Flosky, like most of *Nightmare Abbey's* characters, is introduced by an ironical life-history:

He had been in his youth an enthusiast for liberty, and had hailed the dawn of the French Revolution as the promise of a day that was to banish war and slavery, and every form of vice and misery, from the face of the earth. Because all this was not done, he deduced that nothing was done; and from this deduction, according to his system of logic, he drew a conclusion that worse than nothing was done; that the overthrow of the feudal fortresses of tyranny and superstition was the greatest calamity that had ever befallen mankind; and that their only hope now was to rake the rubbish together, and rebuild it without any of those loopholes by which the light had originally crept in. To qualify himself for a coadjutor in this laudible task, he plunged into the central opacity of Kantian metaphysics, and lay *perdu* several years in transcendental darkness, till the common daylight of common-sense became intolerable to his eyes. He called the sun an *ignis fatuus*; and exhorted all who would listen to his friendly voice, which were about as many as called 'God save King

Richard', to shelter themselves from its delusive radiance in the obscure haunt of Old Philosophy. This word Old had great charms for him.[1]

This is clearly a History of Ideas, and of Coleridge's ideas too. It attributes to Coleridge in exaggerated form the reactions to the French Revolution which Shelley described in his Preface to *The revolt of Islam*:

The sympathies connected with that event extended to every bosom. The most generous and amiable natures were those which participated the most extensively in these sympathies. But such a degree of unmingled good was expected, as it was impossible to realise... The revulsion occasioned by the atrocities of the demagogues and the re-establishment of successive tyrannies in France was terrible... many of the most tender-hearted of the worshippers of the public good have been morally ruined by what a partial glimpse of the events they deplored, appeared to show as the melancholy desolation of all their cherished hopes. Hence gloom and misanthropy have become the characteristics of the age in which we live, the solace of a disappointment that unconsciously finds relief only in the wilful exaggeration of its own despair. This influence has tainted the literature of the age with the hopelessness of the minds from which it flows. Metaphysics,[2] and inquiries into moral and political science, have become little else than vain attempts to revive exploded superstitions, or sophisms like those of Mr. Malthus, calculated to lull the oppressors of mankind into a security of everlasting triumph.[3]

Here is Shelley's 'sacred war', and the sketch of Flosky's life puts Peacock for the moment among the holy Crusaders. Yet (putting aside the rights and wrongs of the Cause) what a sharper swordsman Peacock is! One might even worry the metaphor further and say that, while Peacock is out on the field engaged in close fighting, Shelley is still at home speechifying and moralising. His exposition of the Cause (which I have cut severely in my quotation) is painfully slow, pompous and unspecific, overflowing with melodramatic Scythropian jargon and imagery. Peacock is specific, pinning the abstract reactions on a concrete character.

---

[1] Chapter 1: Halliford, III, 10–11.
[2] 'I ought to except Sir W. Drummond's "Academical Questions"; a volume of very acute and powerful metaphysical criticism.' (Shelley's footnote.)
[3] *Poetical works*, ed. Mary Shelley, 4 vols. (London, 1839), I, 147–8.

The introduction of Flosky, then, gives his mental case-history, tracing what made him what he is. Yet as the resulting character acts and speaks we are little aware of specific ideas. What comes across is a voice, wandering through an uncertain sequence of logic. The obscurity of Flosky's style is in harmony with his obscure meaning. There is no brisk Kantian self-justification such as Moly Mystic offers, but more of gnomic and biblical tones, the tangle of arrogance and false humility, the coy hints and startling connections, that often characterised Coleridge's awkward flirtations with 'the reading public' in *The friend* and the *Lay sermons*. The reader stumbling along behind is never quite sure who is fooling whom. Is Flosky (to use his own idiom) guiding us over complicated terrain with the torch of truth? Or is it an *ignis fatuus*? Does *he* know where we are heading for? Is he perhaps trying to shake us off the trail? Flosky is always ready to confirm our worst suspicions. Poor Mr Listless, struggling with Flosky's proposition that 'Tea, late dinners, and the French Revolution, have played the devil, Mr. Listless, and brought the devil into play', murmurs politely that he 'cannot exactly see the connection of ideas'. Flosky replies that

I should be sorry if you could; I pity the man who can see the connection of his own ideas. Still more do I pity him, the connection of whose ideas any other person can see. Sir, the great evil is, that there is too much commonplace light in our moral and political literature.[1]

What follows is a long defence of 'abstract truth' and 'synthetical reasoning'. It happens to parallel very closely a self-defence that Coleridge once wrote, in reply to a criticism of Southey's. By comparing the relevant passages of Southey, Coleridge and Peacock, we can be more specific in judging the validity of Peacock's parody, and its difference from the stock conservative reaction to Coleridge.

The criticism which Southey expressed to Coleridge in conversation is also recorded for the modern reader in a letter to a third party, Miss Barker:

It is not a little extraordinary that Coleridge, who is fond of logic, and who has an actual love and passion for close, hard thinking, should

[1] Chapter 6: Halliford, III, 48–9.

write in so rambling and inconclusive a manner; while I, who am utterly incapable of that toil of thought in which he delights, never fail to express myself perspicuously, and to the point...Coleridge requested me to write him such a letter upon the faults of the 'Friend' as he might insert and reply to...It described the fault you have remarked as existing in Burke, and having prevented him from ever persuading anybody to his opinions...You read his book, and saw what his opinions were; but they were given in such a way, evolving the causes of everything, and involving the consequences, that you never knew from whence he set out, nor where he was going. So it is with C.; he goes to work like a hound, nosing his way, turning, and twisting, and winding, and doubling, till you get weary with following the mazy movements. My way is, when I see my object, to dart at it like a greyhound.[1]

Southey makes a common enough criticism of Coleridge.[2] Yet one is here reluctant to accept its standpoint, for it stems from habits of mental conservatism. The strong tones of complacency indicate a mind tending to inertia, in the sense of conserving itself from being disturbed by different mental habits. Least of all does it want to be disturbed by Coleridge's example of activity, curiosity, exploration. It might be argued that Southey's concern here is not with those positive aspects of Coleridge, only with his weaknesses. Yet he cannot criticise those weaknesses with any authority because he cannot see the positive aims which are their context and their cause. Southey criticises Coleridge's mind as if it were only attempting the same things as his own. Of course perspicuity and directness come easier to Southey because for him they are ends in themselves, and because they take account of less. The pattern of his logic, and ultimately of his wisdom from experience, is simpler because of what it excludes and ignores for the *sake* of simplicity.

So Southey has no standing as a critic of Coleridge, because he does not comprehend him. I mean 'comprehend' in both senses, which are in fact linked at their deepest. He does not understand Coleridge's mind; nor does he encompass it and look further

[1] 29 Jan. 1810: *Selections from the letters of Southey*, ed. J. W. Warter (London, 1856), II, 188–9.
[2] Hazlitt, among others, echoed Southey by saying that Coleridge was an 'excellent talker, very—if you let him start from no premises and come to no conclusion' (a remark reported by Carlyle, *Life of Sterling*, London, 1851, p. 74).

and wider. Quite the reverse; it is fitting that Coleridge's defence follows Southey in time and encompasses it:

There is no way of arriving at any sciental End but by finding it at every step. The End is in the Means; or the adequacy of each Mean is already its End. Southey once said to me: You are nosing every nettle along the Hedge, while the Greyhound (meaning himself, I presume) wants only to get sight of the Hare, and Flash—strait as a line! he has it in his mouth!—Even so, I replied, might a Cannibal say to an Anatomist, whom he had watched dissecting a body. But the fact is—I do not care two pence for the Hare; but I value most highly the excellencies of scent, patience, discrimination, free Activity; and find a Hare in every Nettle I make myself acquainted with. I follow the Chamois-Hunters, and seem to set out with the same Object. But I am no Hunter of *that* Chamois Goat; but avail myself of the Chace in order to [pursue] a nobler purpose—that of making a road across the Mountain in which Common Sense may hereafter pass backward and forward, without desperate Leaps or Balloons that soar indeed but do not improve the chance of getting onward.[1]

Happily this reply represents Coleridge very favourably in the present discussion. It describes very persuasively his conception of true thinking. At the same time it is Coleridge at his most lively. He picks up with alacrity the metaphor Southey had used smugly, and makes it telling and vivid. It allows him to be humorous—self-directed humour in the context of self-justification, and humour at Southey's smugness. It allows the metaphorical expression of the virtues of what Arnold called 'free play of mind': 'scent, patience, discrimination, free Activity'. True, as Coleridge continues to hunt and nose out the metaphor, it becomes more complicated and fanciful: but it is entirely acceptable because it develops so informally and spontaneously. It demonstrates that free play of mind which Coleridge is defending. And it ends happily in the image of the explorative mind opening up new intellectual territory—'making a road across the Mountain in which Common Sense may hereafter pass backward and forward'.

Yet one may admire the passage and still feel uneasy. Certainly it drowns Southey's criticism: but isn't it a rashly

[1] From the unpublished MS. Egerton 2801, fo. 126: watermark 1822. Printed in *Inquiring spirit, a new presentation of Coleridge*, ed. K. Coburn (London, 1951), pp. 143–4.

extreme reaction? 'I do not care two pence for the Hare'; '[I] find a Hare in every nettle'—these provide sufficient footholds for Peacock's parody. Mr Flosky is table-talking:

Now the enthusiasm for abstract truth is an exceedingly fine thing, as long as the truth, which is the object of the enthusiasm, is so completely abstract as to be altogether out of the reach of the human faculties; and, in that sense, I have myself an enthusiasm for truth, but in no other, for the pleasure of metaphysical investigation lies in the means, not in the end; and if the end could be found, the pleasure of the means would cease. The mind, to be kept in health, must be kept in exercise. The proper exercise of the mind is elaborate reasoning. Analytical reasoning is a base and mechanical process, which takes to pieces and examines, bit by bit, the rude material of knowledge, and extracts therefrom a few hard and obstinate things called facts, every thing in the shape of which I cordially hate. But synthetical reasoning, setting up as its goal some unattainable abstraction, like an imaginary quantity in algebra, and commencing its course with taking for granted some two assertions which cannot be proved, from the union of these two assumed truths produces a third assumption, and so on in infinite series, to the unspeakable benefit of the human intellect. The beauty of this process is, that at every step it strikes out into two branches, in a compound ratio of ramification; so that you are perfectly sure of losing your way, and keeping your mind in perfect health, by the perpetual exercise of an interminable quest; and for these reasons I have christened my eldest son Emanuel Kant Flosky.[1]

The parody is valid because Peacock, unlike Southey, first entertains Coleridge's idea, enters into its spirit before criticising it. Peacock works by keeping close to Coleridge's imagery and train of reasoning, then edging it gradually more and more off course to an absurd conclusion. The passage does not drown Coleridge for us as Coleridge drowns Southey, but establishes itself as an unavoidable partial truth. If Coleridge's passage describes the ideal, Peacock's exposes the attendant dangers and temptations. If the Coleridgean ideal demands extraordinary powers of mind, it can also encourage and camouflage extraordinary weaknesses.

The surprise is that Peacock did not have as his model that

[1] Chapter 6: Halliford, III, 49–50. The final allusion is to the naming of Hartley and Berkeley Coleridge.

particular passage of Coleridge, which comes from an unpublished manuscript. It is uncanny how often, in reading
Coleridge or Shelley, one is pulled up by passages that Peacock
could not have read but which he seems to echo directly, so
well he catches their voice. Perhaps with Mr Flosky's blessing
we may call them *pure anticipated cognitions.*

In that manifesto-speech of Flosky's, the weaknesses exposed
are intellectual ones. But as the novel develops they come home
to us, like Scythrop's, as failings of personality and of human
contact.

Not that Peacock dwells on the human *causes* of Flosky's
mental habits—that is, on the sense we have with Scythrop
that, whatever the philosophical justifications imported from
Königsberg, the real motives can be found nearer home. There
is little hint of the analysis which Coleridge himself made in the
Dejection Ode—

> For not to think of what I needs must feel,
>   But to be still and patient, all I can;
> And haply by abstruse research to steal
>   From my own nature all the natural Man
>   This was my sole resource, my only plan:
> Till that which suits the part infects the whole,
> And now is grown the habit of my Soul.[1]

—and which he frequently elaborated in private to De Quincey
and others. There is no hint at all in *Nightmare Abbey* of such
specific causes as Coleridge's wife and his opium-addiction. This
omission is, I think, a fine example of Peacock's 'good taste'
in two solid senses of that phrase—in human tact and artistic
judgement. With Shelley he could draw on intimate knowledge
so as, paradoxically, to be able to make Scythrop an authentic
but independent creation. Knowing Shelley intimately also
meant that he could judge where and where not the creation
would hurt Shelley personally (Shelley's response in letters
shows that Peacock's judgement on this point was perfect).
On the other hand with the private life of Coleridge whom he

---

[1] In *Sibylline leaves* (London, 1817), p. 241. It is worth noting that the Ode
first appeared in book form while Peacock was planning the novel.

did not know, Peacock could neither get more to work on than hearsay (gossip or slander), nor gauge the effect of a portrait on Coleridge. What touches he did take from Coleridge's private life, he transferred to the creation of Mr Glowry, the glorifier of gloom in the aftermath of a dismal marriage.

But if Peacock does not look back for human causes, he is always anticipating human effects. Even the most respectful reader of *The friend*, the *Lay sermons* or reports of the less coherent lectures, might find himself entertaining the comic possibilities of such a mind engaged in everyday human intercourse. These are just the possibilities Peacock seizes on. Not that he is measuring Coleridge's complex mind by 'the impudent footrule of his own common sense' (Leslie Stephen's phrase for Hazlitt). He does not fall foul of De Quincey's accusation:

Coleridge, to many people, and often I have heard the complaint, seemed to wander; and he seemed then to wander the most when, in fact, his resistance to the wandering instinct was greatest—viz., when the compass and huge circuit by which his illustrations moved travelled furthest into remote regions before they began to revolve. Long before this coming round commenced most people had lost him, and naturally enough supposed that he had lost himself.[1]

Peacock would, I think, have acknowledged this defence of Coleridge when the subjects under discussion demanded intricate paths of thought linking remote areas of knowledge. In this context he would have enjoyed the frustration of Carlyle at Highgate, wanting a simple answer to a complex problem —'[I] tried hard to get something about *Kant* and Co. from him, about "reason" *versus* "understanding", and the like; but in vain',[2] 'you put some question to him...instead of answering this, or decidedly setting out towards answer of it, he would accumulate formidable apparatus, logical swimbladders, transcendental life-preservers and other precautionary and vehiculatory gear, for setting out'.[3] For, whatever he later became, Carlyle appears here the cut-and-dried intellectual wanting, like Mr McCrotchet, the experts to 'settle' the big

[1] 'Coleridge', in *Collected writings*, ed. D. Masson (Edinburgh, 1889), II, 152–3.
[2] *Reminiscences*, ed. C. E. Norton (London, 1887), II, 131.
[3] *Life of Sterling* (London, 1851), p. 73.

topics of the day. But, for even the subtlest genius, there are occasions that demand a simple answer to a simple question. There comes the time when the author of *The golden bowl* has to ask his way to the King's Road, or say a kindly word or two to some children on the beach.[1] And so—Peacock's mind must have speculated—what happens when the transcendental philosopher is asked to 'condescend to talk to a simple girl in intelligible terms'[2] on a factual matter? The speculation leads straight to the encounter between Flosky and Marionetta.

Worried by Scythrop's extreme air of mystery, Marionetta goes to Flosky's apartment to ask for clues. She breaks in upon him rather like the Person from Porlock, for he is sitting with curtains and shutters drawn against the noonday sun 'engaged in the composition of a dismal ballad'.

He sate with 'his eye in a fine frenzy rolling,' and turned his inspired gaze on Marionetta as if she had been the ghastly ladie of a magical vision; then placed his hand before his eyes, with an appearance of manifest pain—shook his head—withdrew his hand—rubbed his eyes, like a waking man—and said, in a tone of ruefulness most jeremitalorically pathetic, 'To what am I to attribute this very unexpected pleasure, my dear Miss O'Carroll?'
Marionetta: I must apologise for intruding on you, Mr. Flosky; but the interest which I—you—take in my cousin Scythrop—
Mr. Flosky: Pardon me, Miss O'Carroll; I do not take any interest in any person or thing on the face of the earth; which sentiment, if you analyse it, you will find to be the quintessence of the most refined philanthropy.
Marionetta: I will take it for granted that this is so, Mr. Flosky; I am not conversant with metaphysical subtleties, but—
Mr. Flosky: Subtleties! my dear Miss O'Carroll. I am sorry to find you participating in the vulgar error of the *reading public*, to whom an unusual collocation of words, involing a juxtaposition of antiperistatical ideas, immediately suggests the notion of hyperoxysophistical paradoxology.

---

[1] Edith Wharton's report of the first incident is too well known to need quoting here. The second incident is described in Jessie Conrad's *Joseph Conrad and his circle* (London, 1935), p. 115: 'Some three of four little girls caught his attention and in his most ingratiating manner he stopped to talk to them. He began by presenting each with some pence and then proceeded to harangue them far above their understanding. The kiddies at last flung the coins on the ground and burst into loud sobbing before they ran away.'
[2] Marionetta's own phrase: chapter 8, Halliford, iii, 75.

Mationetta: Indeed, Mr. Flosky, it suggests no such idea to me. I have
sought you for the purpose of obtaining information.
Mr. Flosky (shaking his head): No one has ever sought me for such
a purpose before.[1]

As Marionetta's questions get more fretful and frustrated, so
Flosky's manner becomes more abstract and abstracted:

Marionetta: Will you oblige me, Mr. Flosky, by giving me a plain
answer to a plain question?
Mr. Flosky: It is impossible, my dear Miss O'Carroll. I never gave
a plain answer to a question in my life.
Marionetta: Do you, or do you not, know what is the matter with
my cousin?
Mr. Flosky: To say that I do not, would be to say that I am ignorant
of something; and God forbid, that a transcendental metaphysician,
who had pure anticipated cognitions of everything, and carries the
whole science of geometry in his head without ever having looked
into Euclid, should fall into so empirical an error as to declare himself
ignorant of anything: to say that I do know, would be to pretend to
positive and circumstantial knowledge touching present matter of
fact, which, when you consider the nature of evidence, and the various
lights in which the same thing may be seen—
Mationetta: I see, Mr. Flosky, that either you have no information,
or are determined not to impart it, and I beg your pardon for having
given you this unnecessary trouble.
Mr. Flosky: My dear Miss O'Carroll, it would have given me great
pleasure to have said anything that would have given you pleasure;
but if any person living could make report of having obtained any
information on any subject from Ferdinando Flosky, my transcendental
reputation would be ruined for ever.[2]

This is a *tour de force* as a comic episode bringing to fruition
the comic creation of Flosky. Yet its force arises from comedy
and criticism reinforcing one another; for personal contact is
to Peacock the significant area in which to criticise Flosky.

However, Peacock's focus is not narrowed to one character:
he brings home Flosky's harmful connections with others,
especially with his 'dearest friend' Scythrop. Scythrop 'had
a strong tendency to the love of mystery, for its own sake, that
is to say, he would employ mystery to serve a purpose, but

[1] *Ibid.* III, 72–4. [2] *Ibid.* pp. 78–9.

would first choose his purpose by its capability of mystery'.[1] In this
he has clearly been encouraged by Flosky, who tells Marionetta
that 'Mystery is the very key-stone of all that is beautiful
in poetry, all that is sacred in faith, and all that is recondite
in transcendental psychology.'[2] Flosky also offers Marionetta
choric comments in the spirit of the age that encourages the
affectation of gloom by Scythrop as well as by Mr Glowry.
'It is the fashion to be unhappy. To have a reason for being so
would be exceedingly commonplace; to be so without any is
the province of genius: the art of being miserable for misery's
sake, has been brought to great perfection in our days.'[3]

This discussion has tried to establish what different aspects of
Flosky interest Peacock, and what relation they have to aspects
of Coleridge. But many readers impatiently return the discussion
to Square One: 'Why didn't he take Coleridge's ideas seriously?'
It is all 'abundantly pleasant', sometimes even 'splendidly
funny', admits Mr Dyson: but 'Did Peacock realise, in fact,
that...Coleridge (to use Mill's phrase) was one of the two
great seminal minds of his age?' The tone and spirit of this
can be countered by a number of other stern rhetorical questions.
Can we hope for any free enquiry or intellectual progress if we
dogmatically mark every dissenting opinion of Coleridge by
an unquestioned standard? Can our age's estimate of Coleridge
be the Victorian one? In particular, are we to be intellectually
bound and gagged by Mill's essay? Does not that essay lack
the qualities that distinguish the earlier essay on Bentham—
the balance of appreciation with criticism, the sense of humour,
the quick feeling for the pretentious or ludicrous, and the
constant reference of specialist fields of study to what Arnold
called 'a central, a truly human point of view'? If we agree
with Arnold that the function of criticism is to cultivate 'a free
disinterested play of mind', 'a current of true and *fresh* ideas',
'a more free speculative treatment of things', then there is
something wanting in Mill's essay and even more so in our
exaggerated respect for it. On the other hand, those evocative
phrases of Arnold do fit the spirit of Peacock, which is not to
lay down a dogmatic and complete account of Coleridge, but

[1] Halliford, III, 71.   [2] *Ibid.* pp. 75–6.   [3] *Ibid.* p. 78.

a provocative 'partial portrait'. It is a sign of our times that by 'provocative' we tend to mean gratuitously irritating, rather than fruitfully stimulating—calling forth free play of mind by boldly setting out one of the many possible views. It is wrong to say that Peacock's portrait was an understandable one given that it was written in 1818 but that it was quickly superseded. We should not be patronising Peacock but using him. In fact, whereas the literary world of 1818 badly needed a sympathetic account of Coleridge to keep its mind in free play, modern Coleridge studies badly need to entertain Peacock's irreverent view.

Although irreverent, his view was far from frivolous. It engaged with as much in Coleridge as did Mill's view. Here in confirmation is a passage from a modern critic which sums up Flosky's clumsy failure to communicate with 'the reading public'. It traces that failure through precisely the vicious circle of impotence, wilfulness and arrogance that interested Peacock:

A serious psychological maladjustment towards his public can be detected...An awareness of the probable unpopularity of his ideas and a certain sense of conscious superiority over his readers made it impossible to address them as intellectual equals. The consciousness that he was in possession of truths denied to others produced the characteristic note of pontification which is evident in early and late works alike. It led to the creation of an air of mystery through the use of out-of-the-way allusions, erudite quotations, unfamiliar words, and technical terms; and to his paying a too 'willing homage to the illustrious obscure'. It led also to the fairly frequent examples of proud self-defence against attacks that had not been and never were to be delivered...An additional hazard was his almost pathological fear of popularity. As long as he was sure that his words were unlikely to be fully understood he could convince himself that they contained invaluable truths. The use of a less complex style might well have attracted more readers; it would certainly have exposed him to the embarrassment of being generally understood.

The point of quoting that passage is that, while it reads like a perceptive analysis of Flosky, it is in fact the conclusion that Mr J. Colmer draws from his close and sympathetic reading of *Coleridge, critic of society*.[1]

[1] Oxford, 1959, p. 173.

Flosky not only illustrates in himself the spirit of the age, but also takes part in general discussions on it. In these he is, like his fellow-guests, the subject of Peacock's great art in altering at will the focus of the novel. Characters who elsewhere stand out in bold idiosyncratic isolation, fit into a chorus where they retain their individuality but the reader is led to attend as much to what is said as *who* says it. With the same skill Peacock can momentarily draw an individual out of the chorus to speak as a particular case—and then sink back into relative impersonality. All this management of voices in a chorus can surely be credited to Peacock's appreciation of opera, and underlines the point made earlier that a writer may learn profoundly from art-forms other than his own, and that real influence is not traceable merely in surface signs (*opera buffa* stage-business, or explicit references to Rossini and Mozart). The art of the chorus is that which Lord Mount Edgcumbe described in a passage Peacock marked in his copy and quoted in his review. Whereas in the time of Metastasio choruses were rare and solo arias the rule: 'In an opera we now require more frequent duos and trios, and a *crashing* finale. In fact, the most difficult problem for the opera poet is the mixing the complicated voices of conflicting passions in one common harmony, without injuring their essence.'[1] In the central chorus or discussion scenes (chapters 5, 6, 7 and 11), this art lets Peacock's account of the Regency move unobtrusively between the particular symptoms and a general diagnosis.

The subject is briefly introduced—and illustrated—in chapter 5, by Mr Flosky and the Honourable Mr Listless. Listless is the average bored and indolent gentleman who rarely laughs because 'the exertion is too much for me'; and who is so mentally lazy that his butler thinks for him: 'Fatout! When did I think of going to Cheltenham, and did not go?'[2] He is no great reader: 'I hope you do not suspect me of being studious. I have finished my education.' Beneath this facetious tone is a real anxiety, for being studious would be then as now a suspicious matter, likely to spread alarm and despondency in any

[1] The Earl of Mount Edgcumbe, *Musical reminiscences* (London, 1834), p. 235.
[2] This draws, of course, on the well-known Windermere anecdote of Beau Brummell.

polite gathering by the threat of 'heavy conversation'. Yet the same conversational etiquette directs that 'there are some fashionable books that one must read, because they are the ingredients of the talk of the day'. And so he receives an express parcel of the latest publications, full of heroic villainy and misanthropy.

Mr. Flosky (turning over the leaves). 'Devilman, a novel.' Hm. Hatred—revenge—misanthropy—and quotations from the Bible. Hm. This is the morbid anatomy of black bile. 'Paul Jones, a poem'. Hm. I see how it is. Paul Jones, an amiable enthusiast—disappointed in his affections—turns pirate from ennui and magnanimity...[1]

Peacock acutely points out that works like Godwin's novels and Byron's tales flatter men like Listless, who confesses that

modern books are very consolatory and congenial to my feelings. There is, as it were, a delightful north-east wind, an intellectual blight breathing through them; a delicious misanthropy and discontent, that demonstrates the nullity of virtue and energy, and puts me in good humour with myself and my sofa.[2]

This reminds us of the vicious circle of literature, taste and manners which is discussed in the contemporary 'Essay on fashionable literature'. When Mr Cypress appears later in the novel, we realise that it is only one step from Listless's fashionable apathy to the spirit of *Childe Harold's pilgrimage*, although there is a contradictory gusto to Cypress's nihilism.

Even Flosky is conditioned by the spirit of the age and the state of the reading public. There is something perversely rigid about his anti-fashionable stance: 'This rage for novelty is the bane of literature. Except my works and those of my particular friends, nothing is good that is not as old as Jeremy Taylor.'[3] Here is one seed of his obscurity and difficulty in communicating, which we have already studied.

The next chapter skilfully leads into the general theme from the particular story of Scythrop and Marionetta. The link is made through Dante, which Scythrop pretends to read while jealous of Listless, with whom Marionetta flirts.

---

[1] Halliford, III, 39. Devilman alludes to Godwin's *Mandeville*, which Shelley said 'shakes the deepest soul' (*Letters*, ed. Jones, I, 523–4).
[2] Halliford, III, 41. [3] *Ibid.*

Marionetta...peeped into his book, and said to him, 'I see you are in the middle of Purgatory.'—'I am in the middle of hell,' said Scythrop furiously...'and I,' said the Honourable Mr. Listless, 'am not reading Dante, and am just now in Paradise,' bowing to Marionetta.[1]

The effect of Listless's inane compliment is to mock Scythrop, whose ostentatious anti-sociable manner is only the reverse side of Listless's social conventionality (as Flosky's anti-popularity is only the perverse reverse of Listless's fashionable taste). This small incident is symptomatic of the rest of Scythrop's behaviour, just as Byron's behaviour at his famous first dinner with Rogers gives a good clue about the psychology of the Byronic hero.[2]

Listless has not read Dante, 'But I find he is growing fashionable, and I am afraid I must read him some wet morning.'[3] He is in fashion, it is decided, because he appeals to modern blue devils: and this leads Flosky, after his parenthetical defence of 'synthetical reasoning', to analyse modern fashionable literature:

the French Revolution has made us shrink from the name of philosophy, and has destroyed...all enthusiasm for political liberty. That part of the *reading public* which shuns the solid food of reason for the light diet of fiction, requires a perpetual adhibition of *sauce piquante* to the palate of its depraved imagination.[4]

So far this echoes Coleridge's and Wordsworth's attacks on the reading public; but Peacock implicates Coleridge himself: '[The reading public] lived upon ghosts, goblins, and skeletons (I and my friend Mr. Sackbut served up a few of the best).'[5] Flosky follows with a sketch of the successive literary rages from 1798 to 1818. The market for the supernatural becoming

---

[1] Halliford, III, 45.
[2] Refusing each course in turn and being asked by the desperate host what he *did* eat and drink, Byron replied, 'Nothing but hard bisquits and soda-water.' [Rogers continues] 'Some days after, meeting Hobhouse, I said to him, "How long will Lord Byron persevere in his present diet?" He replied, "Just as long as you continue to notice it."—I did not know then, what I now know to be a fact—that Byron, after leaving my house, had gone to a Club in St. James's Street, and eaten a hearty meat-supper.' (A. Dyce, *Recollections of the table-talk of Samuel Rogers*, ed. M. Bishop, London, 1952, p. 189).
[3] Halliford, III, 45–6.
[4] *Ibid.* pp. 50–1. [5] *Ibid.* p. 51.

flooded, 'now the delight of our spirits is to dwell on all the vices and blackest passions of our nature, tricked out in the masquerade dress of heroism and benevolence'.[1] The point was often to be made by critics of the Byronic hero.

The only threat to Peacock's sharp but playful diagnosis occurs when Mr Hilary breaks in: 'If we go on this way, we shall have a new art of poetry, of which one of the first rules will be: To remember to forget that there are such things as sunshine and music in the world.'[2] But Listless gracefully averts the danger: 'It seems to be the case with us at present, or we should not have interrupted Miss O'Carroll's music with this exceedingly dry conversation.'[3] And the scene ends with a song, very relevant to Scythrop—

> Why are thy looks so blank, grey friar?...
> But couldst thou think my heart to move
> With that pale and silent scowl?[4]

which reconciles the lovers.

The next discussion, in chapter 7, is led by a new arrival, Mr Asterias the ichthyologist, hot on the trail of a mermaid (who like Flosky's ghost turns out to be Mr Toobad's missing daughter, alias Stella...). He justifies his belief in mermaids by a threadbare and *recherché* catalogue of precedents. But, provoked by Listless's Byronic question as to 'the *cui bono* of all the pains and expense you have incurred',[5] Asterias takes up the position of a genuine scientist-explorer, an amateur in the best sense rather than a blundering eighteenth-century virtuoso-crank, who 'enjoys the disinterested pleasure of enlarging the intellect and increasing the comforts of society'.[6] Only 'the more humane pursuits of philosophy and science... keep alive the better feelings and more valuable energies of our nature',[7] for

A gloomy brow and a tragical voice seem to have been of late the characteristics of fashionable manners: and a morbid, withering,

---

[1] *Ibid.*   [2] *Ibid.* p. 53.   [3] *Ibid.*   [4] *Ibid.* p. 54.
[5] *Ibid.* p. 64. The weary question *Cui bono?* forms the title of the Smith brothers' parody of Byron, in their *Rejected addresses*.
[6] *Ibid.* p. 66.   [7] *Ibid.* p. 65.

deadly, anti-social sirocco, loaded with moral and political despair, breathes through all the groves and valleys of the modern Parnassus; while science moves on in the calm dignity of its course.[1]

This was to be repeated almost verbatim in 'The four ages of poetry'. Yet the similarity brings home the advantages the novel's dramatic discussion-form has over the expository essay. However fruitfully provocative, 'The four ages' can argue in only one direction, dogmatically establish one point of view. In *Nightmare Abbey* the effect is of a 'free play of minds' on the same subject, which is kept in the air bouncing between a range of voices and attitudes of which Asterias's is only one. The subject never comes to rest in one attitude, nor is any one character unqualifiedly endorsed by Peacock. We are never quite sure, for instance, how seriously we can take Asterias's love of science. Doesn't it rest too much on an appetite for experience and action in themselves?

I have made many voyages, Mr. Listless, to remote and barren shores: I have travelled over desert and inhospitable lands: I have defied danger—I have submitted to privation. In the midst of these I have experienced pleasures which I would not at any time have exchanged for that of existing and doing nothing.[2]

This is not Peacock's voice, but has a fanatical note probably intended to mock a similar passage in the Preface to *The revolt of Islam*.[3] Peacock's only clumsy touch in this scene is the closing speech by Mr Hilary to the effect that 'a happy disposition finds materials of enjoyment everywhere'.[4] It is too long and pompous, and receives too much prominence and endorsement. It deadens the 'free speculative treatment' of the subject by pulling it down to a single attitude. It conveys a naïve or complacent idea of 'a happy disposition'—enjoying 'a theatre...crowded with elegance and beauty' and 'gliding at sunset over the bosom of a lonely lake'—which makes Hilary himself a conventional emanation of the spirit of the age.

---

[1] Halliford, III, 65–6.   [2] *Ibid*. pp. 64–5.

[3] Shelley is claiming to have the 'education peculiarly fitted for a Poet': 'I have been familiar from boyhood with mountains and lakes, and the sea, and the solitude of forests: Danger, which sports upon the brink of precipices, has been my playmate. I have trodden the glaciers of the Alps, and lived under the eye of Mount Blanc...' (*Poetical works*, ed. Mary Shelley, p. 149).

[4] Halliford, III, 68.

Luckily the scene does not quite rest there, but concludes with Scythrop's complaint that 'these remarks are rather uncharitable'—these are hard times for 'ardent spirits'.

The fourth discussion-scene (chapter 11) centres on Mr Cypress, calling to say farewell on his way to the Continent. The subject of foreign travel provokes characteristic responses. Cypress asks the Philistine Mr Glowry if he feels

No wish to wander among the venerable remains of the greatness that has passed for ever?
Mr. Glowry: Not a grain.[1]

Nor has Scythrop any wish to 'wander among a few mouldy ruins...and meet at every step the more melancholy ruins of human nature—a degenerate race of stupid and shrivelled slaves, grovelling in the lowest depths of servility and superstition'.[2] Besides, a peer and a genius like Byron has duties in the fight for liberty at home.[3] It is no use Flosky denying all hope of political progress 'after what we have seen in France', for 'a Frenchman is born in harness, ready saddled, bitted and bridled, for any tyrant to ride', while Englishmen are born free.[4] Cypress brushes aside this moral earnestness with supercilious egotism: 'Sir, I have quarrelled with my wife; and a man who has quarrelled with his wife is absolved from all duty to his country. I have written an ode to tell the people as much, and they may take it as they list.'[5] This logical link once asserted, the way is open to blow up one's personal dissatisfactions and failures into a general pessimism, an indictment of life itself. 'I have no hope for myself or for others. Our life is

---

[1] *Ibid.* pp. 101–2.

[2] *Ibid.* p. 102. Peacock is transcribing verbatim a letter from Shelley: 'The people here, though inoffensive enough, seem both in body and soul a miserable race. The men are hardly men, they look like a tribe of stupid and shrivelled slaves.' (20 Apr. 1818: *Letters*, II, 9.) This is a common note in Shelley's Italian letters.

[3] Cf. Shelley: 'The number of English who pass through this town [Milan] is very great. They ought to be in their own country at the present crisis. Their conduct is wholly inexcusable' (from the letter quoted above). Shelley was abroad, he claimed, for health reasons.

[4] Halliford, III, 103–4. Cf. again the central argument of the Preface to *The revolt of Islam.*

[5] *Ibid.* p. 103.

a false nature; it is not in the harmony of things; it is an all-blasting upas...'[1] The phrases and images from *Childe Harold's pilgrimage* are made to sound even more extravagant when strung together in the prose of Cypress's succeeding speeches.

Hilary attacks this pessimism as the offspring of false expectations: 'To expect too much is a disease in the expectant, for which human nature is not responsible.'[2] On love, Hilary says: 'You talk like a Rosicrucian, who will love nothing but a sylph, who does not believe in the existence of a sylph, and who yet quarrels with the whole universe for not containing a sylph.'[3] Of this, which applies strongly to Scythrop, Humphry House says that 'A whole long chapter of Professor Irving Babbitt says little more.'[4]

Hilary's protest that 'the highest wisdom and the highest genius have been invariably accompanied with cheerfulness' is greeted by variations on the theme, 'How can we be cheerful...?' and calls for 'a nice tragical ballad', which is provided by Cypress's *There is a fever of the spirit*.[5] In this and the preceding prose parodies of Byron, Peacock exposes the cant and also the perverse pleasure in Byron's nihilism, together with the cliché and confusion of his imagery. It is a sign of Peacock's quickness and insight that he seized on *Childe Harold's pilgrimage* (particularly canto iv, which had only recently appeared) as the work that both focused and exploited one of the spirits of the age; and that he made about it the central criticisms that most later critics have made.

These scenes give the impression of a comprehensive survey of 'modern gloom' as one of the prevailing spirits of the age. It is comprehensive in that, although a suggestive sketch rather than a survey thick with detail, it characterises convincingly all the relevant areas and representative figures, together with their connections by which the mechanism of fashion and production, supply and demand, is kept in motion. By that vicious circle also studied in the 'Essay on fashionable literature', modern manners and spirits help determine modern literature,

[1] Halliford, iii, 104. [2] *Ibid.* pp. 107–8. [3] *Ibid.* p. 108.
[4] 'The novels of Thomas Love Peacock', *The listener*, xlii (8 Dec. 1949), 998.
[5] Chapter 11: Halliford, iii, 109–11.

which in turn influences manners. Peacock also connects developments in different areas of life and intellectual activity, each with its representative speaker: Flosky prophesies that

> let society only give fair play at one and the same time...to your Cypress' system of morals, and my system of metaphysics, and Scythrop's system of politics, and Mr. Listless' system of manners, and Mr. Toobad's system of religion, and the result will be as fine a mental chaos as even the immortal Kant himself could ever have hoped to see.[1]

Above all, in tracing a common spirit of the age Peacock distinguishes the different levels on which that spirit existed. He distinguishes, for instance, the merely fashionable (in Listless) from the intensely personal (Scythrop, who reads the same rubbish as Listless but absorbs it into his personality, his 'interior structure'). It will be objected that he does not distinguish clearly enough from these the authentically creative—what in the period was represented by the best of Coleridge. But this lies outside Peacock's terms of reference. It is sufficient that, in his dealings with Coleridge as with Byron, he can diagnose the qualities that bind them to the limitations of their age, despite their efforts to stand apart from it. This means that Peacock himself could stand above the period, and have the insight into it which we can normally expect only from the vantage-point of a later period.

*

There is a superficial resemblance between the two novels published in 1818, *Northanger Abbey* and *Nightmare Abbey*, as satires on different forms of romanticism. Dr Jack believes the difference to be that, 'unlike Jane Austen, Peacock is more interested in ideas than in people'. This chapter has tried to show that this is not true, and the real differences lie where Dr Jack finds similarities.

Both novels, says Dr Jack, satirise 'the excesses of modern literature as exemplified in the work of Mrs Radcliffe and the "German" drama of the day'.[2] Mrs Radcliffe and German drama are strongly in the background at Nightmare Abbey, but in

---

[1] *Ibid.* p. 105.   [2] *English literature, 1815–32*, p. 213.

the foreground are *Childe Harold's pilgrimage*, *Mandeville* and *Biographia literaria*. As Flosky points out, ghosts, goblins and skeletons have been out of fashion for years. 'Modern literature' in Peacock's novel is the literature and taste of 1818, not (as with Jane Austen's novel) the turn of the century.

Dr Jack adds that 'in Jane Austen's book a young woman discovers the difference between life in books and life in fact: in Peacock's a young man makes the same discovery'.[1] But in *Northanger Abbey* romance or romanticism belongs only to 'life in books', and an extraordinarily ordinary girl merely confuses it with prosaic if sometimes inhospitable 'real life'. Peacock on the other hand diagnoses inside Scythrop romanticism as it fuses with individual character and directs one's life. To feel the pulse of such a personality, of what might be called lived romanticism, needed more intimate and sympathetic insight than to make fun of 'the excesses of modern literature'. It needed much more than what Dr Jack claims Jane Austen and Peacock share in these two novels, 'a conservative and "eighteenth century" attitude'.[2]

[1] *English literature, 1815–32*, p. 213.   [2] *Ibid.*

8

Three Comparisons
Crabb Robinson, Hazlitt, Byron

These comparisons will draw together the judgements made
in the preceding chapters on Peacock and the Regency. Crabb
Robinson compares most closely as 'common reader' with
Peacock's letters and diaries (chapters 2 and 3); Hazlitt, with
Peacock the literary critic in essays and novels; Byron, with
Peacock as both literary and social critic. More particularly, this
chapter will meet specific challenges to comparison issued by
those writers: for instance, Hazlitt in his criticism of Coleridge,
and Byron in the English Cantos of *Don Juan* which were
influenced by *Melincourt* and *Nightmare Abbey*. By examining
what it was possible for contemporary minds to make of their
age, we can judge more exactly Peacock's relative position in and
grasp of the Regency.

Crabb Robinson

The Regency letters and essays of Peacock, it has been suggested
in chapter 3, are expressions of his chosen rôle of common
reader; and in this he may be compared with Henry Crabb
Robinson. Their response to contemporary literature rarely
issues into formal criticism: the 'Essay on fashionable literature'
and 'The four ages of poetry' may be seen as extensions of
Peacock's discussions by letter with Shelley, while Crabb Robinson gave up his activities as a periodical critic in 1811 and
immediately began his literary diary. Their ways of life were
chosen to accommodate this rôle of common reader: Peacock the
leisured 'Hermit of the Thames' and London visitor, followed
by work at East India House; Crabb Robinson, the legal profession for 'a gentlemanly independence' allowing 'good company with leisure' and a very early retirement.[1]

---

[1] For the phrases quoted here, see above, p. 54.

To consider the virtues of the common reader, and even the possibility of his existence, we have to return to the hackneyed close of Johnson's *Life of Gray*: 'In the character of his Elegy I rejoice to concur with the common reader; for, by the common sense of readers uncorrupted with literary prejudices, after all the refinements of subtilty and the dogmatism of learning, must be finally decided all claim to poetical honours.'[1] The passage is hackneyed because it is so often appealed to nostalgically by modern critics, as if the common reader meant for Johnson the simple reader, the average reader or the taste of the majority. Johnson is invoking not the lowest common denominator of popular taste, but the highest common factor of 'common humanity', 'those general passions and principles by which all minds are agitated, and the whole system of life is kept in motion',[2] to which Shakespeare appeals and on which all new literature should ideally be tested. Certainly this makes the status of common reader open to every individual of integrity,[3] qualified not by outstanding intellectual ability like the members of Johnson's Club, or by skill as a formal critic, but by being 'emotionally educated' and 'emotionally honest'.[4] Yet this is clearly an ideal not often realised. If Johnson rejoiced that with the *Elegy* the verdicts of himself, his ideal 'common reader' and the reality of 'the popular verdict' all coincided, he knew how rarely the reader was 'uncorrupted with literary prejudice'. His final 'rejoice to concur' takes its force from what goes before in the *Life*: Johnson has constantly and violently disagreed with the popular verdict. With two odes, for example, 'though either vulgar ignorance or common sense at first universally rejected them, many have been since persuaded to think themselves delighted'.[5]

[1] *Works* (1825), VIII, 487.
[2] 'Preface to *Shakespeare*', *Works* (1825), V, 106.
[3] 'Readers uncorrupted by literary prejudice' are individual minds uninfluenced by fashion or the majority verdict. 'The common sense' of these is the aggregate of the impression or convictions which these *individual* readers have come independently to hold. It is thus not 'common sense' in the modern sense.
[4] Although the opening of D. H. Lawrence's essay on Galsworthy, from which the quoted phrases come, is becoming as hackneyed as the close of the *Life of Gray*, it is worth alluding to here because Lawrence, like Johnson, insists that the quality of a critic depends on his quality as a reader and ultimately as a human being.   [5] *Works* (1825), VIII, 483.

If Johnson thought the common reader a rare species, could it survive in an age like the Regency when literature and culture were more complex and more specialised than in Johnson's day? Crabb Robinson however presents a perfect specimen, by which we can judge the imperfect specimen Peacock.

Johnson, particularly in the *Life of Gray*, is concerned with the reader's response to new literature, his ability to distinguish the true creative development from fashionable novelty as well as mere conservatism (the 'natural but stale'). A complementary problem is the continual development of the reader's own taste, never hardening into a set of standards of expectation and judgement. For two reasons it is worth turning on this point to a modern writer. One reason is that Dr Leavis has been encouraged by Johnson to take as his norm the reader and not the formal critic: 'By the critic of poetry I understand the complete reader: the ideal critic is the ideal reader',[1] and the critic merely extends the process by 'developing his response into commentary'.[2] A second reason is that, while Dr Leavis describes an ideal which many forces within and outside ourselves work against, it is not a dogmatic requirement but a natural psychological process observed from his own experience and ringing true to ours.

As he ['the critic—the reader of poetry'] matures in experience of the new thing he asks, explicitly and implicitly: 'Where does this come? How does it stand in relation to...? How relatively important does it seem?' And the organization into which it settles as a constituent in becoming 'placed' is an organization of similarly 'placed' things, things that have found their bearings with regard to one another, and not a theoretical system or a system determined by abstract considerations...He doesn't ask, 'How does this accord with these specifications of goodness in poetry?'; he aims to make fully conscious and articulate the immediate sense of value that 'places' the poem.

Of course, the process of 'making fully conscious and articulate' is a process of relating and organizing, and the 'immediate sense of value' should, as the critic matures with experience, represent a growing stability of organization (the problem is to combine stability with growth).[3]

[1] 'Literary criticism and philosophy: a reply', *Scrutiny*, VI (1937), 60.
[2] *Ibid.* p. 61.
[3] *Ibid.*

Crabb Robinson's capacity for development, for stability with growth, and recognition of the genuinely new in literature, is demonstrated by the huge mass of his diaries and correspondence. The following account must be confined largely to excerpts which indicate or comment on his mental habits: to demonstrate those habits in action would need a prohibitive number of quotations recording the multiplicity of his fresh reading and his constant return to and reappraisal of past works. I shall moreover concentrate on the most telling points of comparison with the account of Peacock which it is hoped the reader will be holding in his mind from the foregoing chapters.

Before the turn of the century, Crabb Robinson's taste was what one would expect from a reader born well inside the age of Johnson (1775), who dimly remembered the publication of *John Gilpin*. He wrote in 1843 that

Pope is or rather *was* as great a favourite with me as any one English poet...Referring to an early period of my life, before I had heard of the lyrical Ballads, which caused a little revolution in my taste for poetry, there were four poems which I used to read incessantly... They are of a very different kind and I mention them to show that my taste was *wide*. They were—*The Rape of the Lock*, *Comus*, *The Castle of Indolence* and *The Traveller*.—Next to these were all the Ethic Epistles of Pope.[1]

But his mind was among the few at once open to *Lyrical ballads*: the effect was a 'revolution in my taste for poetry', and he could write later that 'I owe much of the happiness of my life to the effect produced on me first by his [Wordsworth's] works and then by his friendship'.[2] By then Crabb Robinson's recognition of genuine originality, in the face of conservative ridicule from Jeffrey and others, had been confirmed by time: 'this is what distinguishes Wordsworth from the herd of poets. *He lasts*. I love him more now than I did fifty years ago. You will see few men advanced in life who will say the same of Lord Byron, even though they once loved him—that is, as I did Wordsworth, from the beginning.'[3]

[1] *The correspondence of Henry Crabb Robinson with the Wordsworth circle*, ed. E. J. Morley, 2 vols. (Oxford, 1927), I, 518.
[2] *Ibid.* I, 26. [3] *Ibid.* II, 818.

That claim comes from a letter to a young acquaintance James Mottram, which shows another aspect of the common reader: eagerness to share discoveries and help provide new writers with readers. Echoing part of Wordsworth's own 'Supplementary essay' of 1815, Crabb Robinson tells Mottram that 'I made many converts. Wordsworth had to create his public. He formed the taste of the age in a great measure.'[1] Crabb helped create that public by reading aloud, lending copies, and arguing Wordsworth's claims. After one such discussion in a long series of letters to his brother, he could write in 1808, 'You are, and I rejoice at it, a convert to Wordsworth's poetry.'[2] To convert Mottram fifty years later he sent tactful advice on what to read first, with comments that distinguish the best from those acceptable only to uncritical 'Wordsworthians'.[3] The same impulse had made him seek out Wordsworth and other writers and through personal contact give his services as a 'curious, sympathetic, creative reader'.[4] This was an impulse Peacock showed only towards Shelley.

Yet, while the greatest changes in Crabb's taste occurred at the turn of the century, his mind was not arrested there or fixed in an attitude of worship. Wordsworth's egotism and narrowness of taste, repeatedly criticised over the following years, are observed at the first meeting:

Wordsworth at my first tête-à-tête with him spoke freely and praisingly of his own poems, which I never felt to be unbecoming, but the contrary. He said he thought of writing an essay, 'Why bad poetry pleases'...He said he could not respect the mother who could read without emotion his poem, *Once in a lonely hamlet I sojourned*... He wished popularity for his *Two Voices are there, one is of the Sea* as a test of elevation and moral purity.[5]

At the corresponding introduction to Coleridge he was 'deeply impressed by admiration of his genius' but 'equally aware of the infirmities of his character', offering a shrewd account of his conversational strengths and weaknesses.[6] His accurate

---

[1] *Ibid*. II, 818. [2] *Ibid*. I, 50. [3] *Ibid*. II, 818–23.
[4] The phrase of C. F. Harrold, 'Henry Crabb Robinson, a spectator of life', *Sewanee Review*, XXXVI (1928), 49.
[5] Reminiscences for 1808: *On books and their writers*, ed. Morley, I, 10–11.
[6] Reminiscences for 1810: *ibid*. I, 16.

cords of Coleridge's lectures go with complaints at their frequent confusion and repetition; and in conversation he more than once detects that 'his circle of favourite ideas he is confined within as much as any man, and that his speculations have ceased to be living thoughts'.[1] *Political justice* was in 1795 'the book that gave a turn to my mind, and in effect directed the whole course of my life...'.[2] But, while 'no book ever made me feel more generously',[3] his diary references to its author build a picture of meanness and dishonesty.

More positively he responded to the younger poets of the Regency. Keats's *Hyperion*, which we remember Peacock could not find time to read 'if I should live to the age of Methusalem',[4] immediately struck Crabb Robinson as 'a piece of great promise. There is a force, wildness, and originality in the works of this young poet which, if his perilous journey to Italy does not destroy him, promises to place him at the head of the next generation of poets.'[5] Although kept at a distance by the sense of something perverted in Byron, he was quick to recognise that the satires had more power than the serious poems, and was fascinated by his letters as 'a psychological phenomenon'[6] (contrast again Peacock's relative indifference). While finding Shelley as a person, at their only meeting, 'vehement and arrogant and intolerant',[7] he praised his poetry without being alarmed by its atheism, which he could on the contrary diagnose as superficial and provincial: 'the God he denies seems to be after all but the God of the superstitious...he sums up the Christian doctrine, and in such a way that perhaps Wordsworth would say: "This, I disbelieve as much as Shelley, but that is only the caricature and burlesque of Christianity."'[8]

The sequence of diary-entries over twenty or more years, which trace the complex evolution of Crabb Robinson's feelings about Byron and Shelley, would demonstrate two more virtues of the common reader. He has no need to force his impressions

[1] Reminiscences for 1810: *On books and their writers*, I, 219. (The structure of this sentence is a little confused but the sense is clear.)
[2] Reminiscences for 1795: *ibid*. I, 2–3.   [3] *Ibid*. p. 3.
[4] See above, p. 38.   [5] 8 Dec. 1820: *On books and their writers*, I, 258.
[6] 20 Oct. 1832: *ibid*. I, 415.   [7] 6 Nov. 1817: *ibid*. I, 212.
[8] 10 Jan. 1836: *ibid*. II, 479.

into an over-hasty or over-simplified coherence, as the professional critic or academic teacher often must do. On the other hand normal mental habits as well as professional necessity can produce this urge to reach a decision and close the matter—witness Peacock on Shelley or Byron. Crabb Robinson's impulse is rather to explore: even where he is first repelled or bored, his involuntary curiosity leads him back again and again to the writer in question, overcoming prejudices and collecting new impressions and 'fresh knowledge'.

While his taste evolved quite spontaneously, without self-conscious direction, Crabb Robinson was in the right way conscious *of* it. He frequently gauges it by more static tastes. A diary-entry for 1831 reads,

Today I finished Hazlitt's *Conversations of Northcote*. I do not believe that Boswell gives so much good talk in an equal quantity in any part of his *Life of Johnson*...Yet all the elderly people—my friend Amyot, for instance—would think this an outrageous proof of bad taste on my part. I do believe I am younger in my tastes than most men. I can relish novelty and am not yet a *laudator temporis acti*.[1]

He described a *laudator temporis acti* twenty years earlier, when he noted

A visit to Mrs. Buller. Mr. Jerningham with her whom she called the 'last of the old school' to his face, at the same time that she declared she put all Southey's poems in his *Index Expurgatorius*...Mrs. Buller objects to the careless verse in Southey, and she speaks with equal harshness of Scott: his irregular stanzas are a stumbling block to her. She requires an attention to the prescribed rules derived from the older poets. And she recognises no prerogative in genius to dispense with them.[2]

Not that he confuses the fashionable novelties of Southey or Moore with the work of the geniuses of the age. He recognised what Henry James called the 'hatred of art', the offence genius gives, in saying that

Scott has caught all the arts of popularity which Coleridge despises... The mystical sentimentality of Coleridge, however, can never interest the gay and frivolous, who are to be attracted by the quick succession

[1] 16 Dec. 1831: *ibid.* I, 397.
[2] 1 Feb. 1811: *ibid.* I, 22.

171

of commonplace and amusing objects; and for the same reason the deep glances into the innermost nature of man and the original views of the relations of things which Coleridge's works are fraught with are a stumbling-block and an offence to the million, not a charm.[1]

Peacock, in the 'Essay on fashionable literature', made a similar distinction. But his ultimate reaction, which led to 'The four ages of poetry', was to claim that such cultural conditions made genuine poetry impossible, and to save himself the trouble of looking out for it. Those cultural conditions made Crabb Robinson, on the other hand, even more alert for the rare new poem that *was* genuine, and more active in making converts for it. Even when this failed, he did not surrender to the majority verdict: after repeated readings, pressing the claims of 'Peter Bell' to many of his friends, he retired perplexed at Lamb's disagreements.

These are to me inconceivable judgements from Charles Lamb, whose taste in general I acquiesce in, and who is certainly an enthusiast for Wordsworth. But I know no resource against the perplexity arising from the diversities of opinion in those I look up to, but in determination to disregard all opinions and trust to my own unstudied suggestions and natural feelings.[2]

If his own catholic taste in English led him to call Wordsworth's narrow, Crabb Robinson's knowledge of German literature earned him the right to call Wordsworth provincial in his deafness to 'Goethe—whom he depreciated in utter ignorance'.[3] Shelley's atheism too—the account quoted above notes—was provincial. One could piece together from the diaries a criticism of the Romantic poets as a whole that is close to that made by Arnold: they 'did not know enough'.[4] For them both the relevant comparison was with German culture—a more impressive and felt comparison than the 'literature of utility' Peacock relies on in 'The four ages of poetry'.

Nothing brings home more strongly the intellectual provincialism of Regency England than its attitude to contemporary

[1] 9 Oct. 1811: *On books and their writers*, ed. Morley, I, 47–8.
[2] 6 June 1812: *ibid*. I, 103.
[3] 5 Jan. 1836: *ibid*. II, 478.
[4] 'The function of criticism at the present time', *Essays in criticism*, 1st series (London, 1865).

German literature. Kant was known mainly through periodical reviewers as ignorant of Kant's German, let alone his ideas, as Sir William Drummond or Peacock himself. Until Madame de Staël's *De L'Allemagne*, in 1813, Goethe was known almost exclusively as 'the author of Werther', a work of immaturity easily assimilated into the late eighteenth-century English cult of 'sensibility'.[1] *Werther* had in any case been first translated in 1779, and the turn of the century took its excitements from translations of Kotzebue, Klopstock and Wieland. In the face of this popular taste, conservative strongholds like *The anti-Jacobin review* attacked the immorality of all 'German literature' —a phrase that evoked the same stock response as 'Freethinkers' or 'Jacobins'. If those who thrilled to the Germans could not distinguish between Kotzebue and Goethe, neither could the attackers: 'the...author of Werter is avowedly a man of pleasure, and possesses not a single grain of morality'.[2]

Prompted by William Taylor of Norwich, one of the few intelligent students of German, Crabb Robinson went in 1800 as an undergraduate at the University of Jena and remained in the country until 1805. With his irregular and narrow education, and his Calvinistic, middle-class provincial background, he had every excuse for sharing those ignorances and prejudices just described. His triumph was in welcoming all challenges to his assumptions. To him as to Germany Kant's philosophy 'has had a vast effect in freeing the mind from all the shackles of prejudice—Revelation, forms of Government, all, are *criticised*. You may judge how they stand the test.'[3] He found an intellectual standard by which to measure 'my miserably neglected Education—You have no conception to what mortifications my ignorance daily subjects me'.[4] He also found comparisons

---

[1] Professor J.-M. Carré, in *Goethe en Angleterre* (Paris 1920, p. 13) states that *Werther* 'apporte au public anglais une émotion qui n'est pas nouvelle: il touche une corde qu'ont fait vibrer avant lui Rousseau, Ossian et Young. Dans cette émotion il y a de la tristesse, du désenchantement, un vague amour de la nature, l'attendrissement du "promeneur solitaire"; il n'y a pas encore d'élan, de colère, de réaction.'

[2] *The anti-Jacobin review*, IV (1799), Preface, p. xiv.

[3] Letter, 3 March 1802: *Crabb Robinson in Germany, 1800–1805*, ed. E. J. Morley (Oxford, 1929), p. 105. In quoting Robinson's letters I have normalised small points of punctuation and spelling.

[4] 13 Jan. 1802: *ibid.* p. 103.

with his own country's writers: 'I am fully persuaded of the importance of knowing something of foreign literature, even to understand our own. Comparison is the soul of judgement.'[1] Above all the provincial Englishman was able to register English intellectual pronvincialism and lack of disinterestedness, both in the eighteenth century and in the over-simple revolt from it:

Winkleman [sic] on this subject made a remark which is at least worth copying. Your poets and philosophers, said he, have always been *Englishmen* and either patriots or courtiers. They have had views and ends which gave a certain degree of importance to their works...But it has made them incapable of attaining the highest degree of excellence. A pure poet has no other end than to produce a work of art, a pure philosopher no other end than to raise a system of abstract truth...Our poets, our philosophers, are men, not Germans.[2]

Crabb Robinson studied and, through the Brentanos and Madame de Staël, met or even became the friend of many leading German writers, including Goethe. While F. Norman plays him down in these meetings as gauche and easily flattered,[3] Crabb Robinson was at his first dinner-party with Goethe shrewd enough to

distinguish very pointedly a great man from a man of great talents— Schlegel who was at table too, shewed himself to be the latter; he related witty anecdotes, recited epigrams, and shone...But this class of men whose talents are something *they possess* (a property, a thing foreign from and attached to themselves,) is very different from that of those, of whom it should not be said that they *have genius* but that they *are geniuses*...Everything [Goethe] said had the stamp not of his talents but of his sentiments, his permanent habitual feelings, and habits of thinking: and it is knowledge of these which can be acquired alone by personal acquaintance, that is of such vast importance.[4]

'Knowledge' in this last sense is what he missed in Madame de Staël, whom he therefore saw as a mere social collector of geniuses and intellectual collector of 'the latest ideas'.

[1] 13 Nov. 1800: *Crabb Robinson in Germany*, p. 37. [2] 6 July 1801: *ibid.* pp. 73–4.
[3] 'Henry Crabb Robinson and Goethe', part I, *Publications of the English Goethe Society*, new series, VI (London, 1930).
[4] 3 June 1804: *Crabb Robinson in Germany*, pp. 146–7.

I was invited to her in order to be interrogated on the new philosophy. And I saw clearly enough *that I was used*...Madame de Stahl [*sic*] is one of those persons who with a most acute understanding and elegant wit—has nothing else. *She has not the least sense for poetry and is utterly incapable of thinking a philosophical thought*—her philosophy is only a map of observations connected together by a loose logic, and poetry is for her...only rhetoric in verse. She cannot perceive anything in poetry more than *fine passages!!!* And what is an eternal bar to all advances she does not suspect that there is anything above her reach.[1]

Provoked into telling her, 'Madame, vous n'avez pas compris Goethe, et vous ne le comprendrez jamais', he was answered 'Monsieur, je comprends tout ce qui mérite d'être compris; ce que je ne comprends n'est rien.'[2] This was a symbolic confrontation: on her side, proud ignorance beneath superficial curiosity; on his, capacity to learn and grow through awareness of what was still 'above his reach'. Both minds bore appropriate fruits. Exaggerated modesty led Crabb Robinson to give up 'what is not within my reach, viz., pre-eminence as a metaphysical philosopher or a critic',[3] and return to the law. While still in Germany however he wrote for the *Monthly register* a series of articles on Kant and German literature which Professor Wellek shows

deserve...attention not only because of their historical position, but also because of their intrinsic value...they are extraordinarily accurate and vivid. They grasp the central problem of Kant's epistemology and try to give an interpretation of Kant's teaching which is by no means altogether usual and hackneyed even today.[4]

Madame de Staël, helped by garbled versions of Crabb Robinson's articles, produced the bland superficialities of *De L'Allemagne*.[5] It received prominent and respectful reviews in every

[1] 30 Jan. 1804: *ibid.* p. 134.
[2] *Diary, reminiscences and correspondence of Henry Crabb Robinson*, ed. T. Sadler, 3 vols. (London, 1869), I, 177–8.
[3] See above, p. 54.
[4] *Immanuel Kant in England, 1793–1838* (Princeton, 1931), p. 144. The articles began to appear in August 1802. The series planned on Kant were not all published.
[5] French original and English translation both published in 1813. Quoting Mme de Staël's note to Robinson—'si vous aviez un moment de libre pour m'écrire quelque chose sur Kant vous augmenteriez mes richesses

import periodical, written by men like Hazlitt, William Taylor of Norwich and Sir James Mackintosh. The authoress became the literary lion who deposed even Byron. This reception, and the long-held status of the book as an authority on Germany, underlines that continued English provincialism from which Crabb Robinson had released himself. All Peacock could suggest as a release was a return to Drummond, Forsyth and Horne Tooke.

Were it not for its final parenthesis and Crabb Robinson's death a week later, one could almost believe the last diary entry to be planned as a coda and finale, so well does it unite his various qualities as a common reader:

Jan. 31st. During the last two days I have read the first Critical Essay [Arnold's 'The function of criticism at the present time'] on the qualifications of the present age for criticism. He resists the exaggerated scorn for criticism and maintains his point ably. A sense of *creative power*, he declares happiness to be, and [that] Arnold maintains, that genuine criticism is. He thinks of Germany as he ought, and of Goethe with high admiration. On this point I can possibly give him assistance which he will gladly (But I feel incapable to go on)[1]

Here come together his continued openness to new literature during the Victorian period; his admiration for Goethe to balance, as Arnold himself does, that felt for Wordsworth;[2] and his eagerness to help and to discuss. Finally he recognises a justification for the rôle of critic which he himself as common reader had fulfilled. For the criticism Arnold defines is not a professional occupation but a mental habit that belongs to the ideal reader:

judging is often spoken of as the critic's one business; and so in some sense it is; but the judgement which almost insensibly forms itself in a fair and clear mind, along with fresh knowledge is the valuable one; and thus knowledge, and ever fresh knowledge, must be the critic's great concern for himself. . .

morales car je n'entends rien qu'à travers vos idées'—Wellek suggests that the manuscripts he sent her were drafts for the *Monthly register* articles (*Kant in England*, p. 154).

[1] 31 Jan. 1867: *On books and their writers*, ii, 822.

[2] The rough note for the final entry reads, 'Wordsworth and Goethe he honours both' (*ibid.* ii, 822).

...to have the sense of creative activity is the great happiness and the great proof of being alive, and it is not denied to criticism to have it; but then criticism must be sincere, simple, flexible, ardent, ever widening its knowledge. Then it may have, in no contemptible measure, a joyful sense of creative activity; a sense which a man of insight and conscience will prefer to what he might derive from a poor, starved, fragmentary, inadequate creation.[1]

Hazlitt

Crabb Robinson provides a comparison above all with Peacock's letters and biography, for he shows what it was possible for the common *reader* to make of Regency literature. He deliberately renounced the rôle of formal *critic* and so for Peacock's novels and essays we need a complementary comparison, with Hazlitt.

Hazlitt—and his modern supporters—issue Peacock with two specific challenges, for both writers attempt the same two critical tasks. Both attempt a comprehensive interpretation of Regency literature: Humphry House rightly says that Peacock 'was doing in his own medium the same sort of thing that Hazlitt was doing in the essays that were published as *The spirit of the age*'.[2] And both made repeated attempts to characterise the mind of Coleridge. Which has the more insight and authority as a critic?

Mr G. D. Klingopulos has made the strongest claim for Hazlitt:

Hazlitt is significant because he was so completely exposed to the intellectual stresses of his time. He earned the right to be critical of Wordsworth and Coleridge, for no contemporary surpassed him in understanding and praise of their work, and he was utterly disinterested. He had the moral energy that surveys the whole field.[3]

While the particular claim is embedded in the larger one, it is worth beginning by separating it, and examining Hazlitt on Coleridge at some length; particularly as the same critic believes that 'one's sense of Peacock's limitations defines itself around his treatment of Coleridge'.[4]

[1] *Essays in criticism*, 1st series, pp. 37–8 and 40.
[2] *The listener*, XLII (8 Dec. 1949), 998.
[3] 'The spirit of the age in prose', *From Blake to Byron* (London, 1957), p. 148.
[4] *Ibid.* p. 135.

Hazlitt himself claimed the right to criticise Coleridge, but in a more sinister expression than Mr Klingopulos's: 'there is no one who has a better right to say what he thinks of him than I have ."Is there here any dear friend of Caesar? To him I say, that Brutus's love to Caesar was not less than his." But no matter...'[1] As he thinks of the Coleridge of 1798 and reviews Coleridge's works of the 1810s, Hazlitt resolves like Brutus, 'It must be by his death'. Yet unlike Brutus he scarcely pretends to be 'utterly disinterested': the self-righteousness does not disguise the personal spite and pique. The real understanding conveyed in 'My first acquaintance with poets', and in essays on other figures in *The spirit of the age* (where Hazlitt's pride was not directly challenged), is wilfully suppressed in the direct reviews of Coleridge.

The first exhibit is a review in *The examiner* of 'Mr. Coleridge's Lay-Sermon'. Nothing could be less disinterested, for it is in fact a preview, written in advance of publication as 'we can give just as good a guess at the design of this lay-sermon, which is not published, as of *The friend*' and other works that *had* been published.[2] It was clearly intended to help make publication a flop. Having no text as yet to discuss, Hazlitt can give free play to prejudice and ridicule:

No man ever yet gave Mr. Coleridge 'a penny for his thoughts'... A matter of a fact is abhorrent to his nature: the very *air* of truth repels him. He is only saved from the extremities of absurdity by combining them all in his own person. Two things are indispensible to him—to set out from no premises, and to arrive at no conclusion... Innumerable evanescent thoughts dance before him, and dazzle his sight, like insects in the evening sun... *The Friend* is so obscure, that it has been supposed to be written in cypher.[3]

Some of the ridicule is valid, and one or two of the epigrams quoted above are incorporated in the characterisation of Flosky. But Peacock establishes a point swiftly and lightly, and moves to others, building on their connections to make a complete portrait. His mind is always in motion and stimulates free

---

[1] 'On the living poets': *Complete works*, ed. P. P. Howe, 21 vols. (London, 1930–4), v, 165–6.

[2] *The examiner* (8 Sept. 1816): *Works*, ed. Howe, vii, 115.

[3] *Ibid*. pp. 114, 116, 117 and 115n.

play of mind in the reader. Hazlitt repeates variations on one point in sentences as well shaped and carefully chosen as a pile of brick-ends and rubble hurled at a passer-by. He keeps up the volley through the 2,500 or more words of the 'preview' and resumes it in subsequent articles. The reader merely suffers concussion, and for all the frantic energy of abuse Hazlitt's attitude to Coleridge is in a state of stubborn inertia.

When the first Lay Sermon (*The statesman's manual*) did appear, Hazlitt predictably enough found his own expectations confirmed, and reviewed the work in *The examiner*[1] and the *Edinburgh review*.[2] These can be represented by the second, which is an expanded version of the first. It touches on two points which if developed would have made a useful criticism: Coleridge's confused attitude to 'the reading public', and his coy refusals to be specific on (to quote his subtitle) *the Bible the best guide to political skill and foresight*. But Hazlitt surrenders to the more facile pursuit of abuse and dull 'wit', frantically ringing the changes on windmills, shadows, bubbles, waking dreams, mazes, talking in sleep, rainbows on clouds, ravings worse than Joanna Southcott, indecision like swansdown feathers, and the throne of dullness. Here are the hoary old 'standard jokes' of reviewers that Peacock made fun of in his 'Essay on fashionable literature'.[3] The solution offered is equally facile: 'Plain sense and plain speaking would put an end to those "thick-coming fancies" that lull him to repose.'[4]

Mr Klingopulos writes that Hazlitt 'had the independence of judgement of the dissenter'.[5] But when he writes for the *Edinburgh review* he happily surrenders independence not only of judgement but of style to those of the periodical. In reviewing *Biographia literaria* he evaded the need to argue his case by taking cover behind the *Edinburgh review*'s impersonal authoritarian manner which Peacock attacked in his 'Essay'.[6] *The truth is...* and *The plain fact of the matter is...* become frequent phrases in Hazlitt's assertive style, having a function similar to the editorial *we*:

[1] 29 Dec. 1816: *Works*, ed. Howe, VII, 119–28.
[2] Dec. 1816: *ibid.* XVI, 99–114.
[3] See above, p. 34.   [4] *Works*, ed. Howe, XVI, 101.
[5] 'The spirit of the age in prose', *From Blake to Byron*, p. 148.
[6] See above, pp. 33–4.

As for the great German oracle Kant, we must take the liberty to say, that his system appears to us the most wilful and monstrous absurdity that ever was invented. If the French theories of the mind were too chemical, this is too mechanical...[1]

As for any real critical authority behind this authoritarian manner, it is worth noting that Professor René Wellek has demonstrated that

The review which Hazlitt wrote on Coleridge's *Biographia Literaria* is much more than a declaration of antipathy against technicalities the importance of which he did not grasp, but rather a grotesque example of misunderstanding which scarcely can be paralleled from the literature of the time.[2]

Hazlitt's account of Coleridge's own intellectual development is merely a string of the 'standard jokes':

Mr. Coleridge has...from the combined forces of poetic levity and metaphysical bathos, been trying to fly, not in the air, but under ground—playing at hawk and buzzard between sense and nonsense—floating or sinking in fine Kantean categories, in a state of suspended animation 'twixt dreaming and awake—gritting the plain ground of 'history and particular facts' for the first butterfly theory, fancy-bred from the maggots of the brain—going up in an air-balloon fitted with fetid gas from the writings of Jacob Behmen and the mystics...[3]

Having written his anonymous review of *The statesman's manual* for *The examiner*, Hazlitt showed a typically abrupt change of heart—by means of equally typical subterfuge—in an anonymous letter to the editor.[4] Was the reviewer fair, asks the correspondent, who calls himself a 'plain blunt man': can he be describing the Coleridge I heard preach in 1798, the genius who stamped on me 'des impressions que ni le tems ni les circonstances peuvent effacer'? The reminiscence and the quotation from Rousseau indicate that this letter is the germ of the longer tribute to Coleridge written in 1823, 'My first acquaintance with poets'.[5] That essay makes one admire not only Coleridge but Hazlitt as well, for the quality that his reviews suggest he lacked: ability to learn from greater minds rather

[1] *Edinburgh review*, Aug. 1817: *Works*, ed. Howe, XVI, 123.
[2] *Kant in England*, p. 169.   [3] *Works*, ed. Howe, XVI, 118.
[4] *The examiner*, 12 Jan. 1817: *ibid.* VII, 128–9.
[5] *The liberal*, Apr. 1823: *ibid.* XVII, 106–22.

than jeer at their weaknesses. The adverse comments on Coleridge's limited tastes, and his seeming 'unable to keep on in a straight line' in thinking and talking as well as in walking, are justly but gently made. Hazlitt is as ready to criticise his own contrasting journalist's fluency, so different from both Coleridge and his own inarticulacy in 1798 when he tried to compose the thoughts he had stammered out to Coleridge on 'The natural disinterestedness of the human mind',

and shed tears of helpless despondency on the blank unfinished paper. I can write fast enough now. Am I better than I was then? Oh no! One truth discovered, one pang of regret at not being able to express it, is better than all the fluency and flippancy in the world.[1]

Yet the reader is still uneasy. That last passage might read as remorse for his previous reviews of Coleridge. Yet this essay describes the early Coleridge who for Hazlitt has since made nothing of his talents and gone back on his liberal principles.[2] Our idea of Hazlitt's psychology leads us to fear that the admiration for the earlier Coleridge will only serve as fuel for fiercer rage at the later Coleridge. This is exactly what happens in the subsequent essay, first published only a year after 'My first acquaintance with poets' and reprinted in *The spirit of the age* (1825). After a striking and fine opening description of Coleridge's mind as 'tangential'—'scarce a thought can pass through the mind of man, but its sound has at some time passed over his head with rustling pinions'[3]—the essay falls back into a comic idea borrowed from the review of *Biographia literaria*—a facetious imitation in endlessly long sentences of Coleridge's lifelong Cook's Tour of all the world's writers and systems. 'What is become of all this mighty heap of hope, of thought, of learning, and humanity?', comes the sting in the tail; 'It has ended in swallowing doses of oblivion and in writing paragraphs in the *Courier*—Such and so little is the mind of man!'[4] Hazlitt demolishes Coleridge's work section by section. 'If our author's poetry is inferior to his conversation, his prose is utterly abortive.'[5] Yet (despite a brief and un-

---

[1] *Works*, ed. Howe, XVII, 114.
[2] Hazlitt stresses the spirit of Coleridge's Shrewsbury sermon 'upon peace and war; upon church and state—not their alliance, but their separation'.
[3] *Works*, ed. Howe, XI, 29.   [4] *Ibid*. p. 34.   [5] *Ibid*. p. 35.

convincing qualification about its 'brilliancy and richness') it seems that his conversation is also abortive, 'listless talk' in which his faculties 'have gosspied away their time'.[1]

Hazlitt's various essays on Coleridge the thinker and prose-writer can be criticised on two counts. First, they stubbornly deny appreciation of any stage of Coleridge after 1798 ('All that he has done of moment, he had done twenty years ago').[2] It is true, as Mr Klingopulos says, that he 'could not be expected, of course, to have foreseen the influence of Coleridge in nine-teenth-century thought'[3]—although Mr Klingopulos will not make the same allowance for Peacock. Yet 1818 (the year of *Nightmare Abbey* and 'On the living poets') was of all years the time when there was most reason to write off Coleridge as a failure without achievement or influence; whereas by 1825 (the year of *The spirit of the age*) his later prose works and conversation at Highgate were re-establishing him as a key figure of the age. He was beginning to have that influence on particular young men and on the general current of thought that would lead to Mill's verdict. He and his followers were badly in need of the fresh air of criticism; but Hazlitt treats him merely as the wreck of the genius of 1798, a negligible figure in 1825. The second point against Hazlitt is that, while his ridicule of Coleridge is often nominally on the same ground as Peacock's, he is repetitive and dull.[4] Unlike Peacock, he is in complete earnest, possessed by his one idea: when Peacock exaggerates, the intention is to be stimulatingly provocative, whereas Hazlitt's exaggeration impresses itself as pure simple-mindedness.

The account Hazlitt gives us in 'My first acquaintance with poets' of Coleridge reading *Lyrical ballads* to him in 1798 has often been quoted as vivid evidence of the revolutionary effect these poems had on a small number of young men. But Hazlitt's

---

[1] *Works*, ed. Howe, XI 36.
[2] *Ibid.* p. 30.
[3] 'Hazlitt as critic', *Essays in criticism*, VI (Oct. 1956), 402.
[4] Crabb Robinson was 'amused by *The spirit of the age*' but criticised 'his malice, his eternal repetitions, his laboured expansion of his matter *lucri causa* and the occasional bombast, with the bad taste and overloaded ornaments, all of which faults proceed from one source (that he is always thinking as much of his honorarium as his honour)' (*On books and their writers*, I, 322).

taste stuck at 1798. He ignores, for instance, 'The pains of sleep' from the *Christabel* volume of 1816 and the Dejection Ode from *Sibylline leaves* (1817): only 'The ancient mariner', he says, does justice to Coleridge's powers. Even this compliment is full of evasion or innuendo (like Hogg's comments on Shelley's poetry),[1] for the poem 'is high German, and in it he seems to "conceive of poetry but as a drunken dream, reckless, careless, and heedless, of past, present, and to come"'.[2] This brief summary of the poetry in 'On the living poets' is repeated almost word for word in *The spirit of the age*, the only other account being the short review of 'Christabel' in *The examiner*.

It used to be thought, and is still not conclusively disproved, that Hazlitt wrote the review of the 'Christabel' volume in the *Edinburgh review*, the obtuseness and tedious 'wit' of which Peacock attacked in his 'Essay on fashionable literature'.[3] But even if this was by Moore or Jeffrey, Hazlitt's *Examiner* review is in no way more creditable and is as open to Peacock's charges. His attitude seems to me not 'admiration with important reservations'[4] but malice half-covered by evasive placebos—

In parts of Christabel there is a great deal of beauty, both of thought, imagery, and versification; but the effect of the general story is dim, obscure and visionary. The mind, when reading it, is spellbound. The sorceress seems to act without power—Christabel to yield without resistance, the faculties are thrown into a state of metaphysical suspense and theoretical imbecility.[5]

—the bland patronising of the first phrases slide into the 'standard jokes' of reviewers which Peacock derided. Again, the conclusion to part II, for which Peacock offers a perceptive interpretation, Hazlitt proudly announces 'is to us absolutely incomprehensible',[6] just as the *Edinburgh* reviewer quotes the passage 'for the amazement of our readers—premising our frank avowal that we are unable to divine the meaning of any portion of it'.[7] 'Kubla Khan', thinks this reviewer, shares the same 'raving and driv'ling', written while asleep and likely to send the

---

[1] See above, p. 76.   [2] *Works*, ed. Howe, v, 166.
[3] See above, pp. 34–5.
[4] See G. D. Klingopulos, 'Hazlitt as critic', *Essays in criticism*, vi, 402.
[5] *The examiner*, 2 June 1816: *Works*, ed. Howe, iv, 33.
[6] Ibid. p. 34.   [7] *Edinburgh review*, xxvii (Sept. 1816), 63.

reader asleep (more standard jokes!), while Hazlitt's corresponding gibe that 'Kubla Khan' 'only shews that Mr. Coleridge can write better *nonsense* verses than any man in England' makes the addition 'It is not a poem, but a musical composition' a dubious compliment.[1] Of course some such criticism of the dream-world tendencies of 'Christabel' and 'Kubla Khan' would be gladly accepted from a critic who brought to bear a positive ideal of poetry dealing more directly with the human and moral world. But both reviewers ignore an outstanding example of such poetry under their nose in the same volume: 'The pains of sleep' is dismissed by the *Edinburgh* as 'mere raving, without any thing more affecting than a number of incoherent words, expressive of extravagance and incongruity'[2]—while Hazlitt makes no reference at all to the poem.[3]

Hazlitt gives a very broad hint about his motives by singling out for praise and quotation the passage in 'Christabel' on the quarrel of two friends:

> Alas! they had been friends in youth,
> But whispering tongues can poison truth...
> And to be wroth with one we love,
> Doth work like madness in the brain...[4]

He presses the point home by repeating the passage in 'On the living poets' and praising it in *The spirit of the age*. It is (*pace* Mr Klingopulos) a loud enough warning that Hazlitt is utterly *intéressé* in his writings on Coleridge.

If the *parti pris* forces Hazlitt to pretend not to see obvious qualities in Coleridge, this first lie leads to innumerable other lies. In reviewing *Biographia literaria* he has to affect a ludicrous obtuseness, act the plain blunt man. In the face of Coleridge's discussion of poetic diction,

it is unnecessary to say anything, the truth and common sense of the thing being so obvious, and, we apprehend, so generally acknowledged ...Mr. Coleridge bewilders himself sadly in endeavouring to determine

---

[1] *The examiner: Works*, ed. Howe, IV, 33.
[2] *Edinburgh review*, XXVII (Sept. 1816), 66.
[3] At least one other review *did* notice the poem: *The monthly review*, LXXXII (Jan. 1817), 25, said that 'we admire the simplicity of the first two stanzas', which it quoted.
[4] *The examiner: Works*, ed. Howe, IV, 34.

in what the essence of poetry consists—Milton, we think, has told it
in a single line— —'thoughts that voluntary move
Harmonious numbers'.[1]

This is precisely the conservative simple-mindedness that
Peacock ridiculed in Mr Feathernest's definition of poetry.[2]

This simple-mindedness in direct attacks on Coleridge is wilfully
perverse, because in discussing other writers Hazlitt makes
profound indirect use of both Coleridge and Wordsworth. This
point can be introduced most clearly by looking at the treatment
of Wordsworth.

Wordsworth is served no better than Coleridge in direct
criticism. At best (in *The spirit of the age*) Hazlitt timidly and
awkwardly adapts Wordsworth's own phrases from the various
prefaces. At worst (in the articles on *The excursion*)[3] he escapes
into autobiography and personal prejudices about country life
by means of a wilful misreading of Wordsworth's own interest
in rural characters. This and other misreadings are at the
centre of the malicious sketch of a Romantic Revolution, in the
lecture 'On the living poets'. Hazlitt would have us believe
that, taking their cue from the French Revolution, English
poets rose as one man and frantically threw themselves from
the extreme of artifice to that of nature—'rose at once from the
most servile imitation and tamest common-place, to the utmost
pitch of singularity and paradox'.[4] When checked by the specific
instances of Wordsworth and Coleridge (and what other valid
instances were there?), this sketch is not even provocative
exaggeration like Peacock's, but just a senseless falsification.
Together with the equally long attack on Wordsworth's ego-
tistic narrowness of taste, it contradicts rather than balances
the preceding brief paragraph on the *true* revolution made by
Lyrical ballads, the fact that 'they opened a finer and deeper
vein of thought and feeling'.[5]

[1] *Works*, ed. Howe, XVI, 136. [2] See above, p. 123.
[3] *The examiner* (21 and 28 Aug. and 2 Oct. 1814): *Works*, ed. Howe, XIX, 9–25.
[4] *Works*, ed. Howe, V, 161.
[5] *Ibid*. p. 156. After attending the lecture, Crabb Robinson noted: 'He bepraises
Coleridge with outrageous eulogy, at the same time that he reproaches him
bitterly. Praises Wordsworth warmly but in a sentence or two, while he dwells
with malignity on his real or imputed faults.' (*On books and their writers*, I, 222.)

Yet Hazlitt shows that he had understood that true revolution when he turns to other writers. The sketch of Scott which precedes that of Wordsworth in 'On the living poets', and which was so useful to the argument of chapter 1 of the present book, shows a thorough digestion of the idiom and criteria of Wordsworth's criticism as well as the qualities of his poetry. In *The spirit of the age* it is again lack of Wordsworth's inwardness, 'the energies and resources of his own mind',[1] that drives Scott to the external variety of action, costume and scenery. In contrast Byron is fevered and monotonous because of the limitations of his inner resources—'he obstinately and invariably shuts himself up in the Bastile of his own ruling passions'.[2] Wordsworth has provided a central insight around which the varied critical perceptions about lesser writers arrange themselves coherently, and which gives them an authority and dimension we miss in Peacock's similar criticisms.

Even more striking is the effect this appreciation of Wordsworth and Coleridge has on Hazlitt's criticism of philosophers and social thinkers. It is surely an awareness of Coleridge's power of creating ideas and sowing them in the thought of the age—his being what Mill called a 'seminal mind'—that enables Hazlitt to diagnose Bentham's different and more limited powers:

Nor do we think, in point of fact, that Mr. Bentham has given any new or decided impulse to the human mind. He cannot be looked upon in the light of a discoverer in legislation or morals. He has not struck out any great leading principle or parent-truth, from which a number of others might be deduced...Mr. Bentham's *forte* is arrangement...He has methodised, collated, and condensed all the materials prepared to his hand on the subjects of which he treats, in a masterly and scientific manner.[3]

This first point is inseparable from a second, that Bentham's habit of systematising and 'principle of UTILITY' have

not made sufficient allowance for the varieties of human nature, and the caprices and irregularities of the human will. The gentleman is himself a capital logician; and he has been led by this circumstance to consider man as a logical animal. We fear this view of the matter will hardly hold water.[4]

---

[1] *Works*, ed. Howe, XI, 60.   [2] *Ibid*. p. 71.   [3] *Ibid*. pp. 7–8.
[4] *Ibid*. p. 8.

These two points, and even their wording, strikingly anticipate Mill's essay on Bentham. More important, Hazlitt establishes the case against Bentham more persuasively than Mill. He has a much surer grasp of the value of imaginative literature, and is therefore more precise in showing how 'rationalists such as Bentham...had much to learn from the inductive poets. It was the poets who were concrete, the rationalists who were abstract.'[1] But Hazlitt does not *apply* Wordsworth and Coleridge as such, in the manner of ready measuring rods. It is rather that the poets have released Hazlitt's own experience, encouraged him to bring into play his own perceptions of 'the varieties of human nature, and the irregularities of the human will'. His discussion of the criminal mind is a brilliant example.[2] The human perception Hazlitt brings into play, Bentham has suppressed: 'in general habits and in all but his professional pursuits, he is a mere child...He scarcely ever goes out, and sees very little company. He talks a great deal, and listens to nothing but facts.'[3]

If the essays on Byron, Scott and other poets let Hazlitt share the rôle Peacock assumes in *Nightmare Abbey*, as surveyor and valuer of Regency literature and taste, then the essays on Bentham, Godwin, Malthus and lesser figures like Mackintosh let him rival the Peacock of *Melincourt* as mediator in the intellectual conflicts of the Regency. But Hazlitt has more authority as a mediator, as 'a *necessary* figure in the intellectual life of the time'[4] as Mill is some years later, because he has more grasp of the opposing forces. Peacock's mediation in *Melincourt* is inconclusive and frequently vague through lack of this grasp. Forester is less than Shelley, who was himself less than Coleridge or Wordsworth, and Fax is mainly a simple element of Malthus, who himself stood for less than Bentham. Any objection that the mode of a novel cannot be compared with that of an intellectual essay, can be countered by Hazlitt's concluding portrait:

Mr. Bentham relieves his mind sometimes, after the fatigue of study, by playing on a fine old organ, and has a relish for Hogarth's prints.

[1] G. D. Klingopulos, 'The spirit of the age in prose', *From Blake to Byron*, p. 151.
[2] *Works*, ed. Howe, xi, 11 ff.   [3] *Ibid.* p. 6.
[4] G. D. Klingopulos, 'Hazlitt as critic', *Essays in criticism*, iv, 398.

He turns wooden utensils in a lathe for exercise, and fancies he can turn men in the same manner. He has no great fondness for poetry, and can hardly extract a moral out of Shakespeare. His house is warmed and lighted by steam.[1]

This is a relating of character, habits and ideas, a delicate irony and an eye for clinching detail, a feeling for the idiosyncratic figure about (were this a novel) to break into speech and action, that Peacock would have envied.

While *The spirit of the age* has advantages over *Melincourt*, a comparison with *Nightmare Abbey* will produce a more balanced verdict. Hazlitt's book is more wide and varied in scope, but more loose in organisation and insight: Peacock's novel is more narrow in focus, but produces a more coherent and concentrated picture.

Hazlitt's advantage comes out typically in the variety of gradations of conservatism he can diagnose. He can place the antiquarian: 'Mr. Lamb has succeeded not by conforming to the *Spirit of the Age*, but in opposition to it. He does not march boldly along with the crowd, but steals off the pavement to pick his way in the contrary direction.'[2] He taunts the *laudator temporis acti*: Scott

would fain put down the Spirit of the Age. The author of Waverley might just as well get up and make a speech at a dinner at Edinburgh, abusing Mr. Mac-Adam for his improvements in the roads, on the ground that they were nearly *impassable* in many places 'sixty years since'; or object to Mr. Peel's Police-Bill, by insisting that Hounslow-Heath was formerly a scene of greater interest and terror to highwaymen and travellers, and cut a greater figure in the Newgate Calendar than it does at present.[3]

One of the best diagnoses is of the half-anachronistic figure:

Mr. Horne Tooke was one of those...connecting links between a former period and the existing generation. His education and accomplishments...were of the last age; his mind, and the tone of his feelings were *modern*. There was a hard, dry materialism in the very texture of his understanding, varnished over by the external refinements of the old school.[4]

[1] *Works*, ed. Howe, XI, 15.　　[2] *Ibid*. p. 178.
[3] *Ibid*. p. 66.　　[4] *Ibid*. p. 47.

This last essay as a whole denotes in Hazlitt a more delicate sense of orientation in his period, which allows more precision in judging the relative positions of individual figures, than we can find in Peacock. Drastically toned down, Hazlitt's diagnosis might be pondered in relation to Horne Tooke's admiring student, Peacock himself: it reminds us of the particular ways in which Peacock sometimes stands slightly behind or aside from the Regency 'spirit of the age'.[1]

Yet Hazlitt's title hardly gives the work unity: the phrase often recurs only as an over-anxious and quickly dropped attempt to anchor very heterogeneous figures to their period. 'Mr. Wordsworth's genius is a pure emanation of the Spirit of the Age. Had he lived in any other period of the world, he would never have been heard of.'[2] 'The Spirit of the Age was never more fully shown that in its treatment of [Godwin]— its love of paradox and change.'[3] The opinions, and 'the tone of manly explicitness, of *The Edinburgh Review*, are eminently characteristic of the Spirit of the Age...[it] stands upon the ground of opinion; it asserts the supremacy of intellect'.[4] It is in danger of degenerating into a catch-phrase scattered through a miscellany of essays. If the scope of *Nightmare Abbey* is narrow, everything in compensation binds powerfully together around the central core, one central spirit of the age in literature and manners.

Byron

Of the three comparative figures, Byron may seem the most constricted in this context. The range of his writings, the bulk of correspondence and biographical material, and a very active century-and-a-half of criticism, are so enormous that they could only be fully discussed by another parallel work centring on Byron. Rather than set out and discuss it in detail, the present comparison must compress, allude to, and generalise from all that material. Because it centres on Peacock, it must also keep the comparison on Peacock's home ground and

---

[1] Cf. also the account of Tooke's 'mind of a lawyer' (*ibid.* pp. 47–8) with the spirit of *Melincourt*'s engagement with the politics of 1817 (discussed above, pp. 131–2).

[2] *Ibid.* p. 86.   [3] *Ibid.* p. 16.   [4] *Ibid.* p. 127.

select two aspects of Byron, his literary criticism in letters and essays, and his social criticism in the English cantos of *Don Juan*. To select these two aspects on which to challenge him is not unfair, for apart from some sardonic comments by J. J. van Rennes[1] most modern critics have treated the first with solemn respect, and praised the second with modest reservations but without evaluative reference to comparable works like *Nightmare Abbey*.

A complete collection of 'The critical opinions of Lord Byron', on the lines of those made by J. E. Brown for Johnson and M. L. Peacock for Wordsworth, would be a service to Byron studies. But the editor, as he struggled to draw for his Introduction a coherent account of Byron's response to literature, would probably feel he was on a fool's errand. For in his collection he would find the following entry typical. We have seen the reactions of Shelley, Peacock and Crabb Robinson to *Hyperion*; here is Byron's: 'Such writing is [a] sort of mental masturbation—he is always f—gg—g his *Imagination*. I don't mean he is indecent, but viciously soliciting his own ideas into a state, which is neither poetry nor anything else but a Bedlam vision produced by raw pork and opium.'[2] Can a passage like this be called 'literary criticism'? In one sense it can, for the reader of Keats can make use of it. It does engage with the earlier poems if not with *Hyperion*; with their lushness of scene and imagery combined with vulgarity of taste and over-heated tone, that convey deprived inexperienced adolescence—what Yeats saw in Keats as the urchin with nose pressed against the sweetshop window. Yet, if we turn our attention to Byron, it is difficult to know how much credit is due to him. There is no sign that he read Keats with care. Other entries in the 'Critical opinions' would strengthen the suspicion that his reaction was largely that of the sophisticated philistine. 'It is the fashion of the day to lay great stress upon what they call "imagination" and "invention", the two commonest of

---

[1] *Bowles, Byron and the Pope-controversy* (Amsterdam, 1927).

[2] Letter to Murray, 9 Nov. 1820: *Works...letters and journals*, ed. R. E. Prothero, 6 vols. (London, 1898–1901), v, 117. Prothero's asterisks have been replaced with words supplied by T. J. Wise, *A bibliography of the writings...of Byron*, 2 vols. (London, 1932–3), ii, 19.

qualities: an Irish peasant with a little whiskey in his head will imagine and invent more than will furnish forth a modern poem':[1] while this passage follows a defence of Pope's ethical poetry, Byron's standard is more often the fashionable verse of his own day—the reflections and descriptions of Pope's distant imitators and of 'wild' but shallow poets like Scott. Crabb Robinson once noted after a dinner-party: 'Our party consisted of Wordsworth, Coleridge, and Lamb, Moore and Rogers, five poets of very unequal worth and most disproportionate popularity whom the public probably would arrange in the very inverse order.'[2] Byron obligingly confirms:

[Scott] is undoubtedly the Monarch of Parnassus, and the most *English* of bards. I should place Rogers next in the living list (I value him more as the last of the *best* school)—Moore and Campbell both *third*—Southey and Wordworth and Coleridge—the rest...the names are too numerous for the base of the triangle.[3]

It is true that Byron's judgement dates from 1813, and Crabb Robinson's from 1823. A collection from his diaries and letters in the ten years between would show that Byron's valuation of his contemporaries fluctuated. Yet even his decision that compared with Pope 'all of us...are...in the wrong'[4] shows no advance of understanding, for it presumptuously rejects Wordsworth and Coleridge together with his own vulgarisations of Romanticism, and leaves in lonely eminence Crabbe and Rogers as 'the postscript of the Augustans'.[5] This, together with his particular comments on Keats, indicates Byron's mental habits. He is often credited with that quality which, in describing Lady Adeline Fitz-Fulke, he termed mobility—'that vivacious versatility', that 'excessive susceptibility of immediate impressions'.[6] But his literary views have none of the flexibility of Crabb Robinson's, stability combined with growth. Byron's views are usually in a state of quiescence

[1] 'Letter to Murray on Bowles' Strictures on Pope', *Letters and journals*, ed. Prothero, v, 554.
[2] *On books and their writers*, I, 292.
[3] *Letters and journals*, ed. Prothero, II, 343–4.
[4] *Ibid.* IV, 169.   [5] *Ibid.* IV, 197.
[6] *Don Juan*, canto XVI, stanza 97 and note: ed. T. G. Steffan and W. Pratt, 4 vols. (Austin, Texas, 1957), III, 547, and IV, 285.

if not inertia, from which they are roused by abrupt violent explosions of feeling. One is more aware of general emotions than of specific opinions—hurt pride produced *English bards and Scotch reviewers*, while Keats's attack on Pope in *Sleep and poetry* aroused Byron's self-important sense of loyalty. The energy released by the explosion finds no other channel than forceful repetition, which can paradoxically be called a state of mental inertia. Having found a telling insult for Keats he twice repeats it[1] and does not trouble himself for further ideas. His gibes at Wordsworth have the same monotony without the originality, falling back on those standard jokes of the dull reviewer: 'Who can understand him? Let those who do so, make him intelligible. Jacob Behmen, Swedenborg, and Joanna Southcott, are mere types of these arch-apostles of mystery and mysticism.'[2] This comment on *The excursion* conforms to the fashionably acceptable attitude: and on poetry Byron's 'mobility' is mainly confined to susceptibility to fashion, and to flattery. A graceful introduction to, or complimentary letter from, the various villains of *English bards and Scotch reviewers* would turn them instantly into respected colleagues; once the periodicals acknowledge him, he is happy to respect 'Jeffrey and Gifford [as] the monarch-makers in poetry and prose';[3] even Coleridge, appealing to Byron's lordly and patronising sentiments, wins a promise of support over the reviewing of 'Christabel'.[4]

If these are the characteristics of Byron's mind in the 'occasional criticism' in *Letters and journals*, we shall have no false expectations about his attempts at sustained criticism in the controversy with Bowles. That his respect for Pope, as for Johnson,[5] was genuine, can be proved from the enthusiastic tone as well as the interesting critical point of letters like the following:

[1] Cf. 'his is the onanism of poetry' and 'this miserable self-pollutor of the human mind' (*Letters and journals*, ed. Prothero, v, 109, and Wise, *Bibliography of Byron*, ii, 18).

[2] *Letters and journals*, ed. Prothero, iii, 239.

[3] *Ibid.* ii, 322.

[4] *Ibid.* iii, 228–9.

[5] Throughout the letters and diaries Byron continually praises Johnson's works and quotes with respect from them and his conversation. He receives much more attention than Pope.

I will show you more *imagery* in twenty lines of Pope, than in any equal length of quotation in English poesy, and that in places where they least expect it: for instance, in his lines on Sporus—now, do just *read* them over—the subject is of no consequence (whether it be Satire or Epic)—we are talking of *poetry* and *imagery* from *Nature* and *Art*. Now mark the images separately and arithmetically.

        1. The thing of Silk
        2. *Curd* of *Ass's* milk...
  ...23. Pride that *licks the dust*.

Now, is there a line in all the passage without the most *forcible* imagery (for his purpose)? Look at the *variety*, at the *poetry* of the passage— look at the imagination: there is hardly a line from which a *painting* might not be made, and *is*...[1]

Here is a criterion stronger and more genuinely literary than the 'utility' of Peacock's 'Four ages of poetry'. Yet the two open letters to Murray on Bowles give the impression that his motive was mere love of argument, the lone figure 'born for opposition'. He charges at Bowles like a bull, with enraged energy, blind force and weight, but short and narrow in his field of vision and unable to manœuvre. To turn on Byron the kind of imagery he plays with in *Don Juan*, the red rags he charges at turn out to be red herrings. Pages are spent in refuting Bowles's slurs on Pope's private life, and his 'invariable principles of poetry'. The first topic is irrelevant to Pope's poetry, and the second irrelevant to the real crisis in Regency taste and poetry, for it drags discussion back to the era of Warton's *Essay on...Pope* and Young's *Conjectures on original composition*. By the time Byron stops his charge and turned the argument to his own reasons for valuing Pope, he has no energy left for more than a defiant snort:

He is the only poet that never shocks; the only poet whose faultlessness has been made his reproach. Cast your eye over his productions; consider their extent, and contemplate their variety:—pastoral, passion, mock heroic, translation, satire, ethics—all excellent, and often perfect. If his great charm be his *melody*, how comes it that foreigners adore him even in their diluted translations? But I have made this letter too long. Give my compliments to Bowles. Yours ever, very truly, Byron.[2]

---

[1] *Letters and journals*, ed. Prothero, v, 259–60.
[2] *Ibid.* p. 560.

He frequently drifts into a style of oratorical cant without close engagement with the subject: 'Neither time, nor distance, nor grief, nor age, can diminish my veneration for him...His poetry is the Book of Life.'[1] It is the style of Byron in the House of Lords:

'I told them,' he said [to Moore] 'that it was a most flagrant violation of the Constitution—that, if such things were permitted, there was an end of English freedom, and that—' 'But what was this dreadful grievance?' I asked, interrupting him in his eloquence. 'The grievance?' he repeated, pausing as if to consider. 'Oh, *that* I forget.'[2]

Byron is most at home in applying to the poetry of his own day the social criteria and discrimination he had learned at Harrow and Trinity and in 'the monde'.

The grand distinction of the under forms of the new school of poets is their *vulgarity*. By this I do not mean that they are *coarse*, but 'shabby-genteel', as it is termed. A man may be *coarse* and yet not vulgar, and the reverse. Burns is often coarse, but never *vulgar*...It is in their finery that the new under school are *most* vulgar...as what we called at Harrow 'a Sunday blood' might be easily distinguished from a gentleman...[3]

The passage that follows and ends the final letter on Bowles fairly sums up Byron's abilities as a judge of poetry. His criteria will serve to characterise a Leigh Hunt or a Barry Cornwall; but he has no suspicion that their field of validity is limited, that Wordsworth may have been right in arguing that the greatest poetry is beyond the reach of the 'homme du monde'.[4]

Byron was probably encouraged to write the English cantos of *Don Juan*, and to invite comparison with the diagnosis in Peacock's novels of the spirit of the age, by 'John Bull's' pamphlet *Letter to Lord Byron*: 'There is nobody but yourself

---

[1] *Letters and journals*, ed. Prothero, v, 590.
[2] Thomas Moore, *Life of Byron*, 2 vols. (London, 1830), i, 402.
[3] *Letters and journals*, ed. Prothero, v, 591.
[4] See especially Wordsworth's letter to Wilson, ? June 1802: *Early letters of William and Dorothy Wordsworth (1787–1805)*, ed. E. de Selincourt (Oxford, 1935), pp. 292–8.

who has any chance of conveying to posterity a true idea of the *spirit* of England in the days of his Majesty George IV.'[1] He thought this encouragement came from Peacock himself, for Shelley told the latter that 'Lord B. thinks you wrote a pamphlet signed "John Bull": he says he knew it by the style resembling "Melincourt" of which he is a great admirer.'[2] Certainly his admiration of *Melincourt* must have prompted several subjects and techniques of the English cantos, particularly in the house-party at Norman Abbey.

But it is misleading to suggest that 'if we wish to define the quality that sets the English cantos somewhat apart from the rest of *Don Juan*, we should not be too far out in calling it Peacockian'.[3] Their spirit and criteria are rather those we have detected in his literary criticism: the aristocratic man of the world, with touches of the dandy and the rake. Most of their strengths and weaknesses spring from this.

Their greatest strength comes out in a comparison of the London cantos with *Melincourt*. In describing the marriage-market of the *haut monde* which quickly hems in and harasses the fashionable eligible hero and jostles for control of his Turkish protégée, Byron can draw feelingly on his own experience as a sexual and social opportunist sensitive to the menace of social machinery. Under the new propriety the rake has little room to manœuvre. It is 'a low, newspaper, humdrum, lawsuit country', 'commercial, pedantic, moral nation', with the snares of calculating 'cold coquettes', aged coquettes like Lady Pinchbeck turned moral dictators, scheming aunts and menacing brothers:

> Perhaps you'll have a letter from the mother,
>   To say her daughter's feelings are trepann'd;
> Perhaps you'll have a visit from the brother,
>   All strut, and stays, and whiskers, to demand
> What 'your intentions are?'[4]

The girls may do as badly in the sweepstake and win 'Some gentleman, who fights, or writes, or drives'; and here Byron

---

[1] Ed. A. L. Strout (Norman, Oklahoma, 1947), p. 95.
[2] *Letters*, ed. F. L. Jones, 2 vols. (Oxford, 1964), II, 330–1.
[3] M. K. Joseph, *Byron the poet* (London, 1964), p. 173. Joseph here draws on E. F. Boyd, *Byron's Don Juan: a critical study* (New Brunswick, 1945), pp. 155 ff.
[4] *Don Juan*, canto XII, stanza 60: ed. Steffan and Pratt, III, 343.

refers his satire directly back to his own experience and concludes

> I'll not gainsay the generous public's voice
> That the young lady made a monstrous choice.[1]

In comparison the description of the marriage market in *Melincourt* is vague, second-hand and pompous: Peacock's source is literary rather than personal.

Of course that subject is for Peacock only the background against which Anthelia stands out and Forester reacts. But Anthelia herself is an unconvincing and literary figure: the ideal woman exists in Forester's head, and it was a mistake for Peacock to produce her to specification. There is a similar unreality about Byron's corresponding figures: Leila is only a child, and Aurora is a rake's half-sentimental, half-gloating idea of purity. But Byron has the sense not to labour these characters and instead to concentrate on the very different Lady Adeline. In this portrait Byron brings home to us both the acuteness of his reaction to people and its selfishness, its limited field of perception. His viewpoint of the wary rake, hypersensitive to suspicion, menaces, obstacles and others' dubious designs, makes him detect that Lady Adeline's motives in interfering between Juan and Aurora are not disinterested. Yet his own completely *interested* and selfish standpoint means that he cannot enter the woman's mind. A contrast may be drawn with *Don Giovanni*. The opera conveys the rake's furious resentment at, and cynical interpretation of, Donna Elvira's interference. But Mozart himself, while acknowledging the Don's reaction, goes far beyond it to a sympathetic understanding of the woman's complex contradictory feelings. The total understanding of women conveyed in the English cantos is equivalent to Don Giovanni's, not Mozart's.

The English cantos more closely approach *Melincourt* and *Nightmare Abbey* when they describe the Fitz-Fulkes' country house-party. In particular the guests resemble Peacock's crotcheteers in their names and in representing a range of intellectual and social fields. 'Brahmins of the *ton*' like the Countess Crabby and 'Mrs Rabbi, the rich banker's squaw' mix with

---

[1] Canto xii, stanza 38: ed. Steffan and Pratt, iii, 334.

> Dick Dubious, the metaphysician,
>   Who loves philosophy, and a good dinner;
> Angle, the soi-disant mathematician

and the two erudite lawyers and wits Longbow and Strongbow.[1]

But, although Byron takes pains to build up a large collection of these figures (stanzas 79 to 93 of canto XIII), each is only mentioned, then abandoned. He cannot make them a force in his social drama because, unlike Peacock, he could not believe in intellectual specialisms or distinction or eccentricity constituting a force or presence in Regency society. Byron immediately admits that his heart is not in the crotchets he has just described:

> The days of Comedy are gone, alas!
>   When Congreve's fool could vie with Molière's *bête*:
> Society is smooth'd to that excess,
> That manners hardly differ more than dress.

> Our ridicules are kept in the background—
>   Ridiculous enough, but also dull;
> Professions, too, are no more to be found
>   Professional; and there is nought to cull
> Of folly's fruit: for though your fools abound,
>   They're barren, and not worth the pains to pull.
> Society is now one polish'd horde,
> Form'd of two mighty tribes, the *Bores* and the *Bored*.[2]

These lines, especially the last couplet, sum up the scope and spirit of Byron's survey of English society in the house-party cantos. His affinity here is not with Peacock but Count D'Orsay, the aristocratic dandy who clearly reminded Byron in 1823 of himself ten or so years earlier, and who had recently covered the same English social ground—'I know, or knew personally, most of the personages and societies which he describes'.[3] At about the time that Byron was writing the lines on the English 'bores and bored', he was delighted at the confirmation in Count D'Orsay's English Journal,

which is a very extraordinary production, and a most melancholy truth in all that regards high life in England...The most singular thing is, *how* he should have penetrated *not* the *fact*, but the *mystery*

---

[1] Canto XIII, stanza 87: *ibid.* pp. 396–402.
[2] Canto XIII, stanzas 94–5: *ibid.* p. 402.
[3] *Letters and journals*, ed. Prothero, VI, 186–7.

of the English *ennui* at two-and-twenty. I was about the same age when I made the same discovery in almost precisely the same circles . . . but I never could have described it so well. *Il faut être Français*, to effect this.

But he ought also to have been in the country during the hunting season, with 'a select party of distinguished guests', as the papers term it. He ought to have seen the gentlemen after dinner (on the hunting days), and the soirée ensuing thereupon,—and the women looking as if they had hunted, or rather been hunted; and I could have wished that he could have been at a dinner in town, which I recollect at Lord Cowper's—small, but select, and composed of the most amusing people. The desert was hardly on the table, when, out of twelve, I counted *five asleep*; of that five, there were *Tierney*, Lord Lansdowne, and Lord Darnley—I forget the other two, but they were either wits or orators—perhaps poets. . .

Alas, our dearly beloved countrymen have only discovered that they are tired, and not that they are tiresome.[1]

The last sentence echoes the verse-epigram on 'the bores and bored': the whole passage is an essential summary of the house-party cantos.

Within its limits this *ennui* is a valid subject that produces the most telling stanzas. The middle-aged go hunting or shooting 'to make the day more short' and fight off 'That awful yawn which sleep cannot abate'; 'the elderly. . . tumbled books. . . or saunter'd through the gardens piteously',

> Or on the watch their longing eyes would fix,
> Longing at sixty for the hour of six.[2]

The contrast of former ages throws into sharper relief the monotonous conformity of modern life. It has neither the varied brilliance of Congreve's or Molière's age, nor the dirtier colours of Fielding's:

> We have no accomplished blackguards, like Tom Jones,
> But gentlemen in stays, as stiff as stones.[3]

With more grasp and subtlety Byron contrasts the new propriety ('flirtation—but decorous', 'cards, too, but *no* dice') with the more rakish era of which Byron had experienced the tail-end

---

[1] *Letters and journals*, ed. Prothero, VI, 186–7.
[2] *Don Juan*, canto XIII, stanzas 101–2: ed. Steffan and Pratt, III, 405–6.
[3] Canto XIII, stanza 110: *ibid.* p. 409.

in the early 1810s, the era epitomised for Byron by Sheridan.[1]
This strong nostalgia for the bold figures of the previous
generation produces the well-known passage on the theme of
Ubi sunt, beginning

> Where is Napoleon the Grand? God knows:
>   Where little Castlereagh? The devil can tell:
> Where Grattan, Curran, Sheridan...
>
> Where's Brummell? Dish'd. Where's Long Pole
>   Wellesley? Diddled.[2]

Yet, while it is intermittently thrown into relief by this
strong light of contrast, modern monotony and conformity is
in the long run bound to appear a monotonous and indistinct
subject. With that transparency characteristic of *Don Juan*, the
writer freely displaying his workings in the margin, Byron
admits in canto xiv that he cannot find enough dramatic
resources in his subject. The earlier cantos were fool's play—

> Now I could much more easily sketch a harem,
>   A battle, wreck, or history of the heart[3]

for 'surely there's variety': whereas the milieu he is now
committed to describe has

> A dull and family likeness through all ages,
>   Of no great promise for poetic pages.[4]

Why has no-one offered 'a *real* portrait' of the beau monde?—
''Tis that, in fact, there's little to describe'.[5]

More serious, by a series of similar interconnecting confessions, Byron reveals that the artistic impasse goes with
a personal impasse. His life has come to a dead end, and
canto iv begins with six solemn stanzas on suicide. But the
motive is not tragic: he is sated and jaded. The cause of this

---

[1] One way of gauging the change in manners through the Regency is to compare
the descriptions and praise of the aged Sheridan in Byron's letters and journals
with the respectable and largely whitewashed portrait in Moore's *Life of
Sheridan* (1825). Byron in Italy was not, as some critics suggest, out of touch
with the changed standards of propriety: the visits from the Blessingtons, and
from Moore ('too close to the *stove* of society') gave him good samples of
society in the 1820s.
[2] *Don Juan*, canto xi, stanzas 77–8: ed. Steffan and Pratt, iii, 307.
[3] Canto xiv, stanza 21: iii, *ibid.* 419.
[4] Canto xiv, stanza 15: *ibid.* p. 416.   [5] Canto xiv, stanza 20: *ibid.* p. 418.

ennui can in turn be narrowed down to the milieu in which he spent most of his life:

> Doubtless it is a brilliant masquerade;
>   But when of the first sight you have had your fill,
> It palls—at least it did so upon me,
>   This Paradise of Pleasure and *Ennui*.[1]

This is not simply recollected boredom, for Byron hints in the poem at what is very clear in his letters and journals, that after the exciting Venice of *Beppo* he found himself at Ravenna and elsewhere marooned in a milieu as dull and respectable as its counterpart in England. He turned to writing for stimulation and diversion:

> In youth I wrote because my mind was full,
> And now because I feel it growing dull.[2]

Asked why he publishes,

> I ask in turn—Why do you play at cards?
> Why drink? Why read?—To make some hour less dreary.[3]

—so that he equates himself with the Fitz-Fulkes' bored guests killing time until dinner. But—last stage of the vicious circle —writing these cantos is the reverse of stimulating, because their subject is the very society and *ennui* from which writing is intended to be an escape.

This sequence of points, drawn from Byron's own confessions in the verse, enforces W. W. Robson's conclusion that 'great art cannot be made out of a boredom with oneself, which is expressed as a boredom with one's subject-matter'.[4] The sequence, however, suggests a vicious circle, a more intimate relation between the two sources of boredom. It leads one to trace the impasse, the lack of resources, back to the limitations of Byron's experience. Andrew Rutherford calls the description of aristocratic *ennui* 'his deepest insight, conveyed to us in the authentic accents of experience',[5] but the very authenticity depends on the *shallowness* of his experience. His involvement was that of a dandy, who looks to society for amusement, and

---

[1] Canto xiv, stanza 17: *ibid*. p. 417.   [2] Canto xiv, stanza 10: *ibid*. p. 415.
[3] Canto xiv, stanza 11: *ibid*. p. 415.
[4] 'Byron as Poet', *Proceedings of the British Academy*, xliii (1957), 61.
[5] *Byron. A critical study* (London, 1961), p. 212.

expected even poets and others from the cultural fringes to justify themselves as 'the most amusing people'.[1] That was how he anxiously presented himself as entering society, leaving at the door different or deeper criteria and accomplishments. The English cantos have little to report on that society but the man-of-amusement's complaint that he is not being kept amused: they cannot transcend its limitations by conveying how they would strike someone from a different culture (as in *Beppo*) or the strain they would impose on someone of intelligence and ambition (as with Julien Sorel). Nor could Byron, whose own attitude is often near that of the Honourable Mr Listless, and whose own poetry had encouraged that attitude, have produced that characterisation of elegant *ennui* with Peacock's acuteness and detachment.

Byron's experience was limited in breadth as well as depth. The study of his biography and letters confirms the claim of E. D. H. Johnson that 'the poet emerged so rapidly from the obscurity of his solitary youth into the full glare of the *haut monde* that in this quick transition he saw nothing of the intermediate regions where dwell the great middle ranks of a people'.[2] Furthermore his experience of the higher circles was both limited and lacking in discrimination: he found little more at Holland House than at Almack's or the Oxfords' or Melbournes'.

The inferiority of the country-house cantos to *Nightmare Abbey* also betrays that Byron is a poorer artist than Peacock. Despite the example of canto I he is unsure how to do what Peacock did with Shelley and Scythrop; that is, work imaginatively on a character from life so as to re-create him with the impersonal validity of a fictional character. He can only manage direct transcription, which would cause too much scandal: 'I wish to spare 'em, / For reasons which I choose to keep apart'— 'I therefore deal in generalities'.[3] More damaging are his difficulties with the opposite artistic problem, the need every writer has to compensate for lack of first-hand knowledge by

[1] See Byron's description of the dozing dinner-guests (above, p. 198), two of whom were 'wits or orators—perhaps poets'.
[2] 'Don Juan in England', *E.L.H.: a journal of English literary history* (1944), XI, 138.
[3] *Don Juan*, canto XIV, stanzas 21 and 80: ed. Steffan and Pratt, III, 419 and 444.

making his intelligence and imagination work on the glimpses, hints and guesses at his command. Byron frequently boasted of his advantage: 'If [other poets are] admitted into high life for a season, it is merely as *spectators*—they form no part of the Mechanism thereof. Now Moore and I, the one by circumstances, the other by birth...have entered into its pulses and passions, *quarum partes fuimus.*'[1] But Peacock, who only glimpsed that world, could produce the authentic figures of Mr Listless and Mr Cypress. Byron on the other hand flounders when he tries to imagine figures on the fringes of his own milieu, let alone outside it. The attempt at Peacock's range of representative characters, started and dropped in canto XIII, is revived in canto XVI with its architect, picture-dealer and lawyers, and its witty parson exiled from London to the Fens who reminds us of Sydney Smith or of Peacock's fenland Reverend Mr Hilary. But we have to be satisfied with lame hearsay like this:

> ...architect and dealer, were
> Both busy (as a general in his tent
> Writing despatches) in their several stations,
> Exulting in their brilliant lucubrations.[2]

The characters never move or speak: the architect is never heard, unlike the corresponding landscape-gardener of *Headlong Hall*.

This illustrates the more general lack of dramatic creation in the English cantos, compared with Peacock's lively flexibility in switching from description and narration to directly presented dialogue. This, with the slowness of movement and thinness of texture compared with *Nightmare Abbey*, makes it possible to argue that Byron is a more restricted artist than Peacock, because too preoccupied with presenting himself through the narrator. But the more important point suggested by this comparison is that, in the scope of his subject and his attitude to it, Byron not Peacock is the limited Regency figure who fails to transcend the spirit of the age.

[1] *Letters and journals*, ed. Prothero, v, 363.
[2] *Don Juan*, canto XVI, stanza 66: ed. Steffan and Pratt, III, 533.

9

Peacock after the Regency

The decade 1810–20 provided the challenges and shaping experiences that made Peacock's mind and art develop. Peacock
after the Regency may be seen as receding from, losing the
impetus given by, those experiences. As this study is an
investigation of those forces and their results, not an exhaustive
history of Peacock's life and works, the main purpose of the
present chapter is to define further the central concern: Peacock
in the Regency. It will not labour the criticism of the later
novels in their repetitions of earlier successes or their failure
to match them. It will however emphasise the exceptions to this
later reaction and decline: the literary, and more strikingly
the musical, reviews and articles.

*

In his article on 'The *épicier*' Peacock argues that the spirit of
an age and the character of its heroes are related by the
mechanical law of demand and supply. As with politics and
religion,

So with philosophy. An age which demands free enquiry, pushed
without fear or compromise to its legitimate conclusions, turns up
an Epicurus or a Hobbes. In one which likes to put up at a half-way
house, there will be no lack of a Dugald Stewart, or a Macintosh, to
provide it with comfortable entertainment.

So with literature. Among a people disposed to think, their every-
day literature will bear the impress of thought; [and vice-versa].
Milton would be forthcoming if he were wanted; but in our time
Milton was not wanted, and Walter Scott was.[1]

Despite its simplifications this insight, which accounts for the
telling link between Listless and Cypress in *Nightmare Abbey*,
will bear pondering in relation to Regency manners, taste and

[1] *Works*, Halliford Edition, IX, 293–4.

literature. This point about what makes a writer *popular* suggests a complementary one about what is *possible* for him, what intellectual materials he can find in his age. This bears particularly on the class of writers under Peacock's immediate consideration, to which he assigns Pigault-Lebrun and by implication himself: men of talent rather than genius, comic 'novelists of ideas' rather than creative thinkers. Their field, as Arnold puts it, is not 'discovering new ideas' but working with 'the best ideas current at the time'.[1]

Arnold, however, overstates the case by implying the intellectual *passiveness* of such writers. He stresses that their talent depends on 'those materials, those elements, ready for its use', '*current* at the time, not merely accessible'.[2] This denies the effort such a writer shares with any common reader in striving to *gain* access to 'the best that is known and thought'[3] in his time, and to make it inward, so that the resources of the age make contact with his own inner resources.

That Peacock after the Regency lacked these resources and contacts can be shown by taking up the biographical thread from the end of chapter 3, and by developing the disagreement made there with Amarasinghe's view of Peacock's resources: 'Peacock's peculiar merits are reflected in his friendship with Shelley on the one hand and with James Mill on the other.'[4] The later Peacock had the advantage of neither of these friendships. By the time of his appointment at East India House in 1819 and more so by the time he wrote 'The four ages of poetry' in 1820, he and Shelley had become distant both geographically and intellectually. On the other hand the little evidence available suggests that Peacock's reactions to James and John Stuart Mill were bare human tolerance and intellectual distaste.

The son's writings contain the tersest of references to Peacock; the father's, none. On Peacock's side we have only the anecdotes of Sir Edward Strachey:

[1] 'The function of criticism at the present time', *Essays in criticism*, 1st series, p. 5. Arnold's case fits a novelist like Peacock rather better than the poets he is discussing.
[2] *Ibid.* pp. 4 and 5. [3] *Ibid.* p. 37.
[4] *Dryden and Pope in the early nineteenth century* (Cambridge, 1962), p. 179. (See above, p. 55.)

He one day came to my father's room, and said, with mock indignation, 'I will never dine with Mill again, for he asks me to meet only political economists. I dined with him last night, when he had Mushet and MacCulloch, and after dinner, Mushet took a paper out of his pocket, and began to read: "In the infancy of society, when Government was invented to save a percentage—say, of $3\frac{1}{2}$ per cent"—on which he was stopped by MacCulloch with "I will say no such thing," meaning that this was not the proper percentage.' Two or three years later, the story was told in 'Crotchet Castle' in the way the reader knows.[1]

A more puzzling piece of evidence about the later Peacock is that once a week for many years he dined alone with Jeremy Bentham.[2] There is no evidence of what they discussed, and no recognisable fruits in the later novels.

Certainly his work at East India House, especially his part in developing navigational routes and introducing iron steamships, fulfilled the ideal of utility he had pressed on Shelley, let him follow 'some interesting matter connected with the business of life, in the tangible shape of a practical man'.[3] But we soon detect in him the Victorian and modern phenomenon typified by Dickens's Wemmick: the impulse to separate the world of work from the world of home and leisure. Every weekend Peacock went by train through the new suburbs, between the office in Leadenhall Street and his retreat at Halliford-on-Thames. In this home-world, not far from his Regency retreats, he could largely continue his earlier way of life as 'Hermit of the Thames', walking, rowing, dining well and studying Greek. It was largely on these terms, as 'the Laughing Philosopher' or 'the Epicurean Philosopher',[4] that he met friends like the Stracheys or Lord Broughton, and acquaintances like Macaulay, who in 1851 'met Peacock; a clever fellow, and a good scholar...We had out Aristophanes, Æschylus, Sophocles and several other old fellows, and tried each other's quality pretty well. We are both strong enough in

---

[1] Sir Edward Strachey, 'Recollections of Thomas Love Peacock', in *Peacock's Calidore and miscellanea*, ed. R. Garnett (London, 1891), p. 18.
[2] See Grant Duff, *Notes from a diary, 1851–1872* (London, 1897), p. 60.
[3] See above, pp. 72–3.
[4] See Edith Nicholls, 'A biographical notice of Thomas Love Peacock', *Works of Peacock*, ed. H. Cole, 3 vols. (London, 1875), I, xlix.

these matters for gentlemen.'[1] And it was from the same geographical and intellectual retreat that he wrote the later novels.

*

The main stream of Peacock's fiction was interrupted in the 1820s by two attempts at something new: an alliance, more or less uneasy, of satire with romantic folklore.

The second element dominates *Maid Marian* (1822). Peacock has dramatised the stories in Joseph Ritson's collection of Robin Hood ballads with the aid of bustle, farce and facetiousness, of which a fair sample is the military intervention at the wedding (chapter 1):

The earl's bowmen at the door sent in among the assailants a volley of arrows, one of which whizzed past the ear of the abbot, who, in mortal fear of being suddenly translated from a ghostly friar to a friarly ghost, began to roll out of the chapel as fast as his bulk and his holy robes would permit, roaring 'Sacrilege!' with all his monks at his heels, who were, like himself, more intent to go at once than to stand upon the order of their going.[2]

All this, with its accompanying stage-medieval dialogue of knights biding hard by, who cry 'Mass!' and 'Gramercy!' as they deliver shrewd hits, brings back childhood visits to the pantomine. So that, while a number of specific parallels between *Maid Marian* and Scott's *Ivanhoe* used to make scholars talk of plagiarism, the reader will be struck by a more general similarity which brings both books under the criticism of Scott made in *Crotchet Castle*. There is the literature of pantomine, says Dr Folliott, and there is the pantomime of literature; and in both

there is the same variety of character, the same diversity of story, the same copiousness of incident, the same research into costume, the same display of heraldry, falconry, minstrelsy, scenery, monkery ...the same running base of love and battle...As to any sentence worth remembering, any moral or political truth, any thing having a tendency, however remote, to make men wiser or better, to make them think, to make them even think of thinking; they are both precisely alike: nuspiam, nequaquam, nullibi, nullimodus.[3]

[1] G. O. Trevelyan, *Life and letters of Lord Macaulay* (London, 1876), II, 300.
[2] Halliford, III, 6.   [3] Chapter 9: Halliford, IV, 117.

It was natural enough, then, that *Maid Marian* was quickly adapted from a pantomime of literature into an actual panto-mime-operetta with additional scenes grafted on from *Ivanhoe*, and had a long run at Covent Garden.

Maid Marian, Peacock told Shelley in 1818, 'I shall make the vehicle of much oblique satire on all the oppressions that are done under the sun'.[1] Perhaps feeling it had been so oblique in that book as to be missed by most readers, he anxiously underlined the satire in the second romance, *The misfortunes of Elphin* (1829).

We, who live in more enlightened times, amidst the 'gigantic strides of intellect', when offices of public trust are so conscientiously and zealously discharged, and so vigilantly checked and superintended, may wonder at the negligence of Seithenyn; at the sophisms with which, in his liquor, he vindicated his system, and pronounced the eulogium of his old dilapidations.[2]

This particular nudge is unnecessary because it follows an outstanding parody of conservatism in which Seithenyn's defence of the decaying embankment runs exactly parallel with Canning's defences of the Constitution in the years just before the 1832 Reform Bill:

'Prince Seithenyn', said Elphin, 'I have visited you on a subject of deep moment. Reports have been brought to me, that the embankment, which has been so long entrusted to your care, is in a state of dangerous decay.'

'Decay,' said Seithenyn, 'is one thing, and danger is another. Every thing that is old must decay. That the embankment is old, I am free to confess; that it is somewhat rotten in parts, I will not altogether deny; but that it is any the worse for that, I do most sturdily gainsay. It does its business well: it works well: it keeps out the water from the land, and lets in the wine upon the High Commission of Embankment. Cupbearer, fill. Our ancestors were wiser than we: they built it in their wisdom; and, if we should be so rash as to try to mend it, we should only mar it.'

'The stonework,' said Teithrin, 'is sapped and mined: the piles are rotten, broken and dislocated: the floodgates and sluices are leaky and creaky.'

'That is the beauty of it,' said Seithenyn. 'Some parts of it are rotten, and some parts of it are sound.'

[1] Halliford, VIII, 209.   [2] Chapter 4: *ibid.* IV, 43.

'It is well,' said Elphin, 'that some parts are sound: it were better that all were so.'

'So I have heard some people say before,' said Seithenyn; 'perverse people, blind to venerable antiquity: that very unamicable sort of people, who are in the habit of indulging their reason. But I say, the parts that are rotten give elasticity to those that are sound: they give them elasticity, elasticity, elasticity. If it were all sound, it would break by its own obstinate stiffness: the soundness is checked by the rottenness, and the stiffness is balanced by the elasticity...'[1]

But this is a rare passage, occurring early in a novel that soon relaxes into a medley of Welsh myths, an attempt to copy what Scott had done with Scottish folklore and scenery, a conscientiously scholarly pantomime. In his next novel two years later, Peacock returned to the framework of the modern house-party.

In the dominant character of *Crotchet Castle* (1831) one recognises the paradox all his friends found in the later Peacock himself: the Rev. Dr Folliott is well informed but reactionary, superficially lively but basically conservative and unchangeable.

The key to Folliott's emphatic manner is to be found not in his usual confident moments but in the rare occasion when, revealingly and very sympathetically, he is caught off guard. In chapter 7, 'The sleeping Venus', we are told that Mr Crotchet, reading of some magistrates' condemnation of naked statuary, 'determined to fill his house with Venuses of all sizes and kinds'. Folliott, 'very much astonished at this unexpected display', mildly questions Crotchet and finds himself up against a heated Philhellenist who has swallowed whole the contemporary notion of Greek sculpture's 'pure, ideal, intellectual beauty':

Mr. Crotchet: Sir, ancient sculpture is the true art of modesty. But where the Greeks had modesty, we have cant; where they had poetry, we have cant; where they had patriotism, we have cant; where they had anything that exalts, delights, or adorns humanity, we have nothing but cant, cant, cant. And, sir, to show my contempt for cant in all its shapes, I have adorned my house with the Greek Venus, in all her shapes, and am ready to fight her battle against all the societies that were ever instituted for the suppression of truth and beauty.

[1] Chapter 2: Halliford, IV, 15–16.

The Rev. Dr. Folliott: My dear sir, I am afraid you are growing warm. Pray be cool. Nothing contributes so much to good digestion as to be perfectly cool after dinner.[1]

But Folliott himself becomes more and more heated:

Mr. Crotchet: [The Athenians] preferred the society of women who would not have made any scruple about sitting as models to Praxiteles; as you know, sir, very modest women in Italy did to Canova: one of whom, an Italian countess, being asked by an English lady, 'how she could bear it?' answered, 'Very well: there was a good fire in the room.'

The Rev. Dr. Folliott: Sir, the English lady should have asked how the Italian lady's husband could bear it. The phials of my wrath would overflow if poor dear Mrs. Folliott...[2]

Finally thrown completely off-balance intellectually, he throws himself off-balance physically:

The Rev. Dr. Folliott: Would you have allowed Miss Crotchet to sit as a model for Canova?

Mr. Crotchet: Yes, sir.

'God bless my soul, sir!' exclaimed the Reverend Doctor Folliott, throwing himself back into a chair, and flinging up his heels, with the premeditated design of giving emphasis to his exclamation: but by miscalculating his *impetus,* he overbalanced his chair, and laid himself on the carpet in a right angle, of which his back was the base.[3]

Folliott is for once on the defensive and caught off-guard: yet he reacts so emphatically that he might almost appear to be on the offensive. And this relates to his usual habit in conversation, which is to take the initiative and stifle any menace to his control—if necessary breaking in with something cutting before any challenge to his self-assurance or doubts about his intellectual grasp can develop. A mild example of this tactic occurs in chapter 7 itself when he dismisses Crotchet's appeal to Diderot with 'Sir, Diderot is not a man after my heart. Keep to the Greeks, if you please'—after having to ask Crotchet who Diderot was. This is transparent enough: in fact the whole of chapter 7 is successful because Peacock directs his irony at both Folliott and Crotchet. But Folliott threatens the novel

---

[1] *Ibid.* pp. 96–7. [2] *Ibid.* pp. 98–9. [3] *Ibid.* p. 101.

when Peacock over-indulges his liveliness and so lets him overdominate the conversation.

The engaging liveliness comes out in his first entry:

'God bless my soul, sir!' exclaimed the Reverend Doctor Folliott, bursting, one fine May morning, into the breakfast-room at Crotchet Castle, 'I am out of all patience with this march of mind. Here has my house been nearly burned down, by my cook taking it into her head to study hydrostatics, in a sixpenny tract, published by the Steam Intellect Society, and written by a learned friend...My cook must read his rubbish in bed; and as might naturally be expected, she dropped suddenly asleep, overturned the candle, and set the curtains in a blaze.'[1]

But, in the discussion that follows, his liveliness already comes to seem less intellectual energy than 'trenchant ignorance'. His indiscriminate reactionary spirit rejects not only Mac Quedy's political economy but also Skionar's and Kant's philosophy. Despite his scorn for the modern Athens, Folliott has betrayed himself into appearing Mac Quedy's ally in philistinism against Skionar's objections to 'Aristotelian logic'. To look closely at the way this discussion develops: Mac Quedy presses his boast—

Metaphysics, sir, metaphysics. Logic and moral philosophy. There we are at home. The Athenians only sought the way, and we have found it; to all this we have added political economy, the science of sciences.

Folliott retorts:

A hyperbarbarous technology, that no Athenian ear could have borne. Premises assumed without evidence, or in spite of it; and conclusions drawn from them so logically, that they must necessarily be erroneous.

Skionar joins in:

I cannot agree with you, Mr. Mac Quedy, that you have found the true road of metaphysics, which the Athenians only sought. The Germans have found it, sir: the sublime Kant, and his disciples.

Mac Quedy 'makes his own stupidity another's reproach':

I have read the sublime Kant, sir, with an anxious desire to understand him; and I confess I have not succeeded.

---

[1] Chapter 2: Halliford, IV, p. 13.

which Folliott supports with a particularly dismal damp squib:

He wants the two great requisites of head and tail.

Skionar is left to talk to the brick wall of Mac Quedy's 'sheer, honest insensibility':

Transcendentalism is the philosophy of intuition, the development of universal convictions; truths which are inherent in the organisation of mind, which cannot be obliterated, though they may be obscured, by superstitious prejudice on the one hand, and by the Aristotelian logic on the other.

Mr. Mac Quedy: Well, sir, I have no notion of logic obscuring a question.

Mr. Skionar: There is only one true logic, which is the transcendental; and this can prove only the one true philosophy, which is also the transcendental. The logic of your modern Athens can prove every thing equally; and that is, in my opinion, tantamount to proving nothing at all.[1]

With the important figure of Skionar—the opposite of Folliott as much as of Mac Quedy—Peacock is uncertain of purpose. He is far from being an obscure fool like Flosky. In so far as he draws on Coleridge, he may even be Peacock's *peccavi* for the earlier caricatures: 'the poor man has got an ill name by keeping bad company with the idealists-turned-political-sycophants Mr. Wilful Wontsee and Mr. Rumblesack Shantsee'.[2] Skionar is also reminiscent of Shelley, not only in his ideas but in the gentle, reasonable and speculative manner of discussing that Peacock acknowledged in the 'Memoirs' as one side of his friend. In chapter 2 he is almost the novelist's protégé as Forester was in *Melincourt*. Yet, while he lets Skionar have his say, ultimately Peacock does not know what to do with him. After Skionar's speech quoted above, Peacock abandons him and returns to his own intellectual depth by bringing in Mr Crotchet and a minor crank called Mr Firedamp. In the next chapter Skionar talks to Mac Quedy about the difference between perception and calculation, and introduces a Socratic question or two about modern civilisation: but thereafter in the novel he is seldom heard, being replaced by the simpler and less disconcerting Mr Chainmail the medievalist.

[1] *Ibid.* pp. 20–2.   *Ibid.* p. 59.

It is like a Socratic dialogue in which the author connives at the suppression of the Socratic voice.

By allowing this, Peacock leads the novel, despite all its enlivening episodes and subsidiary romantic interests, into an artistic and intellectual impasse, which is most obvious in chapter 10 ('The voyage, continued'). The view of Lechlade Church provokes a three-cornered argument on a subject familiar to readers of *Headlong Hall*. It is of course much livelier than anything in the earlier novel:

Mr. Chainmail: I do not see, in all your boasted improvement, any compensation for the religious charity of the twelfth century...we have no nature, no simplicity, no picturesqueness: everything about us is as artificial and as complicated as our steam-machinery: our poetry is a kaleidoscope of false imagery, expressing no real feeling, portraying no real existence. I do not see any compensation for the poetry of the twelfth century.

Mr. Mac Quedy: I wonder to hear you, Mr. Chainmail, talking of the religious charity of a set of lazy monks and beggarly friars, who were much more occupied with talking than giving; of whom, those who were in earnest did nothing but make themselves, and everyone about them, miserable, with fastings, and penances, and other such trash; and those who were not, did nothing but guzzle and royster, and, having no wives of their own, took very unbecoming liberties with those of honester men. As to your poetry of the twelfth century, it is not good for much.

Mr. Chainmail: It has, at any rate, what ours wants, truth to nature, and simplicity of diction...

The Rev. Dr. Folliott: Let him who loves them read Greek: Greek, Greek, Greek.[1]

But despite all the vigour we are reminded of *Headlong Hall* in the way each speaker represents an extreme and immovable position, each opinionates in turn, and no interchange develops. Peacock's comment is bored and dismissive:

In this manner they glided over the face of the waters, discussing everything and settling nothing. Mr. Mac Quedy and the Reverend Doctor Folliott had many degladations on political economy: wherein each in his own view, Doctor Folliott demolished Mr. Mac Quedy's science, and Mr. Mac Quedy demolished Doctor Folliott's objections.

[1] Halliford, IV, 123–6.

We would print these dialogues if we thought any one would read them; but the world is not yet ripe for this *haute sagesse Pantagrueline*. We must, therefore, content ourselves with an échantillon of one of the Reverend Doctor's perorations [which follows at some length].[1]

This, like the analogous passages in *Don Juan*,[2] is an open admission that Peacock has reached an impasse. He is impatient to reach conclusions and so settles on one point of view (Folliott's); more fundamentally, he is bored with his subject-matter, resorting to impatient summary instead of dramatic presentation.

Peacock's escape from the impasse is much like Byron's. After Folliott's speech he summarises more debates ('Mr. Chainmail fought with Doctor Folliott, the battle of the romantic against the classical in poetry...'),[3] then resorts to the crotchets of Philpot and Trillo, figures as trivial as the corresponding embryos of *Don Juan's* English cantos or of *Headlong Hall*. The chapter ends with the 'love-interest' that largely replaces social discussions in the remainder of the novel.

One should add that the medieval–modern theme does not exist solely in theoretical discussions in the Thames cruise. In the final chapter Chainmail's medieval fantasy, a Christmas wassail at Chainmail Hall, is broken in on by the reality of a pre-Reform-Bill riot. As Captain Swing begins to break down the door the guests find leisure to discuss the reasons for this 'piece of the dark ages we did not bargain for', and lay the blame on Sir Simon Steeltrap who, we were told earlier, 'has enclosed commons and woodlands; abolished cottage-gardens; taken the village cricket-ground into his own park, out of pure regard to the sanctity of Sunday; shut up footpaths and alehouses'.[4] Yet it is Peacock himself who uses the *Hudibras* phrase *rabble-rout*, and has them chased off and the party restored.

Two years after *Crotchet Castle* came the event that told most on the later Peacock: the death of his mother. It was not the kind of experience that gives an impulse to a writer. Emotionally he was paralysed by losing the person to whom he was unusually

---

[1] *Ibid.* pp. 126–7.   [2] See above, pp. 197–201.
[3] Halliford, IV, 128.   [4] Chapter 5: *ibid.* p. 66.

strongly attached and with whom he had always lived, even after marriage. Practically, he lost much of his leisure for writing, for because of his wife's poor health his mother had kept house and raised his children. Her death meant that, except for a few reviews, Peacock wrote nothing for over twenty years.[1]

By the time of *Gryll Grange* (1860) he had retired from East India House and at Halliford could cultivate at leisure an elderly placidity and stability that resisted all change of ideas and habits. Edith Nicholls tells us that

As he advanced in years, his detestation of anything disagreeable made him simply avoid whatever fretted him, laughing off all sorts of ordinary calls upon his leisure time. His love of ease and kindness of heart made it impossible that he could be actively unkind to any one, but he would not be worried, and just got away from anything that annoyed him. He was very fond of his children, and was an indulgent father to them, and he was a kind and affectionate grandfather; he could not bear any one to be unhappy or uncomfortable about him, and this feeling he carried down to the animal creation; his pet cats and dogs were especially cared for by himself.[2]

The account is by one of the granddaughters indulged, she in turn being indulgent and protective towards him.

'Indulgence' also conveys our sense of Dr Opimian, whose domestic life runs closely parallel to Peacock's. 'Mrs. Opimian was domestic', and 'left the Doctor nothing to desire in the service of his table': he in turn is indulgent to her, his servants and pet animals. Self-indulgence characterises Opimian's habits of talking as of eating and drinking. His reaction to every new sign of the times is a simple and overbearing conservatism which the reader is intended to find endearing even when it conflicts with facts or reasoning. In the representative 'Symposium' (chapter 19) he lays down fundamentals familiar to us since *Headlong Hall* ('Science is one thing and wisdom is another');[3] rejects *in toto* all new developments (science, electricity, and 'America; to which we are indebted for nothing but evil')[4] because of their partial abuse or danger; rejects others'

---

[1] For the importance of her death, see Edith Nicholls's 'Biographical notice', *Works*, ed. Cole, I, xli.
[2] *Ibid.* pp. xlix–l.
[3] Halliford, v, 186.   [4] *Ibid.* p. 190.

first-hand knowledge in favour of his own prejudices[1]; refers everything to classical authority,[2] and gauges everybody by their knowledge of the classics.[3]

Yet Opimian, overbearing towards Curryfin (and others) in argument, shows a remarkable curiosity and generosity towards him as a person; and it is Curryfin's own experimenting and enquiring mind which catches Peacock's attention. One might expect him to be as sharply attacked as 'the learned Friend', Lord Brougham, is in *Crotchet Castle*, for he belongs to the Pantopragmatic Society, which promotes 'the real art of talking about an imaginary art of teaching every man of business'. Curryfin's own speciality is lecturing on fish to fishermen and their wives. But we see him not lecturing but satisfying his curiosity and meeting challenges to his ingenuity—breaking in a wild horse, capsizing when testing a design for an infallibly safe sail, trying to skate the figures 898, and just failing to reproduce the 'sonorous vases' of the Greek theatre. Peacock, no doubt with a backward glance at himself fifty years earlier, is clearly taken with this dilettante living in an age when Zimris could no longer be accommodated:

There is a young gentleman who is capable of anything, and who would shine in any pursuit, if he would keep to it. He shines as it is, in almost everything he takes in hand in private society: there is genius even in his failures, as in the case of the theatrical vases; but the world is a field of strong competition, and affords eminence to few in any sphere of exertion, and to those few rarely but in one.[4]

Significantly the speaker is the commonsensical sign-of-the-times Mr MacBorrowdale. It is the same curiosity that governs Curryfin's relations with other people. He is drawn to Miss

[1] Lord Curryfin, who has visited America, objects sensibly to Opimian's generalisations.

[2] Cf. chapter 7: '*Mrs. Opimian:* I think, doctor, you would not maintain any opinion if you had not an authority two thousand years old for it. *The Rev. Dr. Opimian:* Well, my dear, I think most opinions worth mentioning have an authority of about that age.' (Halliford, v, 63.)

[3] '"We have given them [the Americans] wine and classical literature; but I am afraid Bacchus and Minerva have equally "scattered their bounty upon barren ground".' (*Ibid.* p. 191.) Compare Hogg's attack on American vulgarity, 'which in a great measure arises from ignorance of Classical literature', contrasted with the Regency Peacock's more liberal attitude. (See above, p. 29.)

[4] Chapter 21: Halliford, v, 214–15.

Niphet by the challenging sense of enigma and of difference from himself:

> the world seemed to flow under her observation without even ruffling the surface of her interior thoughts. This perplexed his versatile lordship. He thought the young lady would be a subject worth studying: it was clear that she was a character. So far so well. He felt that he should not rest satisfied till he was able to define it.[1]

The novel takes a good deal of its life from his dilemma of choice between Miss Niphet and Miss Gryll. And this runs parallel with Falconer's different kind of dilemma, between an isolated tranquillity and the disturbance of love.

This oscillation of Falconer's brings out the curious way in which the spirit in which the novel is written fluctuates between movement and rest. The character of Falconer takes its charm from Peacock's affectionate recollection of Shelley: while composing the novel he was reading Hogg's *Life of Shelley* and writing his own life of him. But the novel gives too mellow a portrait, blurring the individuality and energy of the young Shelley as recaptured in the 'Memoirs', and remaking him in the image of the elderly Peacock. There is a great deal of common ground between the Peacock who 'would not be worried and just got away from anything that annoyed him', the Dr Opimian whose tastes 'were four: a good library, a good dinner, a pleasant garden, and rural walks',[2] and the Falconer who has 'aimed at living, like an ancient Epicurean, a life of tranquillity...What with classical studies, and rural walks, and a domestic society peculiarly my own, I led what I considered the perfection of life: "days so like each other that they could not be remembered".'[3] Falconer, like his elderly creator, 'placed the *summum bonum* of life in tranquillity, and not in excitement', and faced by 'a disturbing force', love, he 'determined to...avoid exposing himself again to its influence'.[4] Likewise his Greek studies have none of the urgency and élan that characterised Shelley's: his reading deep in the woods and his Greek fantasy in the Tower waited on by seven vestal virgins are merely the fastidious man's escape from the en-

---

[1] Chapter 16: Halliford, v, 157. [2] Chapter 3: *ibid.* p. 19.
[3] Chapter 12: *ibid.* pp. 102–3. [4] *Ibid.* p. 99.

croachment of urban and industrial development—'everything is too deeply tinged with sordid vulgarity'.[1]

Only in passing does Peacock suggest a more urgent psychological pressure behind Falconer's retreat:

Mr. Falconer. I like the immaterial world. I like to live among thoughts and images of the past and the possible, and even of the impossible, now and then.

The Rev. Dr. Opimian. Certainly, there is much in the material world to displease sensitive and imaginative minds; but I do not know anyone who has less cause to complain of it than you have. You are surrounded with all possible comforts, and with all the elements of beauty and of intellectual enjoyment.

Mr. Falconer. It is not my own world that I complain of. It is the world on which I look 'from the loopholes of retreat'...I look with feelings of intense pain on the mass of poverty and crime, of unhealthy, unavailing, unremunerated toil;...of 'all the oppressions that are done under the sun'.[2]

Here the essential psychology of Shelley is touched on and, in different terms, that of the young Wordsworth as worked out in book I of *The excursion*: the hypersensitive mind forced, for self-preservation, to 'avert its eye' and restrict its sympathies. But in *Gryll Grange* it comes to nothing: 'they would have gone off in a discussion on this point, but the French clock warned them to luncheon'.[3] When the topic is resumed, Peacock refers it tellingly to the psychology of the period by the speech of a pointedly named Dr Anodyne on converts to Roman Catholic faith and ritual, and by Falconer's quotation from the religiose Sonnet to the Virgin by 'an orthodox English Churchman', Wordsworth.[4] But this distracts him from investigating further Falconer's psychology; as the novel proceeds his implied extra dimension is ignored, and his escapism is perfectly commensurable with, and comprehensible by, Dr Opimian.

That last comment might appear to be refuted by the chapter (12) that comes immediately after the discussion just examined. For Falconer *is* now disturbed by reality breaking in on the ideal and the tranquil: and it is Dr Opimian who presses him to commit himself to Miss Gryll. But his dilemma has nothing

[1] Chapter 9: *ibid.* p. 79.
[2] Chapter 11: *ibid.* pp. 91–2.
[3] *Ibid.* p. 92.
[4] *Ibid.* pp. 93–4.

of the youthful agitation of Scythrop's; nothing to make him impatient with Opimiam's view of love, which is to 'commit yourself to the current of life', however turbulent, so as to gain the tranquil consolations of old age—a sense of self-justification and achievement, and a family to care for you.

This is perhaps to simplify that fluctuating treatment of love in *Gryll Grange* as a whole which I think leaves most readers with a sense of something haunting and enigmatic. The book springs surprises that suggest Peacock was feeling his way towards a quite different kind of novel. Chapter 27, in which the spinster Miss Ilex confides to Miss Gryll her memory of a lover (who is clearly based on Peacock as a young man),[1] extends the dimensions of the book's discussions of the real and the ideal, and of affection and love; reflects light on Miss Gryll and Falconer; and ends with a kind of victory-in-failure quite different from Opimian's reward of home-comforts.

I find a charm in the recollection far preferable to
The waveless calm, the slumber of the dead
which weighs on the minds of those who have never loved, or loved earnestly.

More characteristic of the novel is the treatment of Falconer's dilemma in chapter 20: generous and curious throughout, but the playful tone impinging on the serious, and the serious varying between the sensitive and the conventionally novelettish. This irregular movement of imagination, this uncertain balance of curiosity and penetration with detachment and complacency, which Peacock displays in the novel—and which he also appears to be appraising in the characters of Opimian, Falconer, Curryfin and Miss Ilex's remembered lover—was best caught by Spedding:

an understanding very quick and bright—not narrow in its range, though wanting in the depth which only deeper purposes impart; a fancy of singular play and delicacy; a light sympathy with the common hopes and fears, joys and sorrows of mankind...just enough for the purposes of observation and intelligent amusement.[2]

*

[1] Compare Edith Nicholls's account of Peacock as 'a universal lover'—a phrase also used by Miss Ilex.
[2] *Edinburgh review*, LXVIII (Jan. 1839), 438. For the full passage, see above, p. 7.

In isolated episodes in *Crotchet Castle* and *Gryll Grange*, especially in those not dominated by Folliott or Opimian, the subjects of 'expression' and 'truth to nature' in poetry and music receive very fresh treatment.[1] These subjects emerge more freely in Peacock's reviews and articles of the 1820s and 1830s, on the insights of which those novel episodes draw.

The best-known of the literary reviews are probably the pair of 'French comic romances' and 'The *épicier*', because Peacock characterises Pigault le Brun in words that fit his own novels. This is from the opening of the first essay:

> Paul de Kock is the legitimate successor of Pigault le Brun...In one respect, his writings present a striking contrast to those of his predecessor. Pigault le Brun began as a writer with the beginning of the French revolution: his successive works are impressed with the political changes of the day: they carry their era in their incidents.[2]

But the most striking aspect of these essays is their social and political exploration of France (and by implication England) after the Revolution and War. The analysis of 'le monde épicier', which quotes Balzac and implies a reading of Stendhal and Constant, leads to this concluding portrait:

> the *épicier*, with his confirmed habit of order, satisfied with any form of government under which he may buy and sell in peace, bringing the vast bulk of his own dead weight to the upholding of any mode of authority which accident has made uppermost at the end of turmoil, and which seems likely to keep prices looking up, and to throw no cloud over his Sunday enjoyment of the picturesque.[3]

However, the third article, which was to deal specifically with Paul de Kock as the *épicier*-novelist, never appeared: and the presentation of le Brun in the first article, while illustrating the catholicity of Peacock's tastes and influences, offers no convincing statement of the value of that particular taste.

Such a statement, in this case concerning one of Peacock's Greek enthusiasms, was provoked by Thomas Moore's *The epicurean*. In exposing the ignorance of Moore's decorative classicism he argues the serious significance of Epicurean philosophy, and approximates it at one point to the Utilitarian:

[1] See especially *Gryll Grange*, chapters 15 and 23 (Halliford, v, 140 ff. and 232 ff.).
[2] Halliford, ix, 255.   [3] *Ibid*. pp. 310–11.

'Thus Epicurus taught, that general utility, or as Bentham expresses it, "the greatest happiness of the greatest number", is the legitimate end of philosophy.'[1] This, while no doubt largely for the benefit of the *Westminster review*'s readers, indicates an attempt to relate and evaluate his allegiances. Although he continued to write for the *Westminster* this attempt, and the implied allegiance to Utilitarian thought, never openly reappeared.

The epicurean was to Peacock merely the average fashionable romance

infinitely acceptable to the ladies 'who make the fortune of new books.' Love, very intense; mystery, somewhat recondite; piety, very profound; and philosophy, sufficiently shallow; with the help of

—new mythological machinery,
And very handsome supernatural scenery;

strung together with an infinity of brilliant and flowery fancies... It is a production in the best style of M. de Chateaubriand.[2]

Its absurdities and confusions can be demolished with ease by quotation and mocking commentary; for example:

I stood before the Pyramids of Memphis, and saw them towering aloft, like the watch-towers of Time, from whose summit when he expires he will look his last.

This is a very infelicitous conceit. The peak of a pyramid must be an uncomfortable dying-bed even for Time. If we attempt to make a picture of this figure, we must imagine the old gentleman dying on tip-toe, and finishing his terrestrial career by rolling down the side of the Pyramid into the sand.[3]

But he brings a second serious standard to bear on Moore's 'flash' style and false imagery. He exposes them by means of all the logic and detailed analysis with which Johnson attacks Gray's Odes; yet (in a typical instance) clinches the matter by a contrast with Wordsworth:

[Moore writes:] 'The swan and the pelican were seen dressing their white plumage in the mirror of its wave.' Whether the pelican uses water as a looking-glass to dress itself by, we have never had an opportunity of determining by observation, but we are very certain that the swan does not... And even if this were, as it is not, the habit

---

[1] Halliford, x, 48–9.　　　[2] *Ibid.* p. 3.　　　[3] *Ibid.* p. 13.

of the swan, it would have been very inconvenient to practise it on the occasion in question, on a lake ruffled by a breeze sufficiently strong to impel a sailing boat with considerable speed. This is to paint from books and imagination, and not from nature. Mr. Wordsworth says of a swan and a lake which he has seen,

> The swan, on still St. Mary's Lake,
> Floats double, swan and shadow.

Mr. Moore says of a swan and lake, which he has not seen, 'The swan dresses its white plumage in the mirror of the ruffled waters.' In the former passage there are picturesquenesses, simplicity and truth: in the latter, a conceit, a misrepresentation and an impossibility.[1]

This passage represents an intelligent conservatism in the face of the merely fashionable development: Peacock's use of Wordsworth against Moore in 1827 is equivalent to Johnson's use of Pope against Gray half a century earlier. He has come to respect much of Wordsworth, but not before his time, and only such as can be assimilated to eighteenth-century or classical canons of correctness.

Predictably enough, the review of Moore's *Letters and journals of Lord Byron* also demonstrates at length that 'Mr. Moore never produces a figure that will stand the test of analysis ...his figurative language [is] chaotic and caleidodoscopical'.[2] What does surprise at first, particularly in something written in 1830, is that he is almost as dismissive of Byron as of his biographer, finding in him neither a titanic force nor 'a psychological phenomenon'.[3] Nor is he even a man of judgement: 'his judgement of individuals is not worth a rush'.[4] Peacock tellingly quotes the anecdote of Byron re-enacting his grand speech to the Lords but forgetting, or pretending to forget, the issue: it could only have occurred between two people whose political opinions were 'a farce'. 'Lord Byron would not have spoken in this strain to Mr. Shelley.'[5] As for Byron's literary opinions, Peacock comments on the hasty changes in *English bards and Scotch reviewers* to show that his

sole standard of judgement of persons was in his own personal feelings of favour and resentment...Sir William Gell [for instance, changed]

---

[1] *Ibid.* pp. 31–2.   [2] *Ibid.* pp. 136 and 137.
[3] Crabb Robinson's verdict: see above, p. 170.
[4] Halliford, IX, 113.   [5] *Ibid.* p. 134.

from coxcomb to classic, by a single stroke of the pen, because...
Lord Byron accidentally became acquainted with him, and so forth.
This was pretty much the way in which he formed his opinions
through life.[1]

Another passage calls his reading shallow and literary ambitions
trivial:

Lord Byron had read enough to produce a general effect with a
multitude of inaccurate recollections. This is the best sort of reading
for those who aim merely at amusing the public: and for the space of
his life before us he aimed at nothing higher.

'I see' he says (October 1810) 'the Lady of the Lake advertised.
Of course, it is in his old ballad style, and pretty. After all, Scott is
the best of them. The end of all scribblement is to amuse, and he
certainly succeeds there.'

And in the same spirit, Captain Medwin reports him to have said:
'The great object is effect, no matter how it is produced.' His reading,
and that of his friend and biographer, are much of a piece in this
respect, and remind us of a French treatise in music, which we saw
advertised the other day, as containing *tout ce qui est nécessaire pour
en parler sans l'avoir étudié*.[2]

This systematic reduction of Byron to the ordinary and
undistinguished is not a case of Peacock failing to appreciate
one of the outstanding figures of his age. It is, rather, a deliberate
protest, for which there are ample grounds, that Byron's
'genius' was of the dubious kind which does not involve the
expected intermediate qualities of strong intelligence, integrity
and self-cultivation. Arnold faced the same paradox when he
wrote that Byron 'was eminent only by his genius, by his
inborn force and fire...except for his genius he was an ordinary
nineteenth-century English gentleman with little culture and
no ideas'.[3] 'Except for his genius'—very often with Byron
genius seems just a matter of superadded energy or flair.

Yet he quotes Byron's attack on 'cant moral, cant religious'
against Moore, who tries to deny or disguise Byron's religious
infidelity. The word *cant* conveys the mass of inert conventional
assumptions, verging on hypocrisy, and the clichés and jargon

---

[1] Halliford, ix, 109. Cf. the point made independently by the present book,
above, p. 192.
[2] *Ibid.* pp. 98–9.   [3] 'Heine': *Essays in criticism*, 1st series, ii, 279.

in which they are passed on. And so Peacock can make a telling link between Moore's ideas and his style, for it is precisely in his discussion of Byron's religion that Moore's style is at its most 'caleidoscopical'. 'This infection, labyrinth, canker, blastment, light that leads astray, cloud, eclipse, etc. etc. so bewilders Mr. Moore with its mere imagination that he loses his own way in a labyrinth of metaphors.'[1] Is the aim to shake the reader himself off the trail of the truth, or is he 'pelting [Byron's] memory with a hailstorm of metaphors, by way of making a good orthodox presentment of himself in the eyes of the religious community'?[2] The conclusion is that Moore's cant is that of the fashionable writer whose only aim is 'to say fine and palatable things',[3] who instinctively 'say[s] of those he wishes to flatter just what he thinks the majority of his readers would wish to have said'.[4]

To expose Moore's sycophancy Peacock quotes from Thomas Jefferson a defence of independent religious judgement which is honourable because honest:

Your own reason is the only oracle given you by heaven, and you are answerable not for the rightness, but uprightness of the decision.[5]

It is in fact in reviewing Jefferson's memoirs that Peacock convinces us that he has found an adequate and concrete standard by which to judge the spirit of his own age and country. He commends the work as

abounding with incitements to moral courage and political honesty; as confirming rational hopes of the progress of knowledge and liberty; as elevating our opinion of human nature; and in all these points counteracting the soul-withering influence of our own frivolous and sycophantic literature.[6]

Even if Peacock overestimates the passages he quotes, he gives substance to the ideal of utility which was invoked in 'The four ages of poetry' but rang hollow in that essay. Here at least he can claim an honourable independence from his age, a conservatism that is not reactionary or philistine.

*

[1] Halliford, IX, 113–14. [2] *Ibid*. p. 116.
[3] *Ibid*. [4] *Ibid*. p. 123.
[5] *Ibid*. p. 120 (Peacock's italics). [6] *Ibid*. pp. 185–6.

Peacock's musical interests first appear in the Regency decade, when he brought Shelley to appreciate the theatre and opera:

In the season of 1817, I persuaded him to accompany me to the opera. The performance was *Don Giovanni*...From this time till he finally left England he was an assiduous frequenter of the Italian Opera. He delighted in the music of Mozart, and especially in the *Nozze di Figaro*, which was performed several times in the early part of 1818.[1]

The interests reappear in the 1830s, when he wrote essays on Bellini and on Lord Mount Edgcumbe's *Musical reminiscences*, and regularly reviewed opera for *The globe* and *The examiner*.

In order to assess the quality of Peacock's reactions, it will first be necessary to give a brief account of the state of music in England in the 1830s. This is drawn mainly from primary sources, from witnesses, reviews, musical periodicals and programmes of the day. Further information has been given by several modern musicologists, in particular by Dr N. Temperley in his 'Instrumental music in England 1800–1850'.[2]

Musical taste and performances divided largely according to the social class of the audiences. In the field of orchestral concerts, the aristocracy subscribed to the annual series of 'Ancient Concerts' or 'Concerts of Ancient Music', organised by a committee of noble or royal 'directors' and forming part of the fashionable London season from 1776 until 1848. In practice, 'ancient' music meant almost exclusively Handel and his Italian contemporaries. In any case no composer could be played who had not been dead for twenty years: the crudity of this rule is shown in the fact that Mozart was introduced in 1824 simply because he died so young, whereas Haydn, whose music was formed in a period that made it more acceptable to conservative tastes, but whose life lasted seventy-seven years, had to wait until 1831. The twenty-year rule was first waived when Beethoven was introduced in 1833. Even after introduction, however, these composers appeared only occasionally among arias and orchestral pieces a hundred years old. In contrast, the Philharmonic Society, founded in 1813, drew its support from professional musicians, and from the middle classes socially excluded from the Ancient Concerts. Its concerts relied heavily on Haydn,

[1] Halliford, I, 82–3. [2] Unpublished Ph.D. thesis (Cambridge, 1959).

Mozart and Beethoven, who by 1830 were already for progressive taste 'the ancients', the revered figures in the background of 'moderns' like Rossini, Spohr and (later) Mendelssohn and Berlioz.[1] It is well known that one of Beethoven's last actions was to dictate a letter of thanks to 'the generous Englishmen' of the Philharmonic Society who had invited him to London and, in his last illness and need, had sent him a loan of £100.[2]

A similar division is found in opera. The King's Theatre, the only international opera-house, was almost exclusively aristocratic in subscribers and mainly Italian in programmes. 'Italian' meant operas with libretti in Italian, performed by a visiting company of Italian singers: for German opera one needed a German company. This mechanical language-barrier partly explains why Mozart's Italian operas, especially *Don Giovanni*, appeared regularly but *Die Entführung aus dem Serail* and *Die Zauberflöte* very rarely. Outside Mozart the word 'Italian' conveyed a musical distinction which was based on superficial musical criteria: Italian opera and above all Rossini were light and lucid in texture, built of arias melodious and leisurely in development, whereas 'the German school' seemed heavy, compressed and abrupt.[3] For this reason the King's Theatre was filled with Rossini, Donizetti, Bellini and many minor contemporaries. The first non-Italian opera given there was *Die Zauberflöte* in 1829, nearly forty years after Mozart's death, and such performances remained very rare after that date. It was, in contrast, the middle-class and knowledgeable musicians, disapproving of the superficiality of the fashionable taste for Italian opera, who championed 'the German school' and agitated for those rare performances of *Die Zauberflöte*,

---

[1] It is worth noting, however, that praise of Beethoven remained ambiguous. He was often called 'wild' and 'eccentric', and seen as restlessly searching for novelty.

[2] While other concerts existed—notably those of the City Amateur Concert Society—they were not a strong power in public taste. Chamber concerts in the modern sense were not initiated until 1835.

[3] 'The German school' thus underwent the criticism previously (and often still) made about Mozart: *The Times* in 1812 had found *La Clemenza di Tito* 'ponderous and laboured, full of disjointed harmonies' and 'scientific discordance' (5 March 1812). It was still true in 1837 that 'the upper classes of this country who are patrons of the Italian opera, are no admirers of Mozart, or of any composer who is voted *passé*. They admire music which is new and of a light character.' (*The musical world*, v (1837), 124.)

Fidelio and *Der Freischütz*.[1] For lighter musical entertainment
they went to Drury Lane or Covent Garden for 'English
operas'—usually a pantomime-like form of spoken play interspersed with songs, for which Peacock's own very popular
Maid Marian needed very little adaptation.

The Ancient Concerts and Italian opera were fashionable
social occasions: hearing the music was secondary. Aristocratic
behaviour was suitably insolent and barbarian in talking,
booing and fighting for seats. The cult of the *prima donna*
meant that operas were compressed or rearranged so as to
form a programme around the 'stars'. Their excessive fees
made the supporting singers and chorus poor and the general
production skimped. Only one rehearsal was normally held,
which the leading singers did not attend, and the actual performance was helped along by an active prompter. Elaborate
stage machinery was demanded by the audience, which was
one reason why the final scene of *Don Giovanni* was almost
invariably omitted, the Don's descent into Hell providing a
perfect theatrical climax.

For these reasons, the reviews in the daily papers mainly
concerned the production, the *prima donna* and the fashionable
audience. They were also brief, as were many of Peacock's for
The examiner, which gave weekly reviews of both opera and
Philharmonic concerts. The only musical periodical of the early
1830s was *The harmonicon*: its only companion, *The quarterly
musical magazine and review*, ended in 1828 and, although a few
others began, they ceased publication almost immediately. The
readership of *The harmonicon* was largely composed of professional musicians, and its editor, W. Ayrton, gave encouragement to young composers. Its reviews, especially Ayrton's,
provide the best comparison with Peacock's.[2]

*

[1] On 'subscription nights' the manager had to present the requests of the aristocratic subscribers: but on 'benefit nights' he could give 'the opportunity to that
large and increasing body of classical amateurs (and which is composed almost
exclusively of the middle class of life) to hear such music as *they* prefer. The
majority of that immense audience that other evening [for *Don Giovanni*,
27 April, 1837], to all appearance, came from the East of Pall Mall.' (*The
musical world*, v, 124; part of the review quoted in previous note.)
[2] *The harmonicon* reviews are unsigned: while Ayrton is believed to have written
the principal reviews, no certain proof exists.

Peacock constantly attacks the ignorance and dishonesty of other reviewers:

> The Times has rare faculties of seeing and hearing. It contrived on Thursday night, to see the whole of Rossini's *Tancredi* though only the first act was performed.[1]

Of Rossini's *Ricciardo e Zoraide*,

> The Morning Post says, 'We have heard the conceptions and feelings of the composer fully worked out and displayed for the first time', from which we may infer it to have been an original conception of Rossini, that his hero should begin his part with a cavatina from *Ermione*, and terminate it with a rondo by Pacini.[2]

Not even *The harmonicon* is innocent:

> It is amusing enough that our friend of the *Harmonicon*...actually censured the English opera management for having restored the original conclusion [to Don Giovanni], which, nevertheless, was not done on any one night of the performance, as we took some pains to ascertain. This is only one instance, among many, which we could accumulate, in which the critics of that candid journal seem to have dispensed with the small preliminary of being present at the performances they criticise.[3]

These exposures of the critics' dishonesty involve exposures of the management's productions, which mangle Rossini for the benefit of the *prima donna* and Mozart for the sake of stage-effects. Peacock can make his charges with authority because of his superior conscientiousness and his superior musical knowledge: unlike some reviewers he can distinguish between Pacini and Rossini, and his knowledge derives from study of the scores and libretti, not just from frequenting the

---

[1] *The examiner* (7 July 1833), p. 421. *All* references to Peacock's music reviews are given to the original. They have not been reprinted in the Halliford Edition or elsewhere, unless otherwise stated.

[2] *Ibid.* (20 Feb. 1831), p. 118.

[3] *Ibid.* (19 June 1831), p. 389. *The harmonicon* review in question (VIII (1830), 354) does attack the producer's judgement 'in retaining the latter part of the opera' as 'the interest of the piece ceases with the hero: all that follows is theatrically tame and redundant'. In fact the production itself broke off at that point. *The harmonicon* lamely defended itself (IX (1831), 182): its report 'was written after witnessing the performance of the opera up to the close of the supper scene, and the entry of the fire and smoke, at which point, considering our duty done, we quitted the theatre'.

King's Theatre. On the conclusion of *Don Giovanni* this knowledge deepens into superior musical and dramatic insight. For *The harmonicon* voiced the overwhelming opinion of the day that it was right to omit the final scene:

the interest of the piece ceases with the disappearance of the hero: all that follows is theatrically tame and redundant.[1]

The manager has, and very wisely, omitted the last scene, which, splendid as is the chorus, is injurious to the effect of the opera as a whole.[2]

Peacock campaigned for a completed performance:

Don Juan's first introduction to a modern English audience was in a pantomime (at Drury Lane we believe), which ended with the infernal regions, a shower of fire, and a dance of devils. Mozart's opera has, properly, no such conclusion. Flames arise—a subterranean chorus is heard—Don Juan sinks into the abyss—the ground closes above him—Leporello remains on the stage: a strongly-marked modulation leads from the key of D minor into that of G major, with a change from common time andante to triple time allegro assai; and the other characters, ignorant of the catastrophe, rush in to seek their revenge:

        'Ah! dov'è il perfido?
        Dov'è l'indegno? &c.'

Leporello explains the adventure, and after a general exclamation, a solemn pause and an exceedingly sweet larghetto movement, in which the dramatis personae dispose of themselves, 'Or che tutti, O mio tesoro', the opera is wound up by a fugue in D major—'Questo è il fin di chi fa mal'; one of the very finest things in dramatic music, and the most appropriate possible termination of the subject; and yet is this most noble composition, this most fitting and genuine conclusion, sacrificed to a dance of devils flashing torches of rosin, for no earthly reason but that so ended the Drury Lane pantomime.[3]

Here musical analysis combines with a grasp of dramatic significance. For Peacock, the hero, despite *The harmonicon*, is not the whole. Nor by implication is Don Giovanni altogether the hero. Mozart's response to him, and our own, is complex or ambiguous: but we have a growing sense, sharpened by the last act and confirmed by the final scene, that Giovanni is not

[1] *The harmonicon*, VIII (Aug. 1830), 354 (almost certainly by Ayrton).
[2] *Ibid.* XI (Mar. 1833), 66.
[3] Review of Lord Mount Edgcumbe, *Musical reminiscences*, in *The London review*, I (1835), 181 (reprinted in Halliford, IX, 238–9).

an ungovernable force of life but a sterile and self-bound figure who interferes with life, tries to destroy it but is destroyed by it. The last scene therefore conveys in confirmation not just a moralistic message that 'evil-doers will be damned' but a deeper and more positive sense that 'life will go on'—life as represented by the triumphant lovers of the final sextet. Of course Peacock does not spell out his interpretation, nor would he choose those terms. But, in suggestive if more strictly musical terms of transitions and contrasts of time, tone and key, he conveys a similar sense of the scene's function as a 'most noble . . . fitting and genuine conclusion'.

If Peacock's musical taste was not superficial, neither was it narrow or conservative. This can best be illustrated by a contrast with Lord Mount Edgcumbe, using as framework his review of the latter's *Musical reminiscences; containing an account of the Italian opera in England from 1773.*

Mount Edgcumbe was a conservative for two reasons. He was aristocratic enough to love 'ancient music', yet too old to share the complementary aristocratic taste for the latest Italian operas and singers. In many passages, which Peacock marked in his copy but of which he quoted only a few in his review, Mount Edgcumbe admits himself to be *laudator temporis acti*: 'so great a change has taken place within a few years that I can no longer receive from it [the Italian opera] any pleasure approaching to that which I used to experience'.[1]

In so far as a critical judgement is involved in his conservatism, this represents it: in time the 'trifling frippery' of modern music will pass away 'and be replaced by one more true to nature, more resembling at least, if not quite reverting to, that simpler kind, which must invariably please all who are susceptible of feeling the genuine, unsophisticated expression of really fine music'.[2] Peacock's review deserves credit for distinguishing negative prejudice for the familiar—'the good old style'[3]—from the positive criteria of simplicity, and making the latter come alive in a really intelligent form. He argues that 'The business, indeed, of the lyrical dramatist is to present,

---

[1] *Musical reminiscences* (London, 1835), 1 (not quoted in Peacock's review).
[2] *Ibid.* p. xi.   [3] *Ibid.*

with the most perfect simplicity, the leading and natural ideas of an impassioned action, divested of all imagery not arising from spontaneous feeling.'[1] So the libretti of Italian opera give, 'with little or no ornament, the language of passion in its simplest form: a clear and strong outline to be filled up by the music'.[2] This is contrasted with the decoration and false imagery of modern English lyrics and poetry, which Peacock perceptively links with the emotional spirit of the 1830s—hardness disguised by cant and show. (By instancing Moore's songs he complements the account of Moore's prose in *The epicurean* and the *Life of Byron*, where he shows that false style betrays false sentiments and cant about, for example, Byron's religion.)

Our old English songs were models of simplicity, but our modern songs are almost all false sentiment, overwhelmed with imagery utterly false to nature...Mr. Moore, with his everlasting 'brilliant and sparkling' metaphors, has contributed to lead the *servum pecus* into this limbo of poetical vanity: But the original cause lies deeper: namely, in a very general diffusion of heartlessness and false pretension.[3]

As with the ideal libretto, so with the music, and with the singers' execution. Among Mount Edgcumbe's lengthy descriptions of famous voices Peacock marked in his copy the praise of Pacchierotti—'his own supreme excellence lay in touching expression'[4]—and the criticism of Mrs Billington: 'She possessed not the feeling to give touching expression, even when she sang with the utmost delicacy and consummate skill.'[5] Peacock drew out this criterion of 'expression—expression— expression' and developed it, with telling illustrations, in his contrast of two prima donnas of 1832: 'both had sweetness and good execution; but Madame Cinti was as cold as an icicle, and Mdlle. Schneider was all feeling and expression'.[6]

It has now been seen that Peacock did not share Mount Edgcumbe's indiscriminate rejection of contemporary Italian opera as 'modern frippery'. He responded to the excitement

---

[1] *London review*, i (1835), 177 (reprinted in Halliford, ix, 230).
[2] *Ibid.* p. 178 (and Halliford, ix, 232).
[3] *Ibid.* p. 179 (and Halliford, ix, 234).   [4] *Musical reminiscences*, p. 13.
[5] *Ibid.* p. 47: quoted by Peacock in *London review*, i (1835), 90.
[6] *Ibid.* p. 83 (and Halliford, ix, 243).

and variety of Rossini, while seeing that Bellini, with a lesser range and more even tenor, had more depth. He finds satisfaction in Bellini, his criterion of simplicity, and very accurately characterises him:

Bellini's forte was in the pathetic; but he has many charming melodies of a more lively character, all tinged, however, in some degree with the tone of melancholy which was natural to his mind. There is...a peculiar beauty and almost classical simplicity in the rhythm of his compositions...[1]

Bellini's great force is in melody...his harmony wants depth and variety: he rather multiplies the repetitions of the chord than gives distinct business to the several components of the score...it has neither the splendid variety of Rossini, nor the consummate combinations of Mozart, nor the torrent of sound of Beethoven, with its mysterious current of murmured undersong.[2]

While it is true that his own reviews of individual operas like *Norma* are not as interesting as this, Peacock's article on Bellini contrasts with the incomprehension of *The harmonicon*, which found him 'feeble stuff', wrote of *Norma* that but for three pieces nothing 'has the slightest pretence to originality, or produces the least effect', and thought reviewing him was 'a wanton waste of ink more valuable than Bellini's opera' itself.[3]

Peacock is again superior in his reaction to Paganini, whom *The harmonicon* greeted purely as a fashionable virtuoso peddling novelties. In its first notice that periodical describes Paganini's technical skill and comments, 'it will be obvious that we think Paganini the most astonishing violinist that ever appeared. But whether we consider him the best is another matter, and a question to be entered into in our next, by which time the present *rage* will be a little abated'.[4] Having sat on the fence until the mob had turned, the periodical offered a sneering notice of 'the grasping Italian' with a longer derogatory article of which the tone is as follows: 'If Paganini really produces so much effect on his single string, à fortiori he would draw forth much more from two. Why not therefore

---

[1] *Ibid.* II (1836), 475 (reprinted in Halliford, IX, 330).
[2] *Ibid.* p. 469 (and Halliford, IX, 321).
[3] XI (July and Aug. 1833), 160 and 183.   [4] IX (July 1831), 81.

employ them?—because he is waxing exceedingly wealthy playing on one only.'[1] In contrast Peacock draws attention to Paganini's genuine extension of musical expression:

Paganini draws forth from his instrument notes and combinations which (in the modern world) none before him have produced or dreamed of: wild and wonderful alike in the strongest bursts of power, and in the softest and sweetest touches, air-drawn and evanescent as the voices of distant birds. The triumph of mechanical skill, astonishing as it is in itself, is the smallest part of the wonder. The real magic is not the novelty of the feat, but the surpassing beauty of the effect...Novelty, of course, enters into the charm of the effect: but the great charm lies deeper than novelty: the perception of surpassing beauty would remain, if that of rarity and strangeness were withdrawn.[2]

Peacock's flexibility of musical taste, his recognition of the genuinely new development in Bellini or Paganini, may be underlined by a comparison of two critical passages. The first is from Mount Edgcumbe's *Reminiscences*: the second, from Peacock's review of that book.

I think I may venture to predict that Rossini will not have ceased to write before he will cease to be remembered, and that his music will be thrown aside as that of many of his predecessors and superiors already is; while the name of Mozart, with those of his two great countrymen Handel and Haydn, will live for ever.[3]

Peacock's passage was clearly suggested by this one, which he marked in his copy, but has two profound differences. For Mount Edgcumbe, Mozart's authority is merely that of the established and familiar figure, comparable to Handel's and Haydn's authority of age, their status as 'ancient music'. For Peacock, Mozart bears the authority of being 'identical with nature': he feelingly describes in Mozart's music the timeless validity that Johnson found in Shakespeare. At the same time, that sense of Mozart's 'authority' does not constrict Peacock's appreciation of lesser or later composers, as it does Mount Edgcumbe's. Rossini deserves a comparison with Paësiello as well as with Mozart.

[1] IX (Aug. 1831), 190.
[2] *The examiner* (12 June 1831), pp. 313–14 (reprinted in Halliford, IX, 444).
[3] Mount Edgcumbe, *Musical reminiscences*, p. 132. Not quoted in the review.

There has been an increase of excitement in the world of reality, and that of imagination has kept it company... There can be no question that Rossini's music is more spirit-stirring than Paësiello's... We were present at the first performance of an opera of Rossini's in England: Il Barbiere di Siviglia, in March 1818. We saw at once that there was a great revolution in dramatic music. Rossini burst on the stage like a torrent, and swept everything before him except Mozart, who stood, and will stand, alone and unshaken, like the Rock of Ages, because his art is like Shakespeare's, identical with nature, based on principles that cannot change till the constitution of the human race itself be changed, and therefore secure of admiration through all time, as the drapery of the Greek statues has been through all the varieties of fashion.[1]

Peacock's grasp of the nature of authority, and of the tact needed in using it, lies behind the allusion to Mount Edgcumbe in the article on Bellini:

Akin to the pedantry of inflexible rules is that of entrenching the want of tact and feeling behind the authority of great names—saying, 'This is nought, because it is not like Mozart, or Haydn, or Beethoven, or Handel, and thus sweeping away all modern music as with the fire of an impregnable battery. All the great names thus used had, in their own day, precisely the same sort of artillery pointed against themselves. When Beethoven was first heard of in England, it was as a madman who wrote crazy music which nobody could perform.'[2]

So with rules: Peacock rejects the expert in favour of the musical equivalent of the common reader without 'prejudices... and the dogmatism of learning':

Musical critics, who hear by rule have laboured to discredit Bellini. Fortunately reputations grow in despite of these systematical doctors. The feelings of the ordinary unsophisticated and unprejudiced hearer are always in advance of their rules; and that which has, in despite of them, been once stamped with popular favour, becomes a standard to the same class of critics of the next generation.[3]

While this suggests too unreserved a trust in 'popular favour' rather than, like Johnson, in the 'common sense' of human nature, it has its justification in that discriminating modernism already

[1] *London review*, I, 183–4 (reprinted in Halliford, IX, 244–5).
[2] *Ibid.*, II, 479 (and Halliford, IX, 336–7).
[3] *Ibid.* p. 478 (and Halliford, IX, 335).

noted in the middle-class audiences of the day. Peacock himself is of course an example of those professional classes and of that intelligent taste. Working at East India House, but with the time and keen interest for reviewing and for the background thought and study, he confirms a point made by Dr Temperley: 'England was the only country which had a professional class with the leisure, independence and influence to back its own opinions.'[1]

'It is fitting that there should be rules in science', says Peacock,

because they are the collected and concentrated experience of ages; but they are not to be converted into pedantic fetters to bind genius through all future time. As there is no possible sequence of sounds to which human passion does not give utterance, so there is no possible consonance and dissonance which will not find its fit place in dramatic music.[2]

It was, above all, Beethoven who was for him the genius who extended the possibilities of music. The full significance of his review of the first English performance of *Fidelio* in 1832 will be clearer if preceded by *The harmonicon*'s more conventional review of the same performance. After commenting on individual singers, *The harmonicon* continues:

But the finest composition, both in conception and dramatic effect, is the chorus of prisoners, which begins the finale of the first act. The performance of this, too, the subdued voices, the crescendoes, the sudden bursts of passion, all show the intelligence of the singers, and the industry of their director...

Feeling then, and most willingly acknowledging, all the beauties we have dwelt on, we must add that, as a whole, *Fidelio* is a heavy opera; there is an absence of variety, a want of two or three light pieces to contrast with the sombre character of the whole, and to relieve. The orchestral accompaniments are most highly and learnedly wrought, but too unremittingly full; every line in the score is literally crammed with notes, till the ear almost aches, and the mind is in a state of exhaustion, from the un-relaxing activity of every instrument in the band. Certainly there may be a redundancy as well as a paucity of harmony. If the Italian School...erred on the side of thinness,

---

[1] 'Instrumental music in England, 1800–1850', i, 32. Dr Temperley suggests this as one reason 'why the revival of Bach began in England as early as in Germany, and much earlier than in any other country'.
[2] *London review*, ii, 478 (and Halliford, ix, 335–6).

that of the German sometimes failed by running into the other extreme, and we reckon Beethoven among those who too often deluge vocal music with accompaniment. What, we may be asked, is the true medium? That, we reply, which may be found by examining the scores of Mozart's operas; and those also of Haydn's *Creation* and his *Seasons*. They are such as Beethoven would have written had he preceded, not followed, those illustrious men. He wished to achieve more than they had accomplished, and occasionally overloaded while he thought he was enriching.

Some short passages interspersed in *Fidelio* will remind the hearers of modulations and effects in Mozart's *Figaro* and in his *Don Giovanni*. These are not intentional, for the independent Beethoven was anything but a plagiarist, and are far from being disagreeable reminiscences; they show that his mind was imbued with the fine traits of his great predecessor.

Let all then true lovers of music hear *Fidelio*; should they think as we do, that its defect is sameness and want of relief—should they even feel the last note as a welcome sound—still, they will have heard enough to amply recompense them for what little trouble and expense they may have incurred. But they must not expect to hear Beethoven's chef d'œuvre; his Christus am Ohlberge, or Mount of Olives, is as a work of genius, superior to the only drama he ever set to music— *Fidelio*. His true greatness, however, is to be sought in his instrumental compositions; there he has no superior, notwithstanding his having followed those who may almost be said to have left no ground for a third to occupy. But though he found 'worlds exhausted', his genius 'imagined new'.[1]

This is not at all hostile. But it is very confused; confused by the new work, and therefore confused in its criteria and uncertain in the direction of its argument. It brings against *Fidelio*, nearly thirty years after its composition, the charge that it is unrelievedly heavy in mood and close-packed in harmonic texture. This was simply the conventional complaint of the day against 'the German school', and one that had sometimes been made at the first performances of Mozart's operas. Yet Mozart and Haydn are here cited as the authorities—illustrating Peacock's dictum that 'that which has, in despite of them [scientific critics] been once stamped with popular favour, becomes a standard to the same class of critics of the next generation'.[2] Beethoven's originality is seen as a gratuitous

---

[1] *The harmonicon*, x (June, 1832), 329.   [2] See above, p. 233.

deviation from classical practice rather than a creative extension of the possibilities of music. The final pointing to such an extension in Beethoven's instrumental music lacks conviction and supporting illustration. The reviewer is most sure of himself in praising the singers, chorus and direction.

Peacock too praised these:[1] but, as he pointed out after the poorer performance of the following year, 'The admiration which this masterpiece of dramatic music excites cannot now be ascribed, in any degree, to transcendent acting, or to anything but the intelligible development of its own intrinsic and indestructible beauty.'[2] The centre of his 1832 review indeed concerns the music:

Beethoven's *Fidelio* is the absolute perfection of dramatic music. It combines the profoundest harmony with melody that speaks to the soul. It carries to a pitch scarcely conceivable the true musical expression of the strongest passions, and the gentlest emotions, in all their shades and contrasts. The playfulness of youthful hope, the heroism of devoted love, the rage of the tyrant, the despair of the captive, the bursting of the sunshine of liberty upon the gloom of the dungeon, which are the great outlines of the feelings successively developed in this opera, are portrayed in music, not merely with truth of expression as that term might be applied to other works, but with a force and reality that makes music an intelligible language, possessing an illimitable power of pouring forth thought in sound. *Fidelio* is, we believe, Beethoven's only opera. It is the sun among the stars. It is not a step in the progress of dramatic music. It is a clear projection of it, a century in advance of its march.[3]

[1] As this praise, in itself superior to *The harmonicon*'s, has never been reprinted, it is worth giving here: 'This opera has been performed in a manner worthy of itself. Madame Schroeder Devrient possesses every requisite of the highest order for the lyrical stage. Her action is perfect nature. Her voice is sweet, clear, powerful, flexible; and above all, it is, both in speaking and singing, more pathetic and heart-touching than any we ever heard. Her intonation is unexceptionably true: her execution is at once highly finished, and of the most beautiful simplicity. The other characters are well sustained. The chorus is admirable. Each individual of it is an actor, discriminated in costume, in the business of the scene, and in the distribution of the music. They sing together, or in parts, with a precision, an expression, a real share and interest in what is going on, to which there has been no parallel in this country. The chorus of prisoners emerging into daylight, may alone be taken as a model of what a chorus ought to be.' (*The examiner* (27 May 1832) p. 340).

[2] *Ibid.* (14 Apr. 1833), p. 230.

[3] *Ibid.* (27 May 1832), p. 340 (and Halliford, IX, 432–3).

This has a tone and rhythm of breathless enthusiasm very rare in Peacock. As rare are the qualities it discerns in Beethoven. *Fidelio* is 'dramatic music' in the sense that *Macbeth* is dramatic poetry, and breaks the old concepts of 'the dress of thought' and truth of expression; rather, the music itself is 'an intelligible language...pouring forth thought in sound'. In this above all the opera is not just one more development in the tradition, it makes a creative leap 'a century in advance'. While Peacock never writes directly of them, all this applies as strikingly to Beethoven's later symphonies and quartets. The passage shows that Peacock found in Beethoven the revolutionary genius in music that he did not find in the literature of his age.

10

Conclusion

No underlining of the account of Peacock is offered here. For, as was stated in the Introduction, the aim has been to reopen his case and to present the complex evidence rather than fix a clear-cut judgement. This aim would be well served by closing the hearing with the very favourable evidence of his music criticism, and in particular the description of *Fidelio* just quoted. But some conclusions should be drawn as to method, critical approaches to a figure like Peacock and his relation to his age. This may be done through a series of essays written by John Stuart Mill, under the title 'The spirit of the age'. They appeared in *The examiner* from January to May 1831—in the exact months when Peacock published *Crotchet Castle*, and began writing music reviews for *The examiner*.

The 'spirit of the age', Mill opens, 'is in some measure a novel expression. I do not believe that it is to be met with in any work exceeding fifty years in antiquity...It is an idea essentially belonging to an age of change.'[1] In such an age,

> Mankind are then divided, into those who are still what they were, and those who have changed: into the men of the present age, and the men of the past. To the former, the spirit of the age is a subject of exultation; to the latter, of terror; to both, of eager and anxious interest. The wisdom of ancestors, and the march of intellect, are bandied from mouth to mouth.[2]

For individual 'men of the present age' the danger is over-optimism, intoxication with any development; for the mass, the evil is 'the *diffusion* of *superficial* knowledge'[3] without real grasp of the bewildering advance and variety of modern thought. But for Mill the alternative, to be men of the past, is no alternative at all. He instances Southey's *Colloquies on society* as 'the musings of a recluse' by one of 'those men who carry

---

[1] *The spirit of the age*, ed. F. A. von Hayek (Chicago, 1942), p. 1.
[2] *Ibid.*   [3] *Ibid.* p. 10.

their eyes in the back of their heads and can see no other portion of the destined track of humanity than that which it has already travelled'.[1] Mill's case against men like Southey is that 'Whatever we may think or affect to think of the present age, we cannot get out of it...to be either useful or at ease, we must even partake its character. No man whose good qualities were mainly those of another age, ever had much influence on his own.'[2]

This is a valid account of the ineffectuality and even the irrelevance of a simply conservative mind; and the description, throughout the essays, of an age of social and intellectual confusion fits both the period of the First Reform Bill and the earlier Regency decade of Peacock's major works. Mill helps to clarify the general issues involved in our judgement of Peacock. Yet, in exchange, our close study of Peacock suggests ways in which Mill has over-simplified those general issues, as a result of his own over-anxiety to find himself intellectually and to master the thought of his age.

This study has brought home the relation to one's age as a timeless and psychological problem. Where Peacock shows simple conservatism it is an inner state of inertia. In so far as this inertia concerns the mind rather than the heart and feelings, his 'judging by common sense' is rarely a matter of holding to the criteria of the previous age or of the eighteenth century, but 'merely another phrase for judging by first appearances'[3] or by lazy prejudice. Similarly, while it is true that many of Peacock's works are deliberate attempts to master and chart the currents of his age, one develops with the age less by 'study' or observation of an external body of facts, than by personal contacts and experiences. Just because lives differ, so we must look for these shaping experiences and contacts in different and sometimes hidden places. We have found them with Peacock in his friendship with Shelley and the crisis and change in his way of life after they grew apart. (With Crabbe one finds the equivalents in his marriage to a chronic manic-depressive, the trauma of his early poverty, his humiliating position at Belvoir and his humiliating experience of non-

---

[1] *Ibid.* p. 3.
[2] *Ibid.* p. 4.
[3] Mill's phrase, *ibid.* p. 28.

conformists.) The fact that the sources of insight are so personal means that a writer may develop at one point, grasp one strand of his age, and not others. It warns us to look for the results in many and perhaps unexpected directions, not just in the (now) most obvious ones.

The warning lets this study end with a reference back to Peacock's Shelleyan novels and to the music criticism.

Select Bibliography

Principles of Selection. This bibliography is not essential for the understanding of the footnotes, which give full reference to editions and works cited or quoted in the text in each chapter. All those editions and works, however, are here collected, together with other works which are not cited in the text but have assisted or influenced the book.

The following are excluded: some works marginal to the subject and quoted only once in the text; and primary and secondary works that have been consulted but have not been of material use (any reader will acknowledge this distinction).

Editions used. A flexible approach has been adopted. Works by the principal figures have normally been cited from modern complete editions. Modern editions of some individual works have been preferred if they have the advantages of a critical text and introduction (e.g. Brett-Smith's edition of Shelley's *Defence of poetry*). In other cases the first edition or first place of appearance has been used.

Arrangement. The bibliography is arranged as follows:

A. GENERAL WORKS ON THE LITERATURE OF THE PERIOD
   1. Regency and Early Victorian Surveys.
   2. Regency Reviewing.
   3. Modern Bibliography and Criticism.
   4. Relations with Germany.
   5. Classical Studies.

B. GENERAL WORKS ON SOCIETY
   1. Contemporary Works.
   2. Modern Studies.

C. GENERAL WORKS ON MUSIC
   1. Contemporary Music Periodicals.
   2. Contemporary Accounts
   3. Modern Works

D. PEACOCK

E. OTHER PRINCIPAL FIGURES
   Byron, Coleridge, Hazlitt, Hogg, Crabb Robinson, Shelley, Southey.

F. MARGINAL AND MISCELLANEOUS WRITERS

SELECT BIBLIOGRAPHY

As the book relates individual writers to their period, the division into general and particular works is difficult and complete cross-reference impracticable.

A. GENERAL WORKS ON THE LITERATURE OF THE PERIOD

I. REGENCY AND EARLY VICTORIAN SURVEYS

W. Hazlitt, 'On the living poets' (1818) and 'The spirit of the age' (1825), in *Complete works*, ed. P. P. Howe, London, 1930–4, vols. V and XI.

R. H. Horne, *A new spirit of the age*, London, 1844.

Bulwer-Lytton, *England and the English*, 2 vols., London, 1834.

J. S. Mill, 'The spirit of the age' (1831), ed. with introductory essay by F. A. von Hayek, Chicago, 1942.

    'Bentham' (1838) and 'Coleridge' (1840), *Mill on Bentham and Coleridge*, ed. with introduction by F. R. Leavis, London, 1950.

Stendhal (H. Beyle), *Selected journalism from the English reviews*, ed. G. Strickland, London, 1959.

T. N. Talford, 'An attempt to estimate the poetical talent of the present age, including a sketch of the history of poetry, and characters of Southey, Crabbe, Scott, Moore, Lord Byron, Campbell, Lamb, Coleridge, and Wordsworth', *The pamphleteer*, May 1815, vol. V.

See also:

P. Hodgart and T. Redpath, edd. *Romantic perspectives: the work of Crabbe, Blake, Wordsworth and Coleridge as seen by their contemporaries and by themselves*, London, 1964.

2. REGENCY REVIEWING

Periodicals and articles are not listed here, but are individually cited in footnotes. The following give information and criticism:

J. Clive, *Scotch reviewers; the Edinburgh review, 1802–1815*, London, 1957.

W. A. Copinger, *On the authorship of the first hundred numbers of the Edinburgh review*, Manchester, 1895 (cf. Schneider *et al.*, below).

R. G. Cox, 'Nineteenth-century periodical criticism', unpublished Cambridge Ph.D. thesis, 1935.

W. Graham, *Tory criticism in the Quarterly review, 1809–53*, Columbia, 1921 (cf. Shine, below).

W. E. Houghton, ed. *The Wellesley index to Victorian periodicals, 1824–1900*, Toronto, 1966.

SELECT BIBLIOGRAPHY

G. L. Nesbitt, *Benthamite reviewing: the Westminster review 1824–36*, New York, 1934.

E. Schneider, I. Griggs and J. D. Kern, 'Early Edinburgh reviewers: a new list', *Modern philology* (1946), vol. XLIII.

H. and H. C. Shine, *The Quarterly review under Gifford: identification of contributors, 1809–24*, Chapel Hill, 1949.

3. MODERN BIBLIOGRAPHY AND CRITICISM

(*a*) *Critical bibliographies*

C. W. and L. H. Houtchens, edd. *The English romantic poets and essayists, a review of research and criticism*, New York, 1957.

T. M. Raysor, ed. *The English romantic poets, a review of research*, revised edition, New York, 1956.

(*b*) *Individual works*

U. Amarasinghe, *Dryden and Pope in the early nineteenth century: a study of changing literary taste, 1800–1830*, Cambridge, 1962.

M. Arnold, 'The function of criticism at the present time', *Essays in criticism*, 1st series, London, 1865.

I. Babbitt, *Rousseau and romanticism*, Boston (Mass.), 1919.

D. Craig, *Scottish literature and the Scottish people, 1680–1830*, London, 1961.

I. Jack, *English literature, 1815–1832* (O[xford] H[istory of] E[nglish] L[iterature], vol. x), Oxford, 1963.

F. R. Leavis, *Revaluation*, London, 1936.

F. E. Pierce, *Currents and eddies in the English romantic generation*, Yale and Oxford, 1918.

W. L. Renwick, *English literature 1789–1815* (O.H.E.L. vol. IX), Oxford, 1963.

R. Wellek, *A history of modern criticism*, vol. II, *The romantic age*, New Haven, 1955.

4. RELATIONS WITH GERMANY

T. Carlyle, 'The state of German literature', *Edinburgh review* (1827), vol. XLVII.

J.-M. Carre, *Goethe en Angleterre*, Paris, 1920.

T. De Quincey, 'Of the English notices of Kant', *Collected writings*, ed. D. Masson, vol. x, Edinburgh, 1890.

W. A. Dunn, *Thomas De Quincey's relation to German literature*, Strasburg, 1900.

F. W. Stokoe, *German influence in the romantic period, 1788–1818*, Cambridge, 1926.

R. Wellek, *Immanuel Kant in England, 1793–1838*, Princeton, 1931.

5. CLASSICAL STUDIES

D. Bush, *Mythology and the romantic tradition in English poetry*, Cambridge, Mass., 1937.

M. L. Clarke, *Greek studies in England 1700–1830*, London, 1945.

H. Levin, *The broken column. A study in romantic Hellenism*, Cambridge, Mass., 1931.

F. Nietzsche on classical studies; selections translated and introduced by W. Arrowsmith, *Arion, a quarterly journal of classical culture*, Univ. of Texas Press, vol. II.

F. E. Pierce, 'The Hellenic current in English nineteenth-century poetry', *Journal of English and Germanic philology* (1917), vol. XVI.

B. GENERAL WORKS ON SOCIETY

1. CONTEMPORARY WORKS

S. Bamford, *Passages in the life of a radical*, 2nd edition, 2 vols. in one, Heywood, Lancs., 1842.

W. Godwin, *Of population*, London, 1820.

C. Knight, *Passages of a working life*, 3 vols., London, 1864–5.

T. Malthus, *An essay on the principle of population* (1798), 4th edition, 2 vols., London, 1807.

Prince Puckler-Muskau, *A tour in England*, 4 vols., London, 1832.

2. MODERN STUDIES

H. A. Boner, *Hungry generations: the nineteenth-century case against Malthusianism*, New York, 1955.

F. K. Brown, *Fathers of the Victorians: the age of Wilberforce*, Cambridge, 1961.

J. H. Clapham, *An economic history of modern Britain: the early railway age, 1820–1850*, London, 1930.

D. V. Class, ed. *Introduction to Malthus*, London, 1953 (two essays by, and modern essays on, Malthus).

E. Halévy, *The growth of philosophical radicalism*, trans. M. Morris, reprinted London, 1952.

  A history of the English people in the nineteenth century. Vol. I, *England in 1815*; vol. II, *The Liberal awakening (1815–1830)*, trans. E. I. Watkin and D. A. Barker, 2nd edition reprinted London, 1961.

E. Moers, *The dandy. Brummell to Beerbohm*, London, 1960.

M. J. Quinlan, *Victorian prelude. A history of English manners, 1700–1830*, New York, 1941.

D. Read, *Peterloo, the 'Massacre' and its background*, Manchester, 1958.

SELECT BIBLIOGRAPHY

L. Stephen, *The English Utilitarians*, 2 vols., reprinted London, 1950.
G. M. Trevelyan, *British history in the nineteenth century and after, 1782–1919*, London, 1937.
G. Wallas, *The life of Francis Place*, revised edition, London, 1918.
R. J. White, *Waterloo to Peterloo*, London, 1957.

C. GENERAL WORKS ON MUSIC

I. CONTEMPORARY MUSIC PERIODICALS

The harmonicon, a journal of music, 1823–33.
The musical world, 1836–90.
The quarterly musical magazine and review, 1818–28.

2. CONTEMPORARY ACCOUNTS

Lord Mount Edgcumbe, *Musical reminiscences; containing an account of the Italian opera in England from 1713. Fourth edition: continued to the present time, and including the festival in Westminster Abbey*, London, 1834.
L. Spohr, *Autobiography*, trans. from the German, London, 1865.

3. MODERN WORKS

G. Grove, *Dictionary of music and musicians*, 5th edition, ed. E. Blom, Oxford, 1954.
E. D. Mackerness, *A social history of English music* (Studies in Social History), London, 1964.
N. Temperley, 'Instrumental music in England 1800–1850', unpublished Cambridge Ph.D. thesis, 1959.
'Mozart's influence on English music', *Music and letters* (1961), vol. XLII.

D. PEACOCK

I. BIBLIOGRAPHIES

Halliford Edition (see below), vol. I, pp. 182–6. (Lists of works and of reviews, books and articles about Peacock.)
B. Read, 'The critical reputation of Peacock, with an enumerative bibliography of works by and about Peacock from February 1800 to June 1958', unpublished Boston University thesis, 1959: available in Xerox prints or microfilm. (Adds minor items to Halliford's lists, but discovers no significant variations of opinion about Peacock.)

2. EDITION

Works, Halliford Edition, ed. H. F. B. Brett-Smith and C. E. Jones, 10 vols., London, 1924–34.

SELECT BIBLIOGRAPHY

3. WORKS NOT IN HALLIFORD

Music reviews in *The globe and traveller* and *The examiner*, 1830–4: complete list in Halliford, IX, pp. 415–20 (Halliford reprints selected passages, *ibid.* pp. 421–45).

Letters in *New Shelley letters*, ed. W. S. Scott, London, 1948.

Letters in *Shelley and his circle, 1773–1822.* The Carl H. Pforzheimer library, ed. K. N. Cameron, 2 vols. (in progress), Cambridge, Mass., 1961– .

Unpublished letters in the Broughton Papers, British Museum Unplaced MSS. 47225.

4. IMPORTANT CONTEMPORARY REVIEWS

'Crotchet Castle' in *Westminster review* (1831), vol. XV.

'Headlong Hall', 'Nightmare Abbey', 'Maid Marian', 'Crotchet Castle' (Standard Novels Edition), *Edinburgh review* (1839), vol. LXVIII.

5. BIOGRAPHY AND CRITICISM

R. Buchanan, 'Thomas Love Peacock: a personal reminiscence', *New quarterly magazine* (1875), vol. IV.

O. W. Campbell, *Peacock* (English novelists), London, 1953.

R. W. Chapman, 'Thomas Love Peacock', *Johnsonian and other essays and reviews*, Oxford, 1953.

C. van Doren, *The life of T. L. Peacock*, London, 1911.

A. M. Freeman, *T. L. Peacock: a critical study*, London, 1911.

F. J. Glasheen, 'Shelley and Peacock', letter to *Times literary supplement*, 18 Oct. 1941.

Lord Houghton, Preface to the *Works of Peacock*, ed. H. Cole, London, 1875, vol. I.

H. House, 'The novels of Thomas Love Peacock', *The listener*, 8 Dec. 1949.

I. Jack, *English literature 1815–32*, Oxford, 1963, chapter VII.

W. F. Kennedy, 'Peacock's economists: some mistaken identities', *Nineteenth-century fiction* (Sept. 1966), vol. XXI.

G. D. Klingopulos, 'The spirit of the age in prose', *From Blake to Byron*, ed. B. Ford (Pelican guide to English literature, vol. V), London, 1957.

J.-J. Mayoux, *Un Epicuréan anglais: Thomas Love Peacock*, Paris, 1933.

E. Nicholls, 'A biographical notice of Thomas Love Peacock, by his grand-daughter', *Works*, ed. H. Cole, London, 1875, vol. I.

M. Praz, *The hero in eclipse in Victorian fiction*, London, 1956. (Part I, 'Romanticism turns bourgeois: Peacock'.)

SELECT BIBLIOGRAPHY

J. B. Priestley, *Thomas Love Peacock* (English men of letters series), London, 1927; new edition, 1967.

P. J. Salz, 'Peacock's use of music in his novels', *Journal of English and Germanic philology* (1955), vol. LIV.

C. H. Soleta, 'Peacock and Shelley', *Notes and queries*, 12 Nov. 1949.

J. I. M. Stewart, *Thomas Love Peacock* (British Council booklets, Writers and their work, no. 156), London, 1963.

Sir E. Strachey, 'Recollections of Thomas Love Peacock', in Peacock's *Calidore and miscellanea*, ed. R. Garnett, London, 1891.

E. OTHER PRINCIPAL FIGURES
BYRON
1. EDITIONS

Works...poetry, ed. E. H. Coleridge, 7 vols., London, 1898–1904.

Byron's 'Don Juan'. A variorum edition, ed. T. G. Steffan and W. W. Pratt, 4 vols., Austin, Texas, 1957.

Thomas Moore, *Letters and journals of Lord Byron: with notices of his life*, 2 vols., London, 1830. (Commonly cited as Moore's *Life of Byron*.)

Works...letters and journals, ed. R. E. Prothero, 6 vols., London, 1898–1901.

Correspondence, ed. John Murray, 2 vols., London, 1922.

Byron: a self-portrait. Letters and diaries, 1798–1824, ed. P. Quennell, 2 vols., London, 1950.

T. J. Wise, *A bibliography of the writings in verse and prose of George Gordon Noel, Baron Byron*, 2 vols., London, 1932–3 (contains fuller versions of some letters, and a discussion of the letters about Keats).

His very self and voice: collected conversations of Lord Byron, ed. E. J. Lovell, New York, 1954 (complete, except that it selects from Lady Blessington and Medwin).

2. CONTEMPORARY ACCOUNTS

Lady Blessington, *Conversations of Lord Byron with the Countess of Blessington*, London, 1834.

T. Guiccioli, *My recollections of Lord Byron: and those of eye-witnesses of his life*, trans. H. E. H. Jerningham, 2 vols., London, 1869.

(J. G. Lockhart), *John Bull's letter to Lord Byron* (1821), ed. A. L. Strout, Norman, Oklahoma, 1947.

T. Medwin, *Conversations of Lord Byron: noted during a residence with his lordship at Pisa, in the years 1821 and 1822*, London, 1824.

SELECT BIBLIOGRAPHY

Stendhal (M. H. Beyle), several articles collected in *Selected journalism*, ed. G. Strickland, London, 1959.

E. J. Trelawny, *Recollections of the last days of Shelley and Byron*, London, 1858.

3. LATER BOOKS AND ARTICLES

M. Arnold, Preface to his selection *The poetry of Byron*, London, 1881: reprinted in his *Essays in criticism*, 2nd series, London, 1888.

S. C. Chew, *Byron in England: his fame and after-fame*, London, 1924.

T. S. Eliot, 'Byron', *On poetry and poets*, London, 1957.

D. V. Erdman, 'Byron and social revolt in England', *Science and poetry* (1947), vol. XI.

'Lord Byron and the genteel reformers', *P.M.L.A.* (1941), vol. LVI.

H. J. C. Grierson, 'Lord Byron: Arnold and Swinburne' and 'Byron and English society' in his *The background to English literature*, London, 1925.

E. D. H. Johnson, 'Don Juan in England', *E.L.H.: a journal of English literary history* (1944), vol. XI.

M. K. Joseph, *Byron the poet*, London, 1964.

F. R. Leavis, 'Byron's satire', *Revaluation*, London, 1936.

L. A. Marchand, *Byron. A biography*, 3 vols., London, 1957.

D. L. Moore, *The late Lord Byron*, London, 1961.

P. Quennell, *Byron, the years of fame*, London, 1935.

Byron in Italy, London, 1941.

J. J. van Rennes, *Bowles, Byron and the Pope controversy*, Amsterdam, 1927.

W. W. Robson, 'Byron as poet', *Proceedings of the British Academy* (1957), vol. XLIII (reprinted in his *Critical essays*, London, 1966).

A. Rutherford, *Byron. A critical study*, Edinburgh, 1961.

COLERIDGE

1. POETRY

Christabel, Kubla Khan, The pains of sleep, London, 1816.

Sibylline leaves, London, 1817.

Poetical works, ed. E. H. Coleridge, 2 vols., Oxford, 1912.

2. PROSE WORKS

The friend. A literary, moral, and political weekly paper...(Penrith, 1809–10), with alterations and additions, 3 vols., London, 1818.

Lectures on Shakespeare: MSS. and reports printed in *Coleridge's Shakespearean criticism*, ed. T. M. Raysor, 2 vols., Cambridge, Mass., 1930.

SELECT BIBLIOGRAPHY

The statesman's manual: or the Bible the best guide to political skill and foresight. A lay sermon addressed to the higher classes of society, London, 1816.

Blessed are ye that sow beside all waters: a lay sermon addressed to the higher and middle classes on the existing distresses and discontents. London, 1817.

Biographia literaria, or biographical sketches of my literary life and opinions, 2 vols., London, 1817.

On method: general introduction to *Encyclopaedia metropolitana,* London, 1817.

3. CONVERSATIONS, NOTEBOOKS AND LETTERS

Specimens of the table-talk of the late Samuel Taylor Coleridge, ed. H. N. Coleridge, 2 vols., London, 1835.

Coleridge the talker: a series of contemporary descriptions and comments, ed. with critical introduction by R. W. Armour and R. F. Howes, Oxford, 1940.

Inquiring spirit: a new presentation of Coleridge from his published and unpublished prose writings, ed. K. Coburn, London, 1951 (draws on as yet unpublished notebooks).

Notebooks, ed. K. Coburn, vols. I–II (two separately bound parts to each volume: in progress), London 1957–62.

4. CONTEMPORARY REVIEWS
(*a*) *Individual*

Christabel (etc.), *Edinburgh review* (1816), vol. XXVII.

Christabel (etc.), *Monthly review* (1817), vol. LXXXII.

'An appeal apologetic from Philip Drunk to Philip Sober' (on 'Christabel'), *The athenaeum,* 2 July 1828 (by John Sterling).

'Coleridge's poetical works', *Blackwood's magazine* (1834), vol. XXXVI (by John Wilson).

'The poetical works', *Quarterly review* (1834), vol. LII (by H. N. Coleridge).

(*b*) *Hazlitt's articles on Coleridge* are collected in his *Works,* ed. Howe, to which references are given in footnotes to this thesis.

(*c*) *On the authorship of the* Edinburgh review *article on 'Christabel',* 1816, vol. XXVII.

P. L. Carver, 'Hazlitt's Contributions to the Edinburgh review', *Review of English studies* (1928), vol. IV.

E. W. Schneider, 'The unknown reviewer of *Christabel*: Jeffrey, Hazlitt, Tom Moore', *P.M.L.A.* (1955), vol. LXX.

H. H. Jordan, *Modern philology* (1956), vol. LIV.

E. W. Schneider, *P.M.L.A.* (1962), vol. LXXVII.

K. Coburn, *Times literary supplement*, 20 May 1965.

(Professor Schneider argues for Moore: Jordan argues for Hazlitt emended by Jeffrey. Professor Coburn produces the following entry from Coleridge's notebooks for Sept.–Oct. 1829: 'A great man is to write an article in the Edinburgh Review. And I am told that it would frighten me, if I heard his name. I do not quite believe this—no! not even tho' it should be Mr. Thomas Moore who had undertaken to strangle the Christabel for Mr. Jeffray [*sic*].' Miss Coburn also finds Miss Schneider's arguments for Moore 'cogent'. The matter can hardly be settled unless relevant letters of Moore or Jeffrey turn up.)

5. BIOGRAPHY AND CRITICISM

Anon. 'Coleridge on politics...a frightened philosopher', *Times literary supplement*, 9 July 1938.

T. Carlyle, *Life of Sterling*, London, 1851.

Reminiscences, ed. C. E. Norton, London, 1887.

J. Colmer, *Coleridge, critic of society*, Oxford, 1959.

T. De Quincey, 'Coleridge', *Collected writings*, ed. D. Masson, Edinburgh, 1889, vol. II.

'Coleridge and opium-eating', *Collected writings*, vol. V, Edinburgh, 1890.

'Conversation and Coleridge', *Posthumous works*, ed. A. H. Japp, London, 1893, vol. II.

H. House, *Coleridge*, London, 1953.

F. R. Leavis, 'Coleridge in criticism', *Scrutiny* (1941), vol. IX.

HAZLITT

I. EDITION

Complete works, ed. P. P. Howe, 21 vols, London, 1930–4.

2. BIOGRAPHY AND CRITICISM

H. Baker, *William Hazlitt*, Cambridge, Mass., 1962.

T. De Quincey, 'Notes on Gilfillan's literary portraits: William Hazlitt', *Collected writings*, ed. D. Masson, Edinburgh, 1890, vol. X.

H. W. Garrod, 'The place of Hazlitt in English criticism', *The profession of poetry and other lectures*, Oxford, 1929.

G. D. Klingopulos, 'Hazlitt as critic', *Essays in criticism* (1956), vol. IV.

'The spirit of the age in prose', *From Blake to Byron* (Pelican guide to English literature, vol. IV), London, 1957.

L. Stephen, 'Hazlitt', *Hours in a library*, 2nd series, London, 1876.

SELECT BIBLIOGRAPHY

HOGG

I. EDITIONS

Memoirs of Prince Alexy Haimatoff (1813), ed. with an introduction and Shelley's review by S. Scott, London (Folio Society), 1952.

New Shelley letters, ed. W. S. Scott, London, 1948. (Correspondence with Shelley, Mary Shelley, Hunt, Peacock, etc.)

After Shelley...the letters of T. J. Hogg to Jane Williams, ed. with a biographical introduction by S. Norman, London, 1934.

Two hundred and nine days: or, the journal of a traveller on the Continent, 2 vols., London, 1827.

Shelley at Oxford (1832), ed. with an introduction by R. A. Streatfield, London, 1904.

The life of Shelley (1858), ed. with an introduction by H. Wolfe, 2 vols., London, 1933.

2. UNCOLLECTED PERIODICAL ESSAYS

'Longus' and 'Apuleius', *The liberal*, 1823.

Review of J. Ebers's 'Seven years of the King's Theatre', *Edinburgh review* (1829), vol. XLIX.

'Recollections of childhood', 'Socratic irony' (two series of articles), *Monthly chronicle* (1839–41), vols. III–VII.

Other essays listed in Lady W. Scott (see below), p. 279.

3. BIOGRAPHY AND CRITICISM

M. Sadleir, 'Shelley's college friend, Thomas Jefferson Hogg. An episode in his later life', *University College record*, 1934.

Lady W. Scott, *Jefferson Hogg*, London, 1951.

HENRY CRABB ROBINSON

I. EDITIONS

Diary, reminiscences and correspondence, ed. T. Sadler, 3 vols., London, 1869.

Blake, Coleridge, Wordsworth, etc., being selections from the remains of Henry Crabb Robinson, ed. E. J. Morley, Manchester, 1922.

Correspondence of Henry Crabb Robinson with the Wordsworth circle (1808–66), ed. E. J. Morley, 2 vols., London, 1927.

Crabb Robinson in Germany, 1800–5: extracts from his correspondence, ed. E. J. Morley, Oxford, 1929.

Henry Crabb Robinson on books and their writers, ed. E. J. Morley, 3 vols., London, 1938.

2. UNCOLLECTED WORKS

Four 'Letters on German literature', *Monthly register* (1802 and 1803), vols. I and II.

Three 'Letters on the philosophy of Kant', *Monthly register* (1802 and 1803), vols. I and II.

'Wordsworth's Prelude', *Christian reformer* (1850), vol. VI.

Two letters about Wordsworth, *Times literary supplement*, 3 Nov. 1927.

Further miscellaneous works are listed in J. M. Baker (see below), pp. 245–8.

3. BOOKS AND ARTICLES

W. Bagehot, 'Crabb Robinson', *Literary studies*, ed. R. H. Hutton, vol. II, London, 1879.

J. M. Baker, *Henry Crabb Robinson of Bury, Jena, The 'Times' and Russell Square*, London, 1937.

C. F. Harrold, 'Henry Crabb Robinson, a spectator of life', *Sewanee review* (1928), vol. XXXVI.

R. W. King, 'Crabb Robinson's opinion of Shelley', *Review of English studies* (1928), vol. IV.

D. G. Larg, 'Henry Crabb Robinson and Madame de Staël', *Review of English studies* (1929), vol. V.

E. J. Morley, *The life and times of Henry Crabb Robinson*, London, 1935.

B. J. Morse, 'Crabb Robinson and Goethe in England', *Englische Studien* (1932), vol. LXVII.

P. Norman, 'Henry Crabb Robinson and Goethe', *English Goethe Society* (1930 and 1931), new series, vols. VII and VIII.

H. G. Wright, 'Henry Crabb Robinson's essay on Blake', *Modern language review* (1927), vol. XXII.

SHELLEY

I. EDITIONS

Poetical works, ed. Mary Shelley, 4 vols., London, 1839.

Complete works (Julian edition), ed. R. Ingpen and W. E. Peck, 10 vols., London, 1926–30.

Verse and prose from the manuscripts, ed. Sir J. E. C. Shelley-Rolls and R. Ingpen, London, 1934.

Shelley's prose (complete, but excluding letters and the two romances), ed. D. L. Clark, Albuquerque, 1954.

'A defence of poetry' in *Peacock's four ages of poetry, Shelley's defence of poetry* [etc], ed. H. F. B. Brett-Smith (Percy reprints no. 3), Oxford, 1921.

SELECT BIBLIOGRAPHY

'A philosophical view of reform' in *Political tracts of Wordsworth, Coleridge and Shelley*, ed. R. J. White, Cambridge, 1953.

Letters, ed. F. L. Jones, 2 vols., Oxford, 1964 (the present 'complete edition').

Shelley and his circle 1773–1822. The Carl H. Pforzheimer library, ed. K. N. Cameron, 2 vols. (in progress), Oxford, 1961– .

2. ACCOUNTS BY CONTEMPORARIES

T. J. Hogg, *Life of Percy Bysshe Shelley* (1858), printed with Peacock's and Trelawny's accounts in *The life of Shelley*, ed. H. Wolfe, 2 vols., London, 1933.

T. Medwin, *The life of Shelley*, 2 vols., London, 1847.

T. L. Peacock, *Memoirs of Shelley* (1858–60), in Halliford, VIII (see Peacock editions above).

E. J. Trelawny, *Recollections of the last days of Shelley and Byron* (1858), reprinted with Hogg, ed. Wolfe, above.

See also

N. I. White, *The unextinguished hearth: Shelley and his contemporary critics*, Durham, N. Carolina, 1938.

3. LATER BOOKS AND ARTICLES

M. Arnold, 'Shelley', *Essays in criticism*, 2nd series, London, 1888.

K. N. Cameron, 'Shelley v. Southey: new light on an old quarrel', *P.M.L.A.* (1942), vol. LVII, pt. 1.

The young Shelley: genesis of a radical, London, 1951.

F. R. Leavis, 'Shelley', *Revaluation*, London, 1936.

J. A. Notopoulos, *The platonism of Shelley*, Duke University Press, 1949.

A. S. Walker, 'Peterloo, Shelley and reform', *P.M.L.A.* (1925), vol. XL.

N. I. White, *Shelley*, 2 vols., London, 1947.

W. B. Yeats, *Autobiographies*, London, 1955 (index lists references to Shelley).

SOUTHEY

I. EDITIONS

Letters from England: by Don Manuel Alvarez Espriella. Translated from the Spanish (an original work in English by Southey; 1807), ed. with introduction by J. Simmons (Cresset library), London, 1951.

Sir Thomas More: or colloquies on the progress and prospects of society, 2 vols., London, 1829.

The life and correspondence of Robert Southey, by C. C. Southey, 6 vols., London, 1849–50.

Selections from the letters of Southey, ed. J. W. Warter, London, 1856 (contains letters not in C. C. Southey's edition).

2. BIOGRAPHY AND CRITICISM

G. D. Carnall, *Robert Southey and his age*, Oxford, 1960.

A. Cobban, *Edmund Burke and the revolt against the eighteenth century*, London, 1929.

R. Williams, *Culture and society*, London, 1958.

F. MARGINAL AND MISCELLANEOUS WRITERS

The following made marginal contributions to the book:

T. De Quincey, *Collected writings*, ed. D. Masson, 14 vols., Edinburgh, 1889–90.

Reminiscences of the English Lake Poets, ed. J. E. Jordan, London, 1961.

J. E. Jordan, *Thomas De Quincey, literary critic: his method and achievement*, Berkeley, 1952.

Sir W. Drummond, *Academical questions*, vol. I (no more published), London, 1805.

S. Johnson, *Works* (Oxford English Classics), 11 vols., Oxford, 1825.

T. Moore, *Memoirs of Sheridan*, London, 1825.

The Epicurean: a tale, London, 1827.

Letters and journals of Lord Byron: with notices of the life, 2 vols., London, 1830.

Poetical works...collected by himself, 10 vols., London, 1840–1.

H. H. Jordan, 'Byron and Moore', *Modern language quarterly* (1948), vol. IX.

S. Rogers, *Recollections of the table-talk of Samuel Rogers*, by A. Dyce, ed. M. Bishop, London, 1952.

J. Horne Tooke, *The diversions of Purley*, London, 1786.

W. Wordsworth, *The excursion*, London, 1814.

The critical opinions of William Wordsworth, ed. M. L. Peacock, Baltimore, 1950.

Index

INDEX